The Lost Ark and the Last Days

IN SEARCH OF
❖ ❖ ❖ ❖ ❖
TEMPLE
TREASURES

Randall Price

HARVEST HOUSE PUBLISHERS
Eugene, Oregon 97402

IN SEARCH OF TEMPLE TREASURES

Copyright © 1994 by Randall Price
Published by Harvest House Publishers
Eugene, Oregon 97402

Library of Congress Cataloging-in-Publication Data

Price, Randall.
    In search of temple treasures: the lost ark and the Last Days / Randall Price.
        p.   cm.
    ISBN 1-56507-277-4
    1. Ark of the Covenant—Miscellanea.   2. Temple of Jerusalem
(Jerusalem)—Miscellanea.   3. Temple Mount (Jerusalem)—Miscellanea.
4. Bible—Prophecies—Temple of Jerusalem.   I. Title.
BM657.A8P75   1994
296.4—dc20   94-11986
                                                                              CIP

94   95   96   97   98   99   00   —   10   9   8   7   6   5   4   3   2   1

To

Jim Williams
Bill and Lorene Williams
Terry and Monica Williams

Whose treasures *of* the earth have made possible my own search for treasures *on* the earth. Thank you, dear friends, your true treasure yet awaits you (Matthew 6:19-21).

In Memory of

Sallie Williams

Whose own quest for the treasure of God's truth brought the greatest of treasures to her family and friends, and enriched my own life beyond measure. Truly, she has received the heavenly treasure of "the crown of life, which the Lord has promised to those who love Him" (James 1:12).

Soli Deo Gloria
("To God alone be the glory")

About the Author

Dr. Randall Price is president of *World of the Bible Ministries, Inc.*, a nonprofit organization serving local churches and the Christian community as an educational equipping facility. His ministry provides a clearer understanding of the Bible and biblical issues through information on the ancient and modern Middle East; Bible prophecy; and historical, cultural, and archaeological studies. He holds a master's degree in Old Testament and Semitic Languages from Dallas Theological Seminary, and a Ph.D. in Hebrew Literature and Middle Eastern Languages, Literatures, and Cultures from the University of Texas at Austin, where he also taught courses in biblical archaeology and the history and culture of modern Israel. He has done graduate studies at the Hebrew University in Jerusalem, has conducted archaeological excavations in Jerusalem and the region of Galilee, and is a certified tour guide to the State of Israel. He has authored several books on the subject of biblical prophecy, including *Ready to Rebuild: The Imminent Plan to Rebuild the Last Days Temple* and *Issues in Dispensationalism*, has appeared nationwide on the CBS television specials *Ancient Secrets of the Bible*, and was the focus of a series about the Temple and its treasures on the nationally acclaimed Christian program *The John Ankerberg Show*.

Acknowledgments

Every book owes its successful completion to many people—this one especially, for it is the product of lives all over the world. To each who had a part I give my most heartfelt thanks—the value of this work would be greatly diminished without each of your unique contributions.

I want to thank my Jewish friends, both in the United States and in Israel, who have often written, called, or spent time in discussing substantive issues with me. While we continue to differ over the central issue of the Messiah, I have learned much from you and wish that the fruitful theological dialogues which we have enjoyed without rancor could be shared by my fellow Christian scholars. After 2,000 years of misunderstanding and miscommunication, such mutual exploration of "the promises to the fathers" could go far in correcting the anti-Semitism that continues to exist within churches that call themselves "Christian" and help Jews more carefully define what being a "Christian" truly means.

I want to thank Dr. Tim LaHaye, one of this generation's foremost Christian leaders, for his friendship, valuable counsel, and especially his willingness to write the foreword. I am most grateful to God that He has set him at the vanguard of the revival of prophetic teaching at this most crucial juncture in world history.

I am grateful to my wife, Beverlee, and my children, Elisabeth, Eleisha, Erin, Emilee, and Jonathan, for allowing me to take time from them to do the research and writing necessary for this book. Our lives were further complicated by the writing of my doctoral dissertation, chapters for two other books, and three moves—all in the same time period! Special thanks to Elisabeth, who in joining me on one of my fact-finding trips in Israel endured long diversions from her desired tours to accommodate my rigorous interview schedule.

My gratitude also goes to my parents, Mr. and Mrs. E.C. Price, and my mother-in-law, Jeri Siddall, whose support and encouragement throughout the project has been greatly appreciated.

Special thanks go to the following people and organizations: members of the Hebrew Study Program Fund, whose prayers and contributions supported me during the initial stages of research; Mrs. Ann Hoch, owner of the Elim Water Company; Mrs. Sandra Ellison and Mr. Cliff Wood for assistance in providing needed work space during the initial phase of collating the research material; and Dr. Gary and Debra Collett for their exceptional hospitality in Jerusalem and assistance in transportation, research, and interviews.

For technical assistance in research, interviews, and photography I wish to thank the following: Drs. Dan Bahat, Meir Ben-Dov, Jim Fleming, Asher Kaufman, Tuvia Sagiv, and Leen Ritmeyer; Mrs. Esther Schlisser of Atara Leyoshna's Temple and Vessels Model Museum for permission to photograph model reconstructions; Mr. Adnan Husseni, Director of the Administration of the Wakf and Islamic Affairs; Mr. Sam al-Wad, Supervisor of Al Haram al Sharief, and Mr. Bassam Abu-Lebdah of the Translation Office (Wakf) for permission and assistance in photography in the Dome of the Rock and interviews; Mr. Fantahune Melaku and Maru Asmare for their assistance in Ethiopian community interviews; Rabbis Shlomo Goren, Mayer Yehuda Getz, Nahman Kahane, and Baruch Ben-Yosef for interviews and technical assistance; Dr. Gershon Salomon and Zev Bar-Tov for special hospitality and interviews; Mr. Menachem Kalisher (and Anat) for continued hospitality, interviews, and translation assistance; Rabbis Yisrael Ariel and Chaim Richman for interviews (1993) and permissions (1992-1993) to photograph exhibitions at the Temple Institute's Visitor's Center; the Wolfson Museum: The Jerusalem Great Synagogue for permission to photograph exhibits; The History of Jerusalem Museum for permission to photograph select exhibits; Mr. Paul Streber for photographic assistance in Israel and being an example of a Christian servant; Mr. David Espurvoa for his work on illustrations; and Mrs. Casey Collins, Mrs. Mary Lou Witcher, and Mrs. Susan Maganá for assistance with transcribing taped interviews.

Special appreciation is extended to Steve Halliday, Steve Miller, and Barbara Sherrill for their editorial expertise; to Bob Hawkins, Jr., president of Harvest House, and Eileen Mason, vice president of editorial, for encouraging and supporting this work; and the fine staff of Harvest House Publishers for seeing it so ably through production.

Questions or comments about the material in this book should be addressed to:

Dr. Randall Price
World of the Bible Ministries, Inc.
110 East Street
San Marcos, TX 78666-7326

Additional related information about the Ark of the Covenant is also available from the author. This includes charts, maps, and an article entitled "The Ark in Eden," which supplements this work and examines allusions to the Ark in the book of Genesis.

Foreword

Ever since Steven Spielberg's box-office hit *Raiders of the Lost Ark*, the world has followed the latest searches for the Ark of the Covenant with heightened interest. In addition, the news of recent archaeological excavations under the Temple Mount have drawn the attention of prophecy students and Bible scholars all over the world—they recognize the significance of these events in relation to the soon coming of the Lord Jesus Christ.

Adding to the excitement are the many stories swirling out of Jerusalem that the Third Temple is on the verge of being built. As a result, interest in the discovery of the Ark has reached near-fever pitch.

There has long been a need for a definitive work that untangles the swirl of fact, rumor, and deception in the light of God's Word. Dr. Randall Price has produced just such a work. It is well written, thoroughly biblical, and extremely fair. There has probably never been a more exhaustive and timely book on this subject. He has dealt with every major story and even tackled the more obscure tales. He has done a great deal of research and is well qualified for this important task. Reading *In Search of Temple Treasures* will help make current efforts to find the Ark much more meaningful.

Any serious student of Bible prophecy and the end times will find this book an invaluable resource in the years to come.

—Dr. Tim LaHaye
PreTrib Research Center

Contents

Preface

Nowhere today is prophetic interpretation more misunderstood than in what is said about the destiny of the Jewish people. Some "scholars" contend that the Jew no longer has a promise from God. Rather, they see Christians as "spiritual Jews" who have inherited all the former promises made to believing Jews in the Old Testament, and the church inheriting the proffered blessings as the "new Israel." Those who believe and teach this perspective hold that the Christian community is the new temple of God and that the only kingdom that we can anticipate is in heaven and not on earth.

As might be expected, these "scholars" deny any significance to modern events in light of the prophetic texts. They declare that these prophecies were fulfilled in and around A.D. 70, or that they had not a historical but a spiritual intent, and therefore they have or will have their consummation only in the church.

Something Missing

When we read the New Testament, however, we are impressed by the fact that Jesus was a Jew (Matthew 1:1), that the disciples were Jews, and that Paul was not only a Jew, but a rabbi (Acts 22:3; 23:6; 26:4-5; Romans 11:1-2; Philippians 3:5). Furthermore, Jesus had declared that salvation was of the Jews (John 4:22) and that He had come only to the lost sheep of the house of Israel (Matthew 15:24). Paul was a loyal Israelite who worshiped in the Temple (Acts 24:11-18), offered sacrifice (Acts 21:26), and declared he had done nothing against the Law of God throughout his entire Christian life (Acts 25:8). Finally, Jesus, Peter, and Paul were united in their profession that they were neither doing nor saying anything that had not already been written in the Old Testament by Moses and the prophets (Luke 24:27; Acts 3:18, 22; 26:22-23).

13

For those who read their Bibles and see only the church, something surely is missing—Israel! Did not Jesus promise a future return for His own people (Matthew 23:39; 26:29)? Did not Paul expound the national restoration of Israel as a vital corrective to presumptuous Gentile Christian faith (Acts 26:6-7; Romans 11:23, 25-29, 31)? Indeed, a resounding *yes* must remind Christians that God's purpose for Israel did not end at A.D. 70, nor can it be fulfilled nationally within a largely Gentile church that is presently losing its spiritual distinctive in the Gentile world.

Because God is not finished with Israel, right-thinking Christians should watch constantly to discover the historical process He is using to complete His promise to this people.

Prophetic Fulfillment and Current Events

I recently received a copy of the official publication of a leading evangelical denomination only to see this headline on the issue's top story: "Scholars see no direct link to prophecy." This generalization was made more specific in the story itself:

> While some radio and TV preachers may see ominous signs of the end times in the newly developing Middle East peace accord, *many Baptist scholars don't see any direct relationship between current events and end-times prophecy.*[1]

Such scholars have argued that the return of Jews to Israel is not *necessarily* a fulfillment of prophecy. They believe that the land could be repossessed by a foreign people, that the Jewish nation could again be dispersed throughout the world, and that at some future time the biblical prophecies could find fulfillment.

Yet for 2,000 years there had been no kind of organized return to the Land until this century, which saw the establishment of an independent Jewish state. From the beginning of the Jewish dispersion, every historian (whether secular or religious) had regarded the probability of such an expected Jewish regathering as miraculous and had interpreted it only in the context of the biblical promise. Today, the very dimension of this return—and of Israeli commitment to defend their right to exist at any cost—argues most convincingly for the fulfillment of the biblical texts.[2]

For some scholars to say that the modern return of Jews to the State of Israel is prophetically irrelevant is to forget the lessons of history itself. Even ultraorthodox Jews, who once opposed Zionism as a secular movement, today contend that a reversal of the Jewish return to Israel would be impossible. They point to the pattern of exile and return in Scripture and say that nowhere is another *Diaspora* (dispersion of the Jews) predicted after the event of return (*see* Isaiah 11:11a). Israelis also argue that in light of the decline in Jewry outside Israel, the explosive rise of anti-Semitism at a level unknown since World War II, and the Islamic world's dedication to destroying the Jewish nation, any suggestion that the Jews could be again scattered among the nations and then return is unthinkable. They view such a proposal as condemning them to another Holocaust. In view of such facts, a modern reversal of the Jewish state could never permit a future fulfillment.

If the modern return of Jews to the State of Israel is part of the fulfillment of God's prophetic plan, then we must begin to consider current events affecting this Land as prophetically significant. From my analysis of the Bible and the land of Israel, nowhere are such events more significant than in the present revival of the Jewish expectation of a Messiah and the establishment of a biblical theocracy in Israel. In a desire to understand this religious phenomenon, I have devoted much time to researching the prophetic issues that underlie this movement.

One of the driving issues, little known or understood by many Christians, is the restoration of the lost Temple treasures, predicted in Jewish writings to occur at the end of the age with the coming of the Messiah. For the past decade modern searches for these treasures have increased in number and gained international attention. Are such searches simply the actions of religious zealots or the sensationalism of crazed Christians? Or do they reflect an actual change of events that is prophetically significant?

Christians and the Temple Treasures

When the author of the book of Hebrews wrote about Old Testament worship, he recalled with reverence the Temple treasures. In his description, one object was set apart from the others with a more elaborate description—the Ark of the Covenant:

> Behind the second veil, there was a tabernacle which is called the Holy of Holies, having a golden altar of incense and the ark of the covenant covered on all sides with gold, in which was a golden jar holding the manna, and Aaron's rod which budded, and the tables of the covenant. And above it were the cherubim of glory overshadowing the mercy seat (Hebrews 9:3-5).

For many Christians, this brief account in the New Testament measures the extent of their knowledge of the holy Ark. Yet when the biblical author had finished these words, he added, "But of these things we cannot now speak in detail" (verse 5). From this statement we can gather that additional details could be known about the Ark and that it was the author's desire that eventually such knowledge should be given to the saints. I am convinced that Scripture does indeed reveal much more about the Ark, both in history and in prophecy, and this book is offered in an attempt to honor that intention of sacred Scripture.

The World at the Hinge of History

Some people might ask, "Wasn't the Ark lost long ago? What significance could it have for us today?" We are living in a pragmatic age in which the study of the past is considered to have little relevance unless a practical application to the present can be demonstrated.

Yet we are also living in a day in which events predicted long ago are rapidly moving toward fulfillment. Changes of great historical significance are taking place all around us with every new day—changes that take on added significance when we examine them in relation to the record of past history. One analyst made this observation:

> It is not that change is new but that the rate of change is unprecedented. More changes have occurred in the past 94 years than in the previous 2,000 years. Changes in the final six years of this decade (from 1994 through 1999) may match if not exceed the changes of the first 94 years of this century.[3]

With such changes occurring so quickly, few of us can grasp the monumental effects on our world and the church. And with each change the world is propelled toward the fulfillment of its ultimate purpose. As this same analyst noted:

> The world is at a hinge of history. This is a time like the time of Christ, the fall of the Roman Empire, the Renaissance, the Reformation, and the Industrial Revolution. The primary similarity is that each one of these hinges swung the world in a new direction. . . . Each introduced a new era unlike the one before. Each was a time of fear and hope, resistance and welcome. There was no going back.[4]

The hinge this time, however, will swing the world into an era unparalleled in all of history. Around the world people are sensing that our planet is on a deadline with destiny. And people who know the Bible are realizing that much of what the Old Testament prophets said concerning the end times daily fills the headlines of our newspapers and nightly flashes across our television screens.

A Crossing of Paths

The direction of my life has led me down a path of exploration I never dreamed I would consider. This path has led me through graduate studies and archaeological excavations in Israel and a doctorate in Middle Eastern studies. During the course of this journey I have lived in Jerusalem, traveled frequently through many countries of the Middle East, and developed friendships and made contacts with many of the leading figures affecting the political and religious aspects of the modern conflict in these lands. I do not mention these things to "qualify" myself, but rather to affirm that what I write comes from a firsthand involvement in the unfolding drama of the destiny of the Middle East.

In my previous book *Ready to Rebuild: The Imminent Plan to Rebuild the Last Days Temple*, written with Thomas Ice, I attempted to go to the principal sources in Israel and permit them to speak for themselves. I have sought to follow that same design in this book about the lost treasures of the Temple and especially the mystery concerning the Ark of the Covenant. I have attempted to research everything published to date on the Ark (which was a monumental task in itself) and made three trips to Israel to personally interview everyone I knew who had some knowledge about the subject. This included secular archaeologists, orthodox rabbis, messianic Jewish activists, Ethiopian priests, and Muslim officials. And most importantly, I have sought to set this wealth of information in an evangelical Christian context with a practical application for the critical days in which we live.

It is my prayer that my exploration will cross paths with your own and that it will awaken you to the reality of the soon appearing of our Savior and encourage your own readiness to meet Him on that day.

—Randall Price

PART ONE

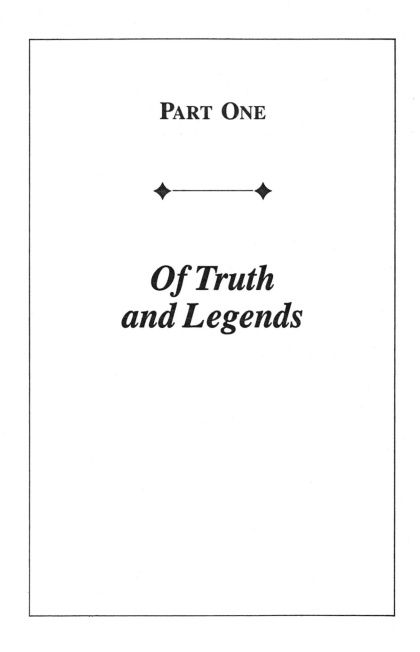

Of Truth and Legends

1

Sign of the End Times

As a child I was irresistibly drawn to tales of high-stakes adventure in far-off, mysterious lands. Some of my favorite books were Robert Louis Stevenson's *Treasure Island* and Traven's *The Treasure of the Sierra Madre*. What these stories and dozens like them have in common is the search for buried treasure.

Perhaps you were like me in daydreaming of exotic voyages to distant shores in search of hidden treasure. What a thrill to think that lost antiquities or unbelievable wealth could be unearthed in some unexplored, secret site! Central to nearly all of these stories is the plot to possess the map or clue that leads to the unclaimed treasure hoard. For the most part, such flights of fancy are the carefully crafted products of fiction, although from time to time we do hear reports of the discovery of an abandoned mine in New Mexico or an undersea wreck loaded with gold and gems.

While every culture has its own tales of legendary loot, the Bible tells a more believable tale of treasures lost in time, perhaps waiting to be uncovered in God's good timing. The biblical accounts of Temple vessels that have disappeared or been captured by invaders are fascinating in themselves. But what launches the drama of the Temple treasures into the realm of prophecy is the expectation of their future return. In this sense, the Bible is a treasure map of time, indicating the era during which the vessels would reappear to function within the rebuilt Temple of the last days (*see* Ezekiel 40–48).

Hints about Things Hidden

The Bible gives only a hint of what may have happened to the Temple treasure. To fill out the picture, we need other clues that permit us to form reasonable theories about their present location and to discern how they may affect the future. Outside the Bible we have such hints preserved in extrabiblical documents that span a four-hundred-year period often called the intertestamental period. While no Scripture was written between the last Old Testament book and the arrival of Jesus, the Jewish nation experienced a number of important historical events and amassed a rich heritage of legends and traditions that reveal significant facets of history and religious practice.

While the extrabiblical literature of this period was not inspired of God, remember that *uninspired does not mean unimportant.* Any writing that comes to us from the time or near the time of the Bible is of immense value. It may give us eyewitness reports of events not covered in Scripture or provide our only source for the experiences of daily life during times now forgotten. For example, we all are aware of the great contribution to biblical understanding that has come to us from the Dead Sea Scrolls and the writings of the first-century Jewish historian Josephus, who lived during the time of Jesus. These—and a whole library of texts known as the Apocrypha and Pseudepigrapha—offer information concerning both the Temple treasures and the end times.

To this we must also add the vast storehouse of learning contained in the Talmud and Mishnah, and the many ancient commentaries (for example, the *Midrash*) rabbis have written on the Bible. Christian scholars are now aware that these sources have long held vital insights about life and religion in both the Old and New Testaments. They have helped resolve

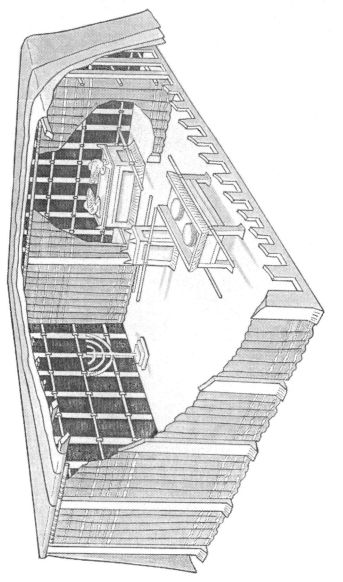

View of the original Temple treasures inside the Tabernacle. These items comprised the furniture or vessels and are identified as: 1) the Golden Table of Showbread, where the priests placed the "bread of the presence" loaves before the Lord; 2) the Great Menorah, which stood six feet tall and remained lit constantly; 3) the Golden Altar of Incense, from which the high priest, on the Day of Atonement, took burning coals and incense into the Holy of Holies; and 4) the Golden Ark of the Covenant, the supremely important place where the presence of God was manifested between the wings of the cherubim.

many unanswered questions and given us a much clearer picture of the life of Jesus as a Jew. Because these works were written to preserve and explain Jewish law, they describe in as complete detail as possible those laws relating to the Temple and its treasures. The judicious use of these works to clarify and confirm New Testament truths should be acceptable to us today just as historical studies reveal they were consulted by Christian scholars in the early church age. The writings of the early church fathers are equally helpful concerning the Temple treasures, as are their thoughts on the last days (influenced in many cases by rabbinic debate).

What the Ancient Sources Say

Jewish sources outside the Bible sought to explain what had happened to the Tabernacle, the Ark of the Covenant, the Great Menorah, the Altar of Incense, and all the most important vessels and treasures of the First and Second Temples. Without these items, they could not envision a complete restoration to glory greater than that of the First Temple (when all of these vessels were present) as predicted by the prophets (see Haggai 2:7-9). Therefore, biblical figures such as Jeremiah and his scribe Baruch were used as spokesmen in these texts. Because Jeremiah had prophesied the destruction of the First Temple and made predictions concerning the final restoration of Israel's glory, in the extrabiblical texts he was made responsible for overseeing the preservation of the Temple's sacred vessels. All of these accounts appear to focus on the last days.[1] Our purpose here is not to evaluate their accuracy, but to study them for what they commonly reveal concerning the tradition of the Temple treasure.

Jeremiah Hides the Temple Vessels

The apocryphal book of 2 Maccabees dates from as early as 163 B.C. and was written to Jews exiled to Egypt.[2] The author envisioned a restored Israel gathered in a rebuilt and purified Temple (1:11, 17; 2:17-18). To assure his readers of the completeness of this restoration, he recounted for them how their fellow Egyptian exile, Jeremiah the prophet, had hidden the Temple treasures. In 2 Maccabees 2:4-8 we learn that at the time of the destruction of the First Temple, Jeremiah took the Tabernacle, the altar of incense, and the Ark to Mount Nebo and sealed them in a secret, unmarked cave. Since these vessels originated with Moses, it was only fitting that they be kept "with him" at the site of his burial. The Greek word for "sealed" in 2 Maccabees 2 has prophetic meaning, being the same word used by the Septuagint (a Greek translation of the Old Testament) in Daniel 12:4, 9 (cf. 8:26)—a text which speaks of a concealment until the end times. The author then has Jeremiah tell his followers that the Temple treasures would remain hidden until the time God regathered Israel and the glorious presence of God appeared in a cloud as it did during the exodus and Solomon's dedication of the First Temple (Exodus 16:10; 1 Kings 8:11). Presumably, this would occur at the rebuilt Temple in Jerusalem.

An anonymous medieval Jewish work entitled *Sepher Yosippon*, based on the writings of Josephus, mentions this same Jeremiah tradition but adds that the secret spot would not be revealed until Jeremiah and Elijah came to return the Ark to its place. This may reflect the Jewish concept of the need for two witnesses to establish all things: thus Jeremiah (who hid the vessels) and Elijah (who reveals all things). Some Jewish traditions thought of Elijah as a restorer of the Temple vessels.[3] He is clearly identified in this role in *Mekilta, Wayassa'*, which comments on Exodus 16:33-34:

> And this is one of the three things which Elijah will, in the future, restore to Israel; the bottle of sprinkling water [containing the ashes of the red heifer], and the bottle of anointing oil. And some

say: Also the rod of Aaron with its ripe almonds and blossoms.

It is tempting here to parallel this idea with the two witnesses of Revelation 11 and their role with the future Temple. Some commentators believe they will come at the beginning of the Tribulation when the rebuilding of the Temple is initiated. If so, this legend may become reality if these two men assist the orthodox Jewish community in the ritual preparations necessary for the restoration of worship.

Two other legends concerning Jeremiah's involvement in hiding the Temple vessels have survived to our time. In the *Life of Jeremiah* (11–19), the prophet takes only the Ark with its sacred contents to a secret place between Mount Nebo and Mount Hor and seals it within a rock. As in the Maccabean story, the Ark will be brought out when Israel is regathered and the glory-cloud appears. In this account, however, the regathering is at Mount Sinai and the resurrected Moses and Aaron are the ones who will bring out the Ark. And in the *Paralipomena of Jeremiah* (3:5-19), Jeremiah (accompanied by Baruch) is commanded by God to take unspecified "holy vessels of the worship-service" and bury them. Again, they will reappear only at the time of Israel's regathering. Of interest in this account is the apparent resumption of sacrifices offered during worship. Perhaps the author was drawing a connection between the reappearance of the Temple vessels and the restoration of Temple worship.

Baruch and the Temple Vessels

Another account of the hidden Temple treasure is recorded in the Second (Syriac) Apocalypse of Baruch (6:5-9). In this version of the story, Baruch sees an angel remove the Temple vessels before the Temple's destruction. Here the vessels include the Ark and its contents, the altar of incense, the priests' clothing and the 48 precious stones that were part of their garments, the veil of the Temple, the ephod, and all the vessels of the Tabernacle. The angel then orders the earth to conceal them until the time of the restoration, when Jerusalem will be forever free. One interesting element in this story is the explanation for the hiding of the vessels: "so that strangers may not get possession of them" (verse 8). This implies that Gentiles should not be the ones to discover the treasures, but Jews alone. In a slightly different tradition (4 Baruch), Jeremiah is told by God to bury the Temple vessels "until the coming of the *Beloved One*." This messianic reference also places the restoration at the end times.

The Samaritan Account of the Hidden Vessels

The Samaritan tradition concerning the hidden Temple vessels is preserved for us by Josephus in his *Antiquities of the Jews* (18. 85-88) and in the Samaritan chronicle called the *Memar Marqah*. The Samaritans were descendants of intermarriages between resident Israelites and Assyrian transplants after the exile of the northern kingdom (about 669 B.C.). The Samaritans had attempted to disrupt the rebuilding of the Second Temple (of Zerubbabel) after they had been rejected by the Judeans from assisting in the project (Ezra 4:1-3). One reason often given for this rejection is that the Jews knew that the Samaritans had their own temple on Mount Gerizim and did not want a rival Temple in Jerusalem (*see* John 4:20, 25). Their offer to assist in building the Temple in Jerusalem was therefore only a ruse.

However, the primary reason Zerubbabel could not allow the Samaritans to participate was that they were foreigners whose religion mixed the Mosaic Law with pagan beliefs. It was this very sort of religion that had brought the destruction of the First Temple and would have threatened the unity of the Judeans and the work of God. Because the Samaritans did not have a part in the Jewish monarchy, they did not accept any of the books of the Bible produced during this time and thus were left with only the Pentateuch (the first five books of the Old Testament). Therefore, the Samaritans developed a competitive version of the Temple treasure tradition to support their own claim against Israel that the Samaritans were heir to true, Mosaic-only worship.[4] Their story may have been influenced by an attempt to refute the Jewish charge based on Genesis 35:2-4 that idols were hidden under Mount Gerizim, rendering it unfit as a place of worship.[5]

Understanding this, we are not surprised to find in Josephus' version of the Samaritan account that Moses is the one who buries the sacred vessels on Mount Gerizim. While Moses does not appear in the last days to recover the treasures, the "prophet like Moses" of Deuteronomy 18:15 (a messianic figure)[6] does—at the time of the future ingathering of refugees at Mount Gerizim. According to the other Samaritan tradition in the *Memar Marqah* (4:11), it is Uzzi the high priest who hides the Temple vessels at the beginning of the era of divine disfavor, which is inaugurated by the death of Moses. In both accounts, Moses, or Moses' prophetic successor, is responsible for the hiding and recovery of the Temple vessels.

More Temple Treasure Traditions

Additional ancient accounts about the Temple treasure agree in general but differ somewhat in the details. For example, while 2 Maccabees 2:1-10 says most of the treasures were preserved, the Jewish historian Eupolemus records that the gold and silver vessels of the Temple were seized as tribute and sent to Babylon, "except for the Ark and the tablets in it. This Jeremiah preserved" (4. 39:5). In the Temple Scroll, the longest of the Dead Sea Scrolls and the most detailed ancient account concerning the Temple, a restored future Temple is described—complete with all the *original* furnishings found in the Tabernacle and First Temple.

Still other Jewish writers state that the Tabernacle, Ark, Menorah, Altar of Incense, and other Temple vessels were all stored within the First Temple and then concealed beneath it before it was destroyed. These vessels apparently remained intact and within the Temple grounds throughout the Second Temple period. This is the popular rabbinic view today, and supposedly has been so ever since A.D. 70 whenever hopes of rebuilding the Temple have arisen. More will be said concerning this tradition in chapter 6.

All of these accounts reveal an early and long historical tradition concerning the Temple treasures. They all have in common the hiding of at least the Ark and they point to the end-time restoration of the vessels by God Himself or a qualified prophetic representative. Now let us consider what the Bible says about the importance of the Temple treasures and the prospect for their future recovery.

No Vessels, No Temple

The Temple vessels were an essential part of the Temple because, like the Temple, they were made according to God's specific command and pattern (Exodus 25:9; 1 Chronicles 28:11-19). These vessels were considered holy and a vital part of the worship of God. It was common in the ancient Near East for a conqueror to place such treasures in the temple of his own god to demonstrate the superiority of his god over that of his vanquished enemies. That's exactly what happened when Nebuchadnezzar took Jerusalem (Daniel 1:2). Later, the desecration of the vessels at a feast hosted by Belshazzar (Daniel 5:1-4) was a direct insult to the God who had declared that "the nations will know that I am the LORD" (Ezekiel 36:23). That same night, God brought about the overthrow of Babylon (Daniel 5:25-31).

God's immediate judgment against Babylon underscores the tremendous sanctity of the Temple vessels. Any violation of this sanctity or common use of the chambers where the treasures were stored was a grave offense (*see* Nehemiah 13:4-9).

To this end they were continually purified (2 Chronicles 29:18) and guarded (1 Chronicles 9:28) to ensure that the Temple service would not be interrupted.

When the First Temple was destroyed, these vessels had to be recovered or remade before the Temple could be rebuilt (Ezra 1:7-11; 3:10-11; 5:14-15; 6:5). At this time we read of the expectation that one of the Temple treasures would be recovered—the Urim and Thummim (Ezra 2:63), which were used to discern the will of God. We also read that other treasures were acquired for the Temple (Ezra 7:14-20; 8:25-34), but these were intended for the Temple treasury, not for Temple worship.

It is the Temple treasures that were vitally connected to the Temple's existence, not the Temple treasury. In fact, although the Temple had been desecrated by foreign idols (Jeremiah 7; Ezekiel 8) and its treasury plundered prior to the Babylonian destruction (2 Kings 24:13), the climactic event spelling the doom of all Jerusalem was the removal of the choicest Temple vessels (2 Chronicles 36:18-19).[7] This passage reveals that the Temple and its vessels are inseparable; therefore the destiny of the two must be prophetically linked as well. Such an idea is endorsed by the pseudepigraphal work Second Baruch, which appears to suggest that the recovered vessels provide a continuity between the destruction of the Temple and its restoration.

Just as the Temple was destroyed first by the Babylonians and later by the Romans (Jeremiah 7:14; Luke 21:5-6, 20-24), so, too, were the Temple vessels taken away (2 Kings 24:13; Jeremiah 27:16-22). Yet, just as the Temple was (and is) to be rebuilt (Daniel 9:16-17, 20-27), so also will these treasures be restored. Support for this deduction may be found in Jeremiah 27:22, which records God's promise concerning this restoration: " 'They shall be carried to Babylon, and they shall be there until the day I visit them,' declares the LORD. 'Then I will bring them back and restore them to this place.' " Isaiah also predicted this restoration of the vessels. But he stated more clearly the idea of divine preservation, which Jeremiah had only implied: "Depart, depart, go out from there. . . . You who carry the vessels of the LORD. But you will not go out in haste, nor will you go as fugitives; for the LORD will go before you, and the God of Israel will be your rear guard" (52:11-12).

Jeremiah and Isaiah were speaking about the first restoration of the Temple when the Jewish people returned from Babylon (Jeremiah 28:1-6), but their prophecies set a pattern for the predicted second return (Isaiah 11:11; Ezekiel 36:24-28) and restoration of the Temple (Ezekiel 37:26-28, 40-48; Daniel 9:27; Zechariah 6:12-15; Matthew 24:15; 2 Thessalonians 2:4; Revelation 11:1-2). Just as Jeremiah and Isaiah predicted the overthrow of Babylon and the restoration of Israel in the past, so also did John predict the same for the future (Revelation 17–20). If the first destruction of 587 B.C. was followed by reconstruction, why not the second destruction in A.D. 70 as well? And if the vessels were part of the Second Temple, should they not be a part of the Third? The Jeremiah text implies that the answer is yes.

This message of restoration was implicitly stated in the detailed description that was given of the Temple vessels when they were plundered (*see* 1 Kings 25:13-17). If the vessels were to be destroyed and forgotten, why preserve them and their features in such detail? The same has been argued for the Temple, for which we have precise measurements that were passed down in the works of Josephus and the Mishnah tractate known as *Middot* ("measurements").

The Lost Treasures and the Last Times

The majority of the legends and traditions about the Temple treasures claim that they were not destroyed or stolen, but hidden away by God to await the end times. The Jewish philosopher Philo, who lived in Alexandria, Egypt, during the first century, personally visited the Temple (*On Providence* 2.

64) and attested that the sacred vessels were a treasure for all time. He explained that the wood of the Ark was undecaying because it contained the incorruptible law and that the Ark and all the furniture of the sanctuary as well as the Temple itself "were ordained not for a limited time, *but for an infinite age.*"[8] Whatever Philo's views about the last days, his belief that the Temple treasures were designed for all the ages assumes that they would return in the future.

One reason the legends proclaimed the recovery of the Temple treasures in the last days was to assure the Jews who lived in exile or under Gentile rule that God's prophetic program had not gone wrong, but was progressing on schedule. It was a way of saying, "What could not be performed today will surely be accomplished tomorrow." These legends were not some sort of psychological ploy to comfort the suffering with a hopeful but unrealistic utopia. These writers fervently believed what the prophets had predicted. They trusted that the God who had once given the order of worship—which required the vessels—would not let His purpose fail.

The legends about the Temple treasures have given the Jewish people a sense of connection with the eternal Israel, whose existence was unaffected by circumstance and whose return was guaranteed by an unconditional and everlasting covenant (Genesis 17:7). They have provided a sense of continuity with the glorious days of Israel's past, when the eternal and the temporal seemed to be one and the Temple and its worship were a holy witness to the world. With the legends, they could look forward to the day when Jews around the world regathered, signaling the time of the redemption, when the Temple would be rebuilt and the hidden Temple vessels returned. This would make possible the restoration of true biblical worship and fulfill the promises made through the prophets of a restored national Israel (Ezekiel 36:18-38; 37:21-28).[9]

The Temple Treasures Today

The conviction that the recovery of the Temple treasures is a vital link to the fulfillment of ancient prophecies has motivated a continuous stream of historians, archaeologists, and treasure-seekers to look for the facts behind the fiction. Some of these men and women eagerly hope that their efforts will one day culminate in the unearthing of these treasures—and that, in light of the Middle East conflict, would be nothing short of earthshaking.

In addition, orthodox Jews in Jerusalem, convinced that the Third Temple will be rebuilt very soon, already have begun remaking the vessels for restored Temple worship. Many of these utensils are presently on display in an exhibit at the Temple Institute.[10] These men have deliberately *not* made at least one of the Temple treasures, however—the Ark of the Covenant—because according to Jewish tradition, it was never actually "lost" but remains hidden, awaiting its day of discovery. This greatest of all Temple treasures is understandably one of the greatest of all stories, a story this book was written to tell.

If you, like me, love a good adventure and the chance to search for secret treasure, then we will find some of that together. But in the chapters to follow we will also come face to face with the Word of the living God, who has acted in history to reveal Himself and has promised to return to this world He made to complete His great plan. The treasure of truth is the greatest treasure of all, and I invite you to accompany me as we consider the truth of the lost Ark and the last days.

2

The Ark Affair

We want to make all mankind again one family of God. We want to make all mankind worshipers of the One God here in Jerusalem on the holy hill, Mount Moriah—the Temple Mount. One of the important things that is connected to this great event is the Ark of the Covenant.[1]

—Gershon Salomon, leader,
the Temple Mount Faithful

An old Jewish maxim states: "Jerusalem is in the center of the world, the Temple Mount is in the center of Jerusalem, and the Temple is in the center of the Mount." We might well add, "And the Ark is in the center of the Temple."

No other single treasure of the Temple held—or holds—the preeminent place of the Ark. It alone bore the great covenant of Moses made at Sinai. It alone once hosted the great glory of God. What could possibly compare with the Ark? To find it would be at once the greatest archaeological, historical, religious, and political discovery of all time! Talmudic scholar Rabbi Liebel Reznick recently wrote about the effect the Ark's return would have on the world:

No other archaeological find would have a greater impact on the destiny of man. What a religious resurgence [this] discovery would cause. How it would cause scholars and laymen to reevaluate the past, examine the present, and speculate on the future cannot be imagined.[2]

With the destruction of the First Temple 2,581 years ago, however, this treasure of treasures disappeared from the biblical record. Ever since then, men have sought to solve the secret of the lost Ark. The story of this ages-long quest, and especially of its escalation in recent years, might accurately be dubbed "The Ark Affair." Certainly with the present conflict in the Middle East over the issue of religious jurisdiction of the holy places in Israel, the return of the Ark to Jerusalem would have international consequences.

Why the Concern?

I am convinced we are living in the last days of the Christian era. The messianic era is on the verge of returning. The ancient prophets predicted this would be a time marked by the Messiah's appearing and the national restoration and spiritual revival of Israel (Zechariah 8:7-8; 12:10–13:2). The Lord Himself promised concerning these coming days:

I will return to Zion and will dwell in the midst of Jerusalem. Then Jerusalem will be called the City of Truth, and the mountain of the LORD of hosts will be called the Holy Mountain (Zechariah 8:3).

Therefore as we come nearer and nearer to this time, we should expect to see international attention focus on the land of Israel and its conflict with surrounding nations (Zechariah 12:2-3). And as I wrote in my earlier book *Ready to Rebuild*, we should also expect to see renewed efforts to revive biblical

Jewish worship and rebuild the Temple in Jerusalem (Zechariah 6:12-15; 14:16-21). Both of these events have now occupied our newscasts to the extent that few today are unaware of their place in the problems of our planet.

Why, then, do we seek to project the Ark into the tense mix of the Middle East? The answer comes from an understanding of the Middle Eastern perspective of the past. For everyone in this region, the issues of the past are of vital concern to the present and form the basis of hope for the future. Part of this past is prophecy, and part of prophecy is the prediction that the Temple treasures would be restored in the last days.

As we have seen in the previous chapter, Jewish concern over the disappearance of the Temple treasures produced a rich tradition that predicted their return for the age of Israel's redemption. For the most part, the writers who provided these legends built their case upon the Old Testament prophets who left clues that could potentially resolve the biblical silence concerning the Ark and the other treasures. Though these extrabiblical writings blend history and an apocalyptic perspective, they may still reflect actual events (though related in legendary proportions).

Even though these writings are not inspired Scripture, their prophecies are generally harmonious with the prophetic program of the Bible. Although orthodox Jews (like many Christians) do not accept the Apocrypha or Pseudepigrapha, they exalt the Talmud above the Bible, interpreting the latter by the former. Because this work teaches that the Ark is hidden and may yet be recovered, the majority of orthodox Jews today anticipate the reappearance of the Ark. Their beliefs are having a significant impact on the present conflict in the Middle East and will continue to in the days ahead. Again, Rabbi Reznick makes the point:

> Jewish tradition has always maintained that the treasures would remain until the coming of the Messiah. Muslim tradition forbids the site [the

Temple Mount] from being explored. Curiosity is
nature's most powerful force. Tradition is God's
immovable object of faith. Here on the Temple
Mount we find the answer to that ancient conun-
drum, "What happens when an irresistible force
meets an immovable object?" for the treasures are
yet to be discovered.[3]

Every student of the Bible, whatever his or her interpretation of prophecy, should recognize that God both controls His
world and will return to it. Consequently, we should become
world-watchers who are eager to see how and when God will
fulfill the details of His plan. This is especially true in a time
when orthodox Israeli Jews—whose actions already have sig-
nificantly affected conflicts in their country—announce their
hope that the Ark will soon reappear along with the Messiah
and the Temple to usher in a new world promised by the
prophets.

A Brief Chronology

Before we move on for a more detailed look at the Ark, let's
get an aerial perspective—the big picture.

The Ark of the Covenant was constructed by the craftsman
Bezalel under the supervision of Moses at Mount Sinai. It was
transported from place to place with the Tabernacle during
Israel's journey through the wilderness and on the conquest
and settlement of the Promised Land.

When King David conquered Jerusalem and made it the
capital of the Jewish nation, he transported the Ark with the
Tabernacle and placed it on a level area—a threshing floor—
situated on the uppermost hill of the mountains of Moriah, a
divine place hallowed from antiquity (2 Samuel 6:1-12, 17).
When David's son, Solomon, became king, he built the First
Temple and placed the sacred Ark within its innermost recesses, known as the Holy of Holies (1 Kings 6:19). The walls

within this room were engraved with the cherubim motif, and on both sides of the Ark were placed huge cherubim overlaid with gold (1 Kings 6:23-29). In the First Temple, the high priest would approach the Ark once a year on the Day of Atonement to bring the sacrificial blood that would obtain another year of pardon for the sins of the Jewish nation.

During the wicked reign of the Judean king Manasseh, the vessels were removed from the Temple and idols put in their place (2 Kings 21:4-7). What happened to the Ark during this period is unknown, but it reappeared a generation later at the time of King Josiah (2 Chronicles 35:3) and was returned to the Holy of Holies after extensive repairs were made to the Temple (2 Kings 22:1-7). About 38 years later, the First Temple was destroyed by the Babylonian commander Nebuzaradan (2 Kings 25:8-9) and all its treasures were presumably looted or destroyed (2 Chronicles 36:19). The Ark, however, was never mentioned among these items.

The Renewed Search

Not until relatively recent times has it been possible to conduct a search for the Ark. Both the physical condition and political situation in the Middle East prevented would-be explorers from such a quest. While some have looked elsewhere, most efforts to recover the Ark have centered on Jerusalem and the ancient site of the Temple. Some people think that a search was made by the Crusaders after they took possession of the Temple Mount and turned the Muslim Dome of the Rock into a church (the *Templum Domini* in the twelfth century). Then there was the ill-fated Parker expedition in 1910, which tunneled underneath the Rock itself. The excavations were interrupted by Muslim authorities and never completed.

So it was not until June 7, 1967, when control of the Temple Mount was returned to the Israelis, that it was possible to consider excavations at the site. This hope was ended a short month later when jurisdiction of the Mount went back to the Muslims. Nevertheless, the years since have seen a revival of the effort to rebuild the Temple along with a renewed search for the Ark.

In the following pages we will investigate both the theories and the claims of those who have sought and currently seek for the Ark. But we will also go further, looking beyond the search for the lost Ark to what the Bible says about the last days. There, hidden within the text of sacred Scripture, we may find clues to the final Ark affair—events that will change the history of the world forever.

3

God in a Box

---

*There I will meet with you; and from above the
mercy seat, from between the two cherubim which
are upon the ark of the testimony, I will speak to you
about all that I will give you in commandment for the
sons of Israel.*

—Exodus 25:22

When I take my children down the cereal aisle at the
supermarket, their choice of breakfast food is based
on a different set of values from mine. I look for the low-fat,
low-sugar, high-vitamin stuff, while they look for the cereal
that has a prize or toy in the box. So long as something other
than cereal is there, they will choose it every time! Of course,
every man has his price, and whenever the stakes are raised to
a free vacation or a $100 bill, I get involved. The chance that
something valuable might be hiding inside that cardboard box
is very alluring. Undoubtedly, the "secret surprise in every
box" marketing strategy has had a lot to do with the success of
Cracker Jack.

Cereal and Cracker Jack are one thing; theology is another.
People do not like spiritual surprises. They prefer that which
is predictable and certain. Perhaps that is one reason why

theologians take such pains to explain the unexplainable, or, as one professor of mine put it, "to unscrew the inscrutable"!

The Mystery of the Ark

When we come to Israel's Ark, we have no choice but to admit we have encountered a great mystery, a *mysterium tremendum*. Here was an object seen by precious few. When it was transported, it had to remain covered throughout its journey. Once it was placed within the Holy of Holies, a specially constructed curtain was hung to prevent anyone from gaining access to it. No one, not even a priest, could enter "beyond the veil"—an expression used idiomatically today to speak of forbidden territory. Only the high priest was allowed to enter the Holy of Holies where the Ark was housed, and even then only once a year. Still, he did not "see" the Ark. The Holy of Holies was a windowless room, which made it pitch-black and impenetrable to the eye. Perhaps that is why the Holy of Holies has been called the "Inner Sanctum," a term used to refer to a dark, terrifying, and mysterious place. To make certain that the high priest did not look upon the Ark, he was commanded by law to carry burning incense, which had to fill the entire room with a veil of smoke before he could approach the mercy seat.

To add to the high anxiety that the nation of Israel felt on this solemn occasion, the high priest had to wear bells on his robe so that the people could hear whether he was still alive once inside the Holy of Holies. Precautions were taken in case the priest should accidentally touch the Ark and be killed or die of some other cause. Just as mountain climbers tie themselves together when they are in treacherous terrain, the high priest was attached by a rope to the priests outside the Holy of Holies. If the unexpected happened, they could withdraw his corpse from within the sacred place without risking their own deaths.

It is easy to see why the Ark was a sacred object of mystery among the Israelites and to the Gentile nations that heard rumors of its destructive powers. It was these very rumors that compelled enemy powers to attack Jerusalem and attempt to pierce the veil and discover the great treasure of the Jews. With this aura of intrigue, it is also easy to understand why the Ark's disappearance from the pages of time so tempts men to search for it. Let's dig now into the cereal box of history to find yet another box—the Ark itself—and to unearth its secrets.

What Did the Ark Look Like?

The Ark itself was of simple construction, yet none of the ancient or rabbinic sources agree on its exact dimensions or design. What we can know is that the Ark was a rectangular box approximately four feet in length and two feet in height and width.[1] This design is indicated in the Hebrew word *'aron*, which means a "box" or "chest."[2] Our English word *ark* comes to us through the Latin *arca*, which likewise means "chest." While we do not make a distinction in English words for *ark,* the Hebrew language uses a different word for *Noah's* Ark (*tebah*).[3]

We can verify the general concept of this chest by comparing the use of the Hebrew word in the Bible with the cultures that had contact with the Israelites and Moses. In Genesis 50:26, for example, the word *'aron* is used for the wooden box or sarcophagus (coffin) in which Joseph was buried while in Egypt. Ancient Egyptian tombs have revealed varied types of chests, some of which are similar in appearance to the Ark of the Covenant. A cedarwood chest, complete with transport poles, was discovered in the tomb of Tutankhamen (1400 B.C.).[4] Because the Ark was made by craftsmen who had lived and worked their entire lives in Egypt, it is possible that the Ark's style was influenced by Egyptian design.[5]

The Ark was constructed with acacia wood, a tree native to the Sinai desert. This wood is so extremely durable that the Greek version of the Old Testament, the Septuagint (LXX), actually translates this word as "incorruptible" or "nondecay-ing" wood. Adding to the imperishable quality of this wood was a layer of gold applied for practical protection and religious symbolism. According to some, the wood was gilded (that is, overlaid like gold leaf).[6] Others say the Hebrew text indicates there were thin boxes of gold on both the inside and outside of the wood box, forming something like a "Chinese box."[7] Thus, the Ark may have been a three-layered box (a gold box, then a wooden box, then a gold box) (*see photo section*).

Above the Ark was a specially constructed slab of gold called the "mercy seat" (Hebrew *kapporet*, "covering"). This slab served as a flat lid for the box and fit into a rim or "crown" of gold that surrounded the top four corners of the outer box. This rim helped hold the lid in place. This was a necessary feature in case the Ark was jostled in transport and the lid accidentally fell off, exposing the contents of the Ark. That might have led to the death of all who looked into the Ark.

The golden lid was topped by two cherubim formed out of one solid piece of gold. As the Jewish commentator Rashi explains it, when the lid was made, apparently a large quantity of gold was poured out and beaten in the middle with a hammer or mallet to make the ends bulge upwards. The cherubim were then formed from these protruding extremities. Before we consider the design of these cherubim, however, we should understand what they were.

Angels and the Ark

What are cherubim? The Bible indicates they are a class of angels like the six-winged seraphim (Isaiah 6:2). There may be an allusion to them in Exodus 32:34, where God tells Moses that He will send His angel before Israel. The worldly portrayal of cherubs as "baby angels" or "cupids" (derived from Graeco-Roman mythology) is inaccurate, because cherubim always appear in Scripture as immensely powerful beings who attend the visible presence of God. They are depicted as composite creatures bearing the form of a winged animal in the lower torso and a human in the upper torso. In Ezekiel 1:6 we read of cherubim each having four faces and four wings. By contrast, the cherubim positioned on the Ark cover had only one face and two wings each.

Throughout the ancient Near East, cherubim are often portrayed as sphinxlike creatures. In Egypt the figure of the Sphinx is a lion-man, while in Babylon it is a bull-man. Some suggest the closest representation we have of the figures that were on the Ark are sphinxlike, ivory cherubim that once were part of King Ahab's palace in Samaria. To what degree these sphinxes depict the Ark's cherubim is difficult to decide. The sphinxes' features probably were influenced by local pagan mythology, while the angels on the Ark were true images of the heavenly reality. Our inability to identify what the cherubim looked like goes back to the time of Jesus, for Josephus, the first-century Jewish writer who recorded an eyewitness description of the Second Temple, said of the cherubim, "No one can tell what they were like."[8] The Talmud (*Yoma* 21a) explains this was because the Ark cherubim were one of five things missing from the Second Temple.[9]

Some rabbis have said that the best explanation for the inclusion of cherubim on the Ark and on the curtains of the Tabernacle and Temple (since such graven images are everywhere else forbidden) was that they served to instill and strengthen faith in the existence of angelic beings.[10] Throughout the Bible, angels are presented as divine messengers who minister first to Israel (God's people) and later to all believers (God's church). Indeed, the Bible states that when the Law was given to Moses on Mount Sinai, angels were present (Deuteronomy 33:2 [LXX]; cf. Acts 7:38). The New Testament also affirms that the Law was "ordained by angels" (Acts 7:53). Perhaps from this experience Moses gained a personal understanding of both the appearance and function of the cherubim.

This angelic function of messenger or intercessor may be inherent in the meaning of the word *cherub* (Hebrew, *keruv*).[11] If the Hebrew meaning is like the Akkadian word *karabu* ("to pray, bless"), then perhaps we are to understand that cherubim served as heavenly intercessors between God and His creation. In this way, the Israelites could be assured that angels were constantly watching over them, because the Ark moved with them everywhere they went.

The Hiding of the Holy

One function of cherubic intercession was to protect sinful man from the all-consuming presence of God's unapproachable glory (*see* 1 Timothy 6:16). In Exodus 33:20 we read that no one could behold God's face (His glory) and live. When God's glory was on top of Mount Sinai, no one, not even an animal, could approach or touch the mountain (Exodus 19:12-24; Hebrews 12:20). If this revelation of God high on a mountaintop could kill instantly, how much more was that likely if He took up residence in the very midst of the Israelite camp! Therefore, the cherubim have a "covering" function. They prevented God's glory from breaking forth upon men. These "covering cherubim" protected Israel while God's presence was manifested at the Ark in the sanctuary.

Later, in Ezekiel 10:4–11:22, we read that the cherubim departed from the Temple with the glory of the Lord. The rabbis believed this removal of the sanctuary's divine protection made it possible for the Babylonians to destroy the Temple in 586 B.C.

In the First Temple, Solomon had constructed two huge cherubim of olive wood that stood 10 cubits (15 feet) high and had a wingspan of 20 cubits (30 feet).[12] These great cherubim were made to cover (or overshadow) the Ark and its poles (1 Kings 8:7-8; 2 Chronicles 5:8). In contrast to the two solid gold cherubim on the Ark, these were overlaid with gold, stood on their feet, and looked out toward the entrance of the

Holy of Holies, which faced east. As larger types of the Ark's cherubim, they may have functioned symbolically in a similar protective manner as guardians of the Ark.

The Wings of Witness

The most important feature of the cherubim was their wings. As we will see, the wings were directly related to the revelation of God in the Tabernacle and Temple, and as such might be considered "wings of witness." Along with their guardianship role, the other primary function of these creatures was to provide a means by which God could "come down" in a theophany (divine appearance). In passages such as Psalm 18:10, God comes down to earth riding on a cherub, while in other texts the cherubim are suggested by such images as a "chariot" (1 Chronicles 28:18; Isaiah 66:15; Jeremiah 4:13), "clouds" (Exodus 19:9; Leviticus 16:2; cf. Exodus 16:10; 40:34; Psalm 104:3; Isaiah 19:1), and "wind" (Psalm 18:10; 104:3; cf. Deuteronomy 33:26; Psalm 68:34). Apparently such divine manifestations among men required the company of such angelic beings. In like manner, an angelic entourage bore testimony to the nature of the Messiah when they, with the glory of God, attended Jesus' birth (Luke 2:9-14).

In the book of Ezekiel, the wings of the cherubim who leave the Temple are in constant motion, moving in harmony with God's departing presence. By contrast, the cherubim who covered the mercy seat of the Ark are stationary; their wings are at rest. Why the difference? In the first instance, God's omnipresence was being indicated by motion; He can be anywhere He chooses at any time. In the case of the Ark, however, God's presence was localized. Perhaps this depicted His *abiding* in the midst of His people.[13]

Various accounts describe the cherubim wings as being raised above or level with their heads. Yet the word translated "upward," "on high," or "above" (Hebrew *lema'lah*) in Exodus 25:20 and 37:9 actually indicates the wings were spread *horizontally* near their heads rather than vertically above their heads (*see photo section*). [14]

A Throne and a Footstool

The outstretched wings on the cover of the Ark touched one another and apparently formed the seat of a celestial throne, while the Ark beneath served as its footstool. The Ark as God's footstool might have served as a "contact point" between heaven (the throne between the cherubim) and earth. If the Ark was a visible (or tangible) footstool for the invisible (or intangible) throne of God when He "descended" to earth, then we can understand the mobile character of the Ark. Wherever God's presence was to be temporally manifested—whether at Sinai, in the wilderness, in Israel, on the battlefield, or in a foreign land such as Philistia—the Ark had to be available for the Lord of heaven to "rest His feet" on earth. This idea is suggested by the various passages that picture the Lord of hosts as sitting enthroned *above* the cherubim (1 Samuel 4:4; 2 Samuel 6:2; 2 Kings 19:15; Psalm 80:1; 99:1; Isaiah 37:16); the parallels in King David's words, "The Ark of the covenant of the LORD and . . . the footstool of our God" (1 Chronicles 28:2); and Psalm 132:7-8: "Let us worship at His *footstool*. . . . Thou and the *ark* of Thy strength."

The throne and footstool concept is well attested by many contemporary texts and artifacts and especially by the religious art of Israel's closest neighbors, Syria and Palestine. [15] At Byblus, Hamath, and Megiddo archaeologists have found representations of a king seated on a throne and flanked by lion-man cherubim. [16] The cherubim of the Megiddo ivories also depict this imagery and are of particular interest because they reflect Phoenician craftsmanship such as was employed in building both the First and Second Temples (1 Kings 5; Ezra 3:7). This symbolism of the cherubim's design was to denote the divine status of the one enthroned, riding upon a heavenly chariot powered by angels (*see* 2 Samuel 22:11; Psalm 18:10).

(It is possible this symbolism may lie behind a future act of the Antichrist in the Temple, but let us reserve that for chapter 14.)

The cherubim represented a special place between heaven and earth where the glory of God could be manifested among men. During the days of the Tabernacle, this dwelling of the divine presence appeared over the cherubim as a cloud during the daylight hours and as a pillar of fire at night (Exodus 40:34-38). During the First Temple era, however, God's glory could not be seen; it was manifested only within the Holy of Holies. The Talmud (*Shabbat* 22b) tells us that burning lamps were used outside the veil to testify to the fact "that the *Shekinah* abides in the midst of Israel."

The Value of the Ark

Some have sought to make the Ark a priceless object based solely on its net worth in gold. But nowhere are we told how much gold was used to make the Ark. One rabbinic sage, based on a statement in Exodus 37:24, believed that only one talent (3,000 shekels) of gold was used for both the Ark and its cover.[17] If this were so, the gold used would equal about 20 pounds—certainly valuable, but not priceless. The real value of the Ark is in what it contains.

Inside the Ark

Remember the illustration of the cereal box? What made an ordinary box of cereal (especially one I didn't like) worth buying was the prize that might be hidden inside. While the Ark was basically an ordinary box, it's what was inside that counts.

The Ark contained sacred objects that demonstrated God's presence among the Israelites in the desert. These were to serve as witnesses to future generations of Israelites—witnesses of God's covenant with His people (*see* Hebrews 9:4).

Pagan shrines held images of their gods, but in the Ark no such images were present. Instead, there were objects representing God's activity among His people. These objects included the stone tablets on which were carved the Ten Commandments (Exodus 25:16), the entire Pentateuch written by Moses (Deuteronomy 31:24-26), the staff of Aaron the high priest that had miraculously budded and borne ripe almonds (Numbers 17:8-10), and a golden pot of the last trace of the heavenly manna that fed the Israelites during their 40-year sojourn in the desert (Exodus 16:32-35).[18] While all of these were present at one time or another inside, beside, or in front of the Ark, only the tablets of the Law and the Torah remained permanent fixtures (2 Chronicles 5:10).[19] It is the presence of these items that makes the Ark of supreme importance to the Jewish people. Rabbi Shlomo Goren, the former Ashkenazi Chief Rabbi of all Israel, explains:

> The Ark—the 'Aron Ha-brit—includes the Ten Commandments, [i.e.,] the broken and unbroken Tablets, and the entire scroll written by Moses. It includes every item that is important for the history of the Jews, and it is the highest stage of sanctity we can have.[20]

The tablets of the Law were probably two inscribed stone flakes not much larger than the size of a man's hand, while the Torah was written using ink on Egyptian papyrus.[21] Two rabbinic sages, Rabbi Meir and Rabbi Yehuda, debated whether these stones and the scroll were placed side by side within the Ark (Meir) or, if in the fortieth year of the desert sojourn, a shelf was attached to an exterior side of the Ark to hold the Torah scroll (Yehuda).[22]

Whatever the placement of these documents, if the Ark represented God's footstool, then we may be able to understand their position in relation to the Ark from a similar custom prevalent in other ancient Near Eastern cultures.[23] It was common in those days to put documents and agreements between rival kingdoms "at the feet" of their god in their sanctuary. This god acted as the guardian of treaties and supervised their implementation. Egyptian records tell us of a pact between Ramses II and Hattusilis III that was sealed by depositing the treaty at the feet of both the Hittite king's god Teshup and the pharaoh's god Ra. This custom may have been in the prophet Samuel's mind when he recorded the ordinances of the kingdom and set them "before the LORD" at the foot of the Ark (1 Samuel 10:25). Perhaps King Hezekiah was also acting in accordance with this custom when he "spread . . . out before the LORD" the threatening letter of the Assyrian Rabshakeh (Isaiah 37:14).

Testimonies of Judgment

The faces of the cherubim faced one another (as if in communion) and were inclined downward toward the mercy seat (Exodus 25:20; 37:9). As they looked continually at the objects within the Ark, they beheld items which reminded them of acts of rebellion against God. The broken tablets of the Ten Commandments (Exodus 32:19) were a witness to the great spiritual defection and breaking of the covenant by the people—a defection which almost cost them their existence as Abraham's seed (Exodus 32:10; Deuteronomy 9:14). The pot of manna recalled the violations committed against its gathering (Exodus 16:20) and the complaints against its provision (Numbers 11:6). The rod of Aaron was a visible reminder of the treasonous spirit that sought to replace God's appointed leadership (Numbers 16).

Each incident represented by these objects was followed by judgment. After the breaking of the tablets, 3,000 Israelites died at the hands of the Levites. After the complaint over the manna, a severe plague destroyed the greedy individuals among the tribes. When Korah and his company rebelled, an earthquake wiped out his family and supporters and a plague killed an additional 14,700 Israelites.

Because God knew that Israel would continue to sin (Deuteronomy 31:27-29), these objects—and particularly the Torah scroll—were deposited in the Ark as a legal declaration against Israel's future violations of the covenant (Deuteronomy 31:26). Therefore, when the cherubim looked down into the Ark, they saw the defiling sins of Israel which spoke of God's deserved judgment.

Testimonies of Grace

On the other hand, each of these objects also represented the grace of God. Along with the broken tablets was a second set of tablets indicating God's gracious will to continue in His covenant with Israel (Exodus 34:1-28). The pot of manna revealed God's loyal love in that He continued His constant care of the nation by giving her "daily bread" until everyone finally reached the Promised Land (Exodus 16:35; Joshua 5:12). Aaron's budded rod was graciously given to validate God's proper priesthood (Numbers 17:5; 18:6-9, 23) and to preserve the lives of those who would otherwise have perished for their complaints (Numbers 17:10). Finally, the book of the Law was present with the Ark to testify to every successive generation (Deuteronomy 4:9) that God had chosen the nation not because of anything she had done but because of His own sovereign love and gracious choice (Deuteronomy 7:6-9).

This testimony of grace that was connected with each object in the Ark assured Israel of the possibility of divine forgiveness, which ultimately was obtained on the Day of Atonement when the high priest sprinkled the blood of the guilt offering upon the mercy seat. The very word for "mercy seat" (*kapporet*, "covering") survives to this day in the Jewish holiday *Yom Kippur*, an annual day of atonement. As the blood covered the lid of the Ark, it symbolically covered the sin represented by the objects inside. Thus, when God looked down from between the cherubim, He saw only the expiatory blood. Though He sat on a throne of justice, it now became a throne of grace. The Ark, then, was theology in a box: It was an ever-present testimony of the eternal truth that God will be gracious to those who come to Him in His appointed way.

Understanding the Untouchable

Those who understood the theology of the Ark knew that God was a holy God and that they were unholy people. The Ark, which represented God's presence, was to be treated as holy, and no one was to look upon or touch it. Even the Levites who transported the Ark had to cover it with a cloth without touching it in the process. Many people are disturbed by these extreme regulations. Why couldn't people merely gaze at the Ark as did the Beth-shemeshites (1 Samuel 6:19) or touch it—even to keep it from falling—as did Uzzah (2 Samuel 6:6-7)?

Some have said the Ark was untouchable because it was an ancient battery charged with high voltage. Anyone who disturbed its energy flow would be electrocuted instantly. Henry Soltau, a scholar of the last century who wrote about the Temple vessels, believed that those who looked into the Ark were killed because the contents of the Ark were exposed, and inside were the tablets of the Law, which was "the ministration of death," and so would have brought "destruction to the thousands of Israel."[24]

Such conclusions, however, import a physical consequence to a spiritual reality—spiritual death based on the Law's demand for righteousness (see 2 Corinthians 3:6). The Law is "holy, and just, and good" (Romans 7:12 KJV), whereas we are unholy, unjust, and evil. It was God's unmet requirement (as codified in the Law) that brought death, not the tablets themselves (see Romans 2:12-16; 3:19-20; 5:13-14, 20; 7:7-11).

Death in connection with the Ark came not because of anything inherent or within the structure of the Ark but because touching or looking upon it was a trespass against God's holiness. One of the categories of serious sin in the Old Testament was "violation (Hebrew, *ma'al*) of the holy things" that were set apart exclusively to God, the sanctuary, or the priests (Leviticus 5:15). The explanation for this commandment is given in Leviticus 10:3: "It is what the LORD spoke, saying, 'By those who come near Me I will be treated as holy, and before all the people I will be honored.'"

The men of Beth-shemesh may well have been killed because they sought to dishonor God by their action of peering into the Ark. This is the insight offered by *Targum Jonathan on the Prophets*, in which two explanations are given in the interpretive reading of the biblical passage—one in the text and the other in the margin. The body text says that the men of Beth-shemesh "rejoiced that they had gazed upon the Ark of the Lord *when it was uncovered*." The margin text says that the men died "because *they rejoiced at Israel's misfortunes and despised the Ark* of the Lord when it was uncovered." The emphasis in the text is upon the blasphemous act of the men enjoying the sight of the "naked" Ark because beholding the Ark was akin to beholding God Himself. The emphasis in the margin text is upon the treasonous act of coveting the destruction of their fellow Jews—an act of derision because it mocked the power of the Ark, which was pledged to protect God's people. Both readings betray an ulterior motive to defame God's glory; thus, the men were worthy of divine punishment.

The Extent of Holiness

We must not assume that the Ark alone was to be regarded with honor as a physical representation of God's holiness. *All* the vessels within the Temple belonged in this category. For the priests to misappropriate any of these items, as Nadab and Abihu did (Leviticus 10:1-2), or for an unqualified person to use them was to invite certain death (Numbers 1:51; 3:10, 38; 18:7). Achan brought such judgment on himself when he confiscated some of the spoils of Jericho, which were under a ban (that is, they were considered sacred property [Joshua 7:15]). This also happened to the Levites of the house of Korah who sought to be priests (Numbers 16–18). Even good Judean kings, such as Uzziah, were not exempt. He was punished when he offered incense within the Temple (2 Chronicles 26:16-19). This kind of sin was considered the primary reason for the downfall of Judah and the destruction of the First Temple because "they defiled the house of the LORD which He had sanctified in Jerusalem" (2 Chronicles 36:14).

It may be difficult for us to understand how touching or even looking upon an object could be an act worthy of death. Our problem, in part, comes from living in an age in which *nothing* is considered sacred. Not only is there a lack of reverence for things associated with God, but such things are viewed with suspicion and are mocked and slandered. Such universal sin is a sign that the Holy One will soon come to judge this world. If God did not spare His own chosen people for such offense, why would He pardon a pagan populace?

Approaching God and the Ark

The Ark reminds us that the Holy One can be approached only in holiness. We cannot come to God as we are in ourselves any more than the common Israelite could trespass God's sanctity and live. We cannot come with professed religion alone; those who wore the priestly robes and violated God's laws died as well. We can come only if we are holy. God made such holiness possible for us through the sacrifice of Christ: "We have been sanctified through the offering of the body of Jesus Christ once for all" (Hebrews 10:10). Jesus as our holy Savior has made us acceptable to God by covering our sins with His blood, and has further qualified us to serve God as priests. Because of the holy work of Christ, those who have faith in Jesus are now considered holy to the Lord: "you are not your own, for you have been bought with a price: therefore glorify

God in your body" (1 Corinthians 6:19-20). In light of that,
Christians are commanded to not contaminate themselves
with unholy things (1 Corinthians 5:7-13; 6:9-18; 2 Corinthians 6:14–7:3; 1 Peter 1:14-16).

The Purpose of the Ark

The aim of the Ark was to manifest God on earth. This is
seen by the various terms used of the Ark, such as: "The ark of
the LORD, the LORD of all the earth" (Joshua 3:13); "The ark of
the God of Israel" (1 Samuel 5:7); and "The ark of the LORD
God" (1 Kings 2:26). God's dwelling with man was made
possible only on the basis of a covenant, which is reflected by
other names the Ark bore: "The ark of the testimony" (Exodus 25:22) and "The ark of the covenant" (Numbers 10:33;
Judges 20:27). Because the Law forbade the making of images
of God, the next best thing would be an object that represented
God's character. While the glory-cloud (called in later Jewish
literature the *Shekinah*) for a time confirmed God's presence,
the tablets of the Law within the Ark were, for all time, a
revelation of God through His Word. Conservative scholars
have made this point well:

> What would have been better adapted to make
> the presence of God felt as a reality than the stone
> tablets with the Ten Words, through which the Lord
> had made known to His people His ethical charac-
> ter? For the words on these tablets were a kind of
> spiritual portrait of the God of Israel, who could not
> be pictured in bodily form, but whose living, holy
> presence was a vital element in His people's daily
> life.[25]

Perhaps for this reason the tablets were repeatedly said to
have been "written by the finger of God" (Exodus 31:18;
32:15-16; 34:1, 28; Deuteronomy 9:10). More than any other

communication from God to men, the tablets were direct evidence of God and of His relationship to Israel.

The Activities of the Ark

The Ark performed a number of functions at the same time.[26] These activities were primarily related to God's people, but also to others who associated with Israel. In 1 Samuel 6:10–7:2 this association is negative, as those at war with Israel capture the Ark and suffer its destructive power. But in 1 Kings 8:41-43 this association is positive, as those outside of Israel pray toward the Temple, which houses the Ark. This is important to observe, because if the Ark has a prophetic destiny, it will take place first with respect to the Jewish people, and eventually will include Gentiles as well. What are some of these functions of the Ark that have made it the mystery of the ages?

A Passageway of Power

First, the Ark served as a channel of God's power among His people. In this sense the Ark was a passageway of divine power, because it served as an extension of God wherever it went. We see this demonstrated when the Ark was brought to the Jordan River, where the waters immediately parted so the Israelites could cross (Joshua 3:8–4:11). God used this incident to show He was with this new generation of Jews just as He had been with their fathers at the crossing of the Red Sea. We see this again at Jericho when the Ark led the way in the supernatural destruction of that city (Joshua 6:6-21). Likewise, whenever the Ark was brought onto a battlefield, both Israel and her enemies attributed the outcome of the battle to the Ark (Numbers 14:44-45; 1 Samuel 4:8, 17-22; 5:2-12; 2 Samuel 11:11). God's power as mediated through the Ark could be either for cursing or for blessing. When the Ark was treated without regard to God's specific commandments, those involved were cursed—for example, the men of Beth-shemesh or Uzzah—and instant death resulted. On the other hand, when people like Abinadab (1 Samuel 7:1-2) and Obed-edom (2 Samuel 6:11-12) properly cared for the Ark at their homes, the result was blessing.

A Gateway to God

Just as the Ark channeled God's power, so it also revealed His will. A veritable "gateway to God," the Ark was a means by which divine guidance was given to men. In Exodus 25:22, God told Moses that He would meet with him at the Ark and speak to him there. Numbers 7:89 also depicts Moses coming to the Ark and hearing the voice of God speaking from between the cherubim. For this reason, some have called the Ark a "divination or oracle box."[27]

It has been suggested that the high priest, with his ephod, his breastplate, and the Urim and Thummim, was able to receive divine communication from God by approaching the Ark.[28] It is also possible that when the tribal leaders and Levites assembled before Joshua and Eleazar the high priest at Shiloh for a divine decision, it was because the Ark was stationed there (Joshua 21:1-2). In the days of the judges the Ark was apparently used for this purpose, because Judges 20:27 notes that "the sons of Israel inquired of the LORD (for the ark of the covenant of God was there [at Bethel] in those days . . .)." In addition, the boy Samuel, sleeping near the Ark, was summoned and spoken to by God (1 Samuel 3:3-21).

The Greatest Treasure of All

When we at last get to the bottom of this box we call the Ark, we have really discovered the greatest treasure of all—God. Imagine, God in a box! In saying this, it's important to point out that God was *never* contained or boxed in by the Ark. King Solomon made this clear in 1 Kings 8:27 when he acknowledged: "Will God indeed dwell on the earth? Behold, heaven and the highest heaven cannot contain Thee, how much less this house which I have built!" Solomon was quite aware that when his prayers were directed to the Ark, God would hear in His dwelling place in heaven (1 Kings 8:30). The Ark was merely a means of *manifesting* God's presence on earth, for God in His omnipresence fills both heaven and earth (Isaiah 66:1) and remains in His heavenly Temple (Psalm 11:4; 20:6).

I trust that you have found the Ark to be a worthwhile prize. It is bigger than most of us dream, and it has a great store of additional surprises packed away inside!

4

The Hinge of History

We are simply passing through history. This—this is history![1]

—Belloq to Indiana Jones in
Raiders of the Lost Ark

In the preface I referred to the Ark as a possible hinge for future history. This is rather likely in light of the biblical record. Many times the Ark is revealed as a pivotal instrument in the transition to new chapters in God's sovereign plan. A survey of biblical events connected with the Ark can be found in any work on Old Testament history. Let's concentrate on those texts in which the Ark plays a dominant role and seek to discern how history turns upon these events. As you read, keep in mind that the history of the Ark parallels the history of Israel, who was called to be a light to the nations. What light does the Ark shed on this history as it journeyed through time with the people of God?

The Ark at the Exodus

The history of the Ark begins during the period known as the exodus. During this era the descendants of Abraham forsook their status as seminomadic and servile clans to assume their predestined place as a nation (Genesis 12:2). The Ark, a symbol of Israel's unique covenantal relationship with God (2 Chronicles 6:11), took on its significance right from the beginning of Israel's identity as a nation. This was demonstrated in two ways: First, the Ark bore the constitution of Israel's favored-nation status, which we find recorded in Amos 3:2: "You only have I chosen among all the families of the earth." Second, through the Ark God showed that He was willing to share Israel's wilderness experience and to be their companion through the journey to the Promised Land (Deuteronomy 4:7; 32:10-12; Joshua 1:5).

The Ark was first revealed to Moses on Mount Sinai (Exodus 25:8-22). It was to be the first and preeminent piece of the Tabernacle's furniture. Through it alone God was to meet with Moses and manifest His sovereign plan. So as Israel was formed into a new national entity and moved forward to fulfill its purpose as the people of God, the Ark went with them as a sign and seal of God's power to perform His promise.

The Ark and the Conquest

As the exodus concluded, the conquest began. Constituted as a nation at Sinai, now the people would begin to function as a nation once they acquired the land God had given to Abraham. In the battle to possess the land the Ark was at the forefront, assuring these untrained warriors that God would go before them and conquer their enemies.

As the Ark traveled and camped with the Israelites, its usual position was in the middle of the assembled tribes (Numbers 2:17; 10:14-28). This was to remind Israel that God was fulfilling His promise to dwell in their midst. But this may have also caused the Israelites to assume that they were somehow protecting the Ark by encompassing it on every side. Any such thought would be dramatically reversed at the entrance to the Holy Land. In Joshua 3:3-4 we are told that before the crossing of the Jordan River, the Ark was repositioned at the head of the tribes and all Israel was commanded to follow the Ark. The reason given is so "that you may know the way by which you shall go, for you have not passed this way before" (verse 4).

Thus, the Ark provided both divine guidance and powerful protection for the Israelites. It also served as a focus for their faith in an unknown and untried place. In this way the nation was taught that it was not Israel who protected the Ark, but the Ark that protected Israel. God was not to be in the background of their lives, but at the forefront—the One who must be followed by faith when passing through the deep waters of life.

To confirm this truth, the Ark divided the waters of the Jordan just as God had parted the Red Sea at the crossing of these Israelites' ancestors (Joshua 3:14-17; cf. Exodus 14:21-22). Notice that the waters were stopped as far as 15 miles upstream (verses 15-16). This happened during flood season when the Jordan was overflowing its banks. For the waters to part as they did was indeed a miracle comparable to that performed at the exodus.

The Ark led the way before the Israelite army at Jericho. As the presence of the God of all creation was announced by the seventh trumpet blast on the seven trumpets on the seventh day, the walls of the city came down (Joshua 6:4-20). Through this encounter and others to come, the people learned that to fight without the Ark of God meant sure defeat, a lesson unlearned by their faithless forefathers (Numbers 14:44-45). After learning a similar lesson of obedience at Ai (Joshua 7:1–8:29), the nation renewed its loyalty to the Mosaic covenant at Joshua's altar on Mount Ebal and the Ark was placed in the valley between the tribes divided on the twin mountains of Ebal and Gerizim (Joshua 8:30-35).

It may be no coincidence that the Ark appeared in history at Israel's first entrance into the land as a nation and disappeared at its first exit as a nation. In the first event it was accompanied by Israel's faith, and thus the nation conquered. In the last event Israel had lost its faith, and thus the nation was conquered. The hinge of history truly swung upon the Ark.

The Ark and the Judges

The next major turning point in Israel's history was during the distressing days of the judges, when "everyone did what was right in his own eyes" (Judges 21:25). The movement in this case was from a theocracy—in which God ruled the nation directly through His spiritual representatives—to a monarchy—in which God ruled indirectly through a political representative, the king. The Ark again had a major role in a period of transition.

First Samuel 6–7 describes the capture of the Ark, a tragedy brought about by the nation's misplaced faith. God is a jealous God (Deuteronomy 6:15) and will tolerate no rivals—even when it involves His own Ark, which had been transformed into a magic talisman by a desperate people (1 Samuel 4:3). God had called Israel to be a light to the Gentile nations that surrounded her. This witness was intended to affirm God's superiority and sovereignty, but was effective only as long as the people lived in holiness and obedience to God's laws.

In 1 Samuel 2–3 the loss of the Ark coincides with the loss of holiness and obedience on the part of God's servants. The capture of the Ark is preceded by the capture of the hearts of the high priest and his priestly sons to overindulgence, apathy, unbridled lust, and spiritual rebellion. Furthermore, we are told in this account that "word from the LORD was rare in those days" (3:1). The theocracy had failed because God's rule was not evident in His own priests, who were to rule over His nation. God therefore rejected the high priest Eli's family line with the famous admonition: "For those who honor Me I will honor, and those who despise Me will be lightly esteemed" (2:30). Because Israel could not follow Eli's worthless sons, they rebelled against God's direct rule and asked for a king like the other nations (1 Samuel 8:3-5).

The Ark, which had been turned into a sort of charm, could not fulfill its calling to demonstrate God's sovereignty through such people. Therefore, to show Israel it was abandoning God (1 Samuel 8:7) and to carry on the mission of witness before the nations, the Lord permitted the Ark to be captured by the Philistines. On Israel's side, the departure of the Ark is paralleled by the departure of Eli, as news of its loss leads to his death (4:18). There seems to be a literary connection between Eli's fall from his chair (1 Samuel 1:9; 4:13, 18) and the fall of God's throne (the cherubim with the Ark) to the enemy. It was not God who had left His people, but His people who had left Him. This drama of departure is put in full relief as Eli's daughter-in-law, distressed at her family deaths and the Ark's capture, gives birth prematurely and in testimony to their plight, names the child "Ichabod," which means "The glory [the Ark] has departed from Israel" (4:19-21).

On the Philistine side, the arrival of the Ark was the arrival of defeat. When the Ark was placed in the Philistine temples as a sign of conquest by their gods, instead the Ark ended up conquering their gods by making them fall over. Thus the Philistines learned what they had previously voiced: that no god could stand before the Ark (4:8; 5:1-5). In addition, these enemies of God could not escape the plagues that befell them in every city to which the Ark was brought (5:6-12). This identified their punishment with that of the Egyptians, who had likewise defied God and His people Israel.

When the Ark was returned to Israel for the beginning of the monarchy, it was sent by a now-fearful adversary who acknowledged the Ark as a testimony of the sovereignty of Israel's God (6:1-3, 7-12). The Ark was returned with gifts of appeasement to Israel (6:8, 15-18), who unfortunately had not yet learned the lessons its enemies had painfully mastered. As soon as the Ark reached the border of Israel at Beth-shemesh, a number of the men in that city lined up to take turns peering into it.[2] As a result all these men died and great fear fell on Israel, whose cry echoed that of the Philistines: "Who is able to stand before the LORD, this holy God? And to whom shall He go up from us?" (6:20). Rather than repent and draw near to God, the people wanted to put God as far away from them as possible. This attitude toward the Ark eventually came to be shared by the first king of Israel as well.

The Ark and the Monarchy

King Saul

Saul was made the first king of Israel after the nation had rejected God's kingship. The people applied worldly standards and selected him because he stood taller and looked more handsome than anyone else (1 Samuel 9:2; contrast this with the spiritual standard used to choose David, 1 Samuel 16:7). Saul, from the beginning of the monarchy, reveals the vast difference between the rule of man and the rule of God. During his entire reign, there is but one recorded instance where he resorts to the Ark (1 Samuel 14:18). Yet even here, the Greek translation of the Old Testament substitutes the term "ephod" for "Ark" in this passage, so there is some uncertainty as to whether Saul actually called for the Ark at all. However, 1 Chronicles 13:3 sheds light on Saul's relation to the Ark when it reports this testimony from the leaders of Israel: "Let us bring back the ark of our God to us, *for we did not seek it in the days of Saul*" (emphasis added).

King David

David's heart was in tune with God's (1 Samuel 13:14). After the conquest of Jerusalem, his thoughts immediately turned to the Ark. His desire was to build a Temple that, like the Tabernacle, would be designed for the sole purpose of housing the Ark. It appears that his spiritual insight concerning the need for a permanent home for the Ark was drawn from deep meditation on Scripture and his experiences (*see* Psalm 132). Interestingly, this insight and desire to house the Ark was lost for a time when David lapsed into sin with Bathsheba (2 Samuel 11). On that occasion, God used Bathsheba's husband to show David his decline. Although the king of Israel attempted to cover his adultery by getting Uriah to sleep with his wife, this Gentile declared that he would not go up to his house while the Ark remained in a tent (2 Samuel 11:11).

At Kiriath-jearim, where the Ark had been brought after the disaster at Beth-shemesh, it was properly attended by a qualified priest, Abinadab, and his three sons, Eleazer, Uzzah, and Ahio. The transportation of the Ark from Kiriath-jearim to Jerusalem in the same manner as it had been brought by the Philistines (on an oxcart) was not according to God's specific instruction to the Levites (1 Chronicles 15:15). Only the Kohathites were to transport the Ark, and they were to do so by placing its poles on their shoulders (Exodus 25:14-15; Numbers 3:30-31; 4:15; 7:9). Whether David understood this is uncertain, but ultimately this violation led to the death of Uzzah.

It is possible that God allowed this delay in the transfer of the Ark to teach Israel that the final decision regarding its location was with God and not with man.[3] Even David could not dictate the movement of the Ark; if it came to Jerusalem, it would not be by the king's whim but by God's will. After the death of Uzzah, David left the Ark in the charge of a Philistine named Obed-edom (2 Samuel 6:10). Again, a Gentile was used to teach the king of Israel a lesson. The fact that it did not destroy his house was confirmation to David that the direction toward Jerusalem was the direction of blessing (2 Samuel 6:11-12).

Israel's change from a self-centered administration (Saul's) to a spiritual administration (David's) is illustrated by David's personally donning the priestly ephod and escorting the Ark to Jerusalem in joyous celebration (2 Samuel 6:14; cf. 1 Samuel 2:18). When Saul sought to take the place of the priest, the

Lord removed the kingdom from him (1 Samuel 13:8-14). But when David took the priest's role, God promised to establish his kingdom forever (2 Samuel 7:16). The difference may be observed in their hearts. Saul explained that he forced himself to act (1 Samuel 13:12), whereas David did it willingly, even at the cost of being misunderstood and maligned (2 Samuel 6:20-21; 1 Chronicles 15:29). Saul had no concern for proper procedure or for God's commandments (1 Samuel 13:13), but David was careful to obey the law of the Ark (1 Chronicles 15:2, 12-15) and to do what he did "before the LORD" (2 Samuel 6:21; cf. 1 Chronicles 16:29). Further, Saul had *usurped* the priestly prerogative, but David had *joined* with the priest (1 Chronicles 15:25-27).

Scholars have found in documents from the ancient Near East a possible explanation for the contrast between the actions of Saul and David concerning the Ark. In the royal inscriptions of Mesopotamia, the legitimate king of Israel is portrayed as the restorer of the forgotten "cult." This is consistent with David's vow to not rest until the Ark was restored to prominence (Psalm 132). Because Psalm 132 portrays the Ark's procession into Jerusalem and it cites 2 Chronicles 6:41-42 (which mentions the Ark's installation in the Temple and David's faithfulness), there may be some biblical support for the Mesopotamian inscription. The Ark was central to the recognition and establishment of a king after God's own heart.

For this reason, David's bringing of the Ark to Jerusalem is viewed as a climactic new exodus. The captivity of the Ark in Philistia paralleled the captivity of Israel in Egypt; the miraculous actions of the Ark among the Philistines paralleled God's miracles in Egypt; and finally, the Ark's entrance into Jerusalem as "the promised place" (2 Samuel 7:10; 1 Chronicles 17:9) paralleled Israel's entrance into Canaan, the Promised Land. Notice that when David fled Jerusalem after Absalom's usurption of the throne, he refused to allow the Ark to be removed from the city and thereby diminish its status as a holy place.

King Solomon

Solomon's construction of the Temple and the Ark's placement within it marked a new beginning in the relationship between God and His people. The dedication of the Temple by Solomon was the high point of his spiritual career and a major transition in Israel's history. For the first time, the nation was at peace on every side. The kingdoms of Israel and Judah were consolidated and unified with Jerusalem as their capital. And the Ark had ceased its wanderings among the tribes to take its home in the Temple (2 Samuel 7:6; Psalm 132:13-14).[4] To connect the Temple with the Tabernacle and provide a continuity from the days of the exodus to Solomon's day, God's glory returned to take its place between the wings of the cherubim (1 Kings 8:10-11; 2 Chronicles 5:13-14; 7:1-3).

Once the Ark was brought into the Temple it was to remain there and all prayer was to be directed toward it from every place on earth (1 Kings 8:30, 41-43; 2 Chronicles 6:20). This explains the absence of the Ark in Israeli military engagements after the time of Solomon.[5] No longer would the Ark go to the battlefield; instead, the soldiers on the battlefield were to pray toward the Ark (1 Kings 8:44-45). If they were suffering defeat, they knew it was because of sin, and they would then come to the Ark with their penitent supplications (2 Chronicles 6:24-25). At long last, the Ark, like the nation, seemed to experience a time of rest during the days of Solomon and for a short time thereafter. But things were about to change.

The Ark and the Apostasy

Israel's last major turn upon the hinge of the Ark comes during the great civil war that divided the kingdom between the north (Israel) and the south (Judah). King Solomon's compromise with the religions of his foreign wives started the nation on this path of spiritual defection and decline (1 Kings 11:1-28). The prophet Ahijah predicted that Solomon's sin had set in motion a process that would ultimately tear the kingdom in two (1 Kings 11:29-35). When Israel did secede from Judah, it compromised or limited the northern kingdom's access to the Lord's presence at the Ark in Jerusalem, which was located in the southern kingdom (1 Kings 12:27).

To satisfy Israel's need for a sanctuary, Jeroboam constructed alternate worship sites at Dan and Bethel, which were located at the northern and southern borders of the new kingdom (1 Kings 12:28-29). Jeroboam also substituted a rival to the Ark at each of his new religious centers. He reasoned that because the Ark had come from Sinai, a place associated with the covenant and Israelite origins, he needed to use another religious symbol from this site. Therefore he chose the golden calf (1 Kings 12:28), which had been made by the high priest Aaron and which Aaron had associated with the worship of the true God (Exodus 32:1-6). This was a smart move; to the uninformed Israelite, this symbol had the authority of the Aaronic priesthood and was part of the exodus tradition. When the calves were dedicated, Jeroboam even used the same injunction that Aaron had pronounced (1 Kings 12:28b; cf. Exodus 32:4).

While by this action the northern kingdom obtained access to a historical sanctuary, it also inherited the history of corruption and judgment that was part and parcel to it (*see* Exodus 32:8-10). At Sinai the people needed Moses to intercede and save them from annihilation (Exodus 32:11-35). This time, however, there was no way to appease God's wrath, for that was possible only through legitimate priests officiating at the Ark (Leviticus 16:29-34). It wasn't long before the Assyrians exiled the Israelites, leaving only the southern kingdom of Judah and the Ark.

After the demise of the north, apostasy returned to Judah to inflict a greater desecration than Israel had ever known. The apex of this apostasy came with the reign of King Manasseh, who renovated the Israelite sanctuary according to a pagan design. Apparently this was done by removing all the temple vessels and replacing them with pagan idols, referred to in the biblical text as "the abominations of the nations" (2 Kings 21:2; 2 Chronicles 33:2). The text implies that in place of the Ark he put an image of the Canaanite fertility goddess Asherah (2 Kings 21:7; 2 Chronicles 33:7). If this were so, then it is theorized that he must have destroyed the Ark,[6] but, as we will see in the next chapter, this is improbable. Despite Manasseh's replacement of the Ark, we find it still in existence when we come to the time of Manasseh's grandson, Josiah (2 Chronicles 35:3).

The Ark's Last Appearance

Josiah was a godly king who sought to make spiritual and political reforms based on the Bible. He began by renovating and purifying the Temple that Manasseh had desecrated (2 Chronicles 34:8-33). As part of this necessary reform, he ordered the Ark returned to the Temple by the faithful Levites, whose job was to transport it whenever it had to be moved (2 Chronicles 35:3). This verse records the last mention of the Ark in the Old Testament; there is nothing but silence concerning its location from this point onward. Later events in Judah may or may not have included the Ark. Eventually the monarchy came to an end and the sin of Manasseh was blamed for Judah's fall and the loss of the Temple and all that it contained.

The Ark on the Arch?

After the exile, a Jewish remnant returned to Judah and rebuilt the Temple. The testimony of the Bible and Jewish historical and rabbinic sources are united, however, in affirming that the Ark was *not* present in the Holy of Holies in the Second Temple. Some have thought that the Romans, who burned the Temple in A.D. 70 and took many of the Temple vessels, might also have taken the Ark. This is supposed by some to have been either a remade Ark or the original Ark, which had been preserved somewhere in hiding within the Temple. The confusion over which Temple treasures were taken by the Romans is reflected in the writings of German historian Ferdinand Gregorovius, renowned for his history of the Roman empire in the Middle Ages. In 1853 he wrote a poem entitled "Lament of the Children of Israel in Rome" and published a treatise called "The Ghetto and the Jews of Rome." In both this poem and treatise he declared that the Ark appears in relief on the Arch of Triumph in Rome. This arch depicts the Roman emperor Titus' triumphal procession through the streets of Rome with the spoils of the Jewish Temple after its destruction in A.D. 70. In his treatise Gregorovius states:

> In the passageway of the Arch, through which no Jew will pass, the holy vessels of the Temple at Jerusalem which were carried in Titus' triumphal procession are to be distinguished: the seven-branched candelabrum, the golden table of the shewbread, the Ark in which the Law was kept, and the silver trumpets of the jubilee.[7]

Because Gregorovius included the table of showbread in his list, it is difficult to understand why he would also include the Ark. There is only one object on the relief that might be mistaken for the Ark, and that is the table of showbread. There are simply not enough objects in the picture to accommodate his list! He exemplifies those who mistakenly believe the Ark is pictured on the Arch. In the final analysis, Rome came and conquered, but it did not capture the Ark.

The history of the Temple ended with no return of the Ark. Even so, the disappearance of the Ark in the biblical text is a hinge upon which the rest of history turns, for the search for the Ark has been a continuing historical pursuit ever since.

5

What Happened to the Ark?

There is no report that the Ark was carried away or destroyed or hidden. There is not even any comment such as, "And then the Ark disappeared and we do not know what happened to it" or, "And no one knows where it is to this day." The most important object in the world, in the biblical view, simply ceases to be in the story.[1]

—Richard Elliot Friedman

Silence is golden," so the poets say. But for those who wonder about the golden Ark, silence is galling. How could Israel's greatest treasure—the center of its national worship, the very reason for the Temple's existence, and above all, the place of God's presence—simply vanish in time without a trace? According to Hebrew University professor Menahem Haran, "its disappearance is one of the enigmas in the history of the First Temple."[2] How could the Jews in the Bible who so revered the Ark leave no record of their lament over its loss or expectation of its recovery? It is important that we answer this question before we consider any future reappearance of the Ark. The reason for this has been stated by Terence Fretheim:

It has long been recognized that the ark virtually disappears from historical sources after Solomon places it in the temple (1 Kings 8). This has led some scholars to adopt an agnostic attitude toward any subsequent use to which the ark may have been put.[3]

If the future of the Ark is in doubt because of its past, then it is necessary for us to consider its disappearance more carefully. In this chapter we will attempt to read between the lines of history and Scripture to determine whether the Bible really is as silent as it has been assumed. Then as we weigh the available evidence, perhaps we will be able to move closer to answering the age-old question, What happened to the Ark?

Initial Considerations

Historians and archaeologists generally assume that the story of the Ark came to an end sometime during the period of the monarchy, since there is no mention of it thereafter. There *is* one statement from a record composed after the exile that implies the Ark was present "to this day" (2 Chronicles 5:9), but the meaning of "to this day" has been debated. The Gemara in *Yoma* 53b, commenting on Mishnah *Yoma* 5:2, said that Rabbi Eliezer and Rabbi Simeon ben Yohai disputed with Rabbi Judah ben Il'ai about the fate of the Ark. The former contended that the Ark had gone into exile in Babylon (citing 2 Chronicles 36:10; Isaiah 39:6; Lamentations 1:6). The latter held that the Ark was buried in its own place (citing 1 Kings 8:8). Rabbi Judah defended his position by using the phrase in 1 Kings 8:8 "they are there to this day" to mean "forever." The other rabbis disproved this interpretation of the phrase and thus won the argument.

The statement in 2 Chronicles 5:9, which is in agreement with the "winning" rabbis, most likely refers to an earlier time when the Temple was standing (a hundred years before). Apparently it was taken from the parallel passage in 1 Kings

8:8, which Rabbi Judah had used in his argument. "To this day" means "the day of the Temple."

As the above dispute reveals, there are a number of historical proposals for what happened to the Ark. Let us consider several of these explanations.

Theories About the Ark's Fate

The Attack by Pharaoh Shishak

Shortly after the death of Solomon and the division of the nation under his son Rehoboam (about 926 B.C.), the weakened southern kingdom of Judah was invaded by the Egyptian pharaoh Sheshonk I (Shishak). The biblical text states quite clearly that he "came up against Jerusalem" and that he "took away the treasures of the house of the LORD" (1 Kings 14:25-26).

At the Temple of Karnak in Luxor, Egypt, Shishak's own account of his triumph is recorded. There we learn that he presented the spoils of his Palestinian campaign as a dedicatory offering to his patron god, Amun. In addition, when Shishak's tomb was discovered in Tanis in 1939, both his sarcophagus and mummy were found lavishly adorned with gold. Perhaps the source of some of this gold may be attributed to Solomon's Temple, since the pharaoh's plunder from there included 500 shields of beaten gold (1 Kings 10:16-17). Some scholars have thought that Shishak's gold provides evidence that the Ark was taken, presented to Amun, and then melted down to be recast for royal use. This theory received popular exposure when Steven Spielberg adopted it to explain the Ark's location in the first Indiana Jones film.

There are significant difficulties with this theory. First, if Shishak did raid Jerusalem, it is clear that he did not enter the Temple's outer division, the Holy Place, much less the inner division, the Holy of Holies. However, there is no data from the Bible or extrabiblical texts that he entered Jerusalem at all! Shishak's own record of the 156 cities he captured did not mention Jerusalem. The statements in 1 Kings 14:25-26 that he "came against Jerusalem" and "took away [from] the house of the LORD" may only mean that he exacted tribute from the city.[4] The Judean king Jeroboam would have willingly paid Shishak, since he owed the Pharaoh a debt for granting him political asylum when Solomon had sought to assassinate him (1 Kings 11:34-35, 40).

Second, what was given in tribute was "the treasures of the house of the LORD and the treasures of the king's house" (1 Kings 14:26). These items were stored in the Temple treasury outside the Temple proper, in a part of the palace complex called the House of Lebanon (1 Kings 7:1-12; 10:17). Based on the repeated association of the "treasuries" with "the king's house" in the Bible, we may assume that these storehouses were similar in nature. Since the text does not list any of the specific vessels that were taken, it is most probable that Shishak's spoil consisted only of nonritual objects or of vessels not in present use in the Temple service. First Kings 7:51 tells us that in these treasuries were also kept the spoils of war taken from defeated enemies (*see* 2 Samuel 8:7-12). While this "treasure" was certainly valuable and was dedicated to the Lord, it did not at all compare with the sanctity of the Temple vessels and the Ark.

Third, if Shishak had taken *all* the Temple treasures, then why do we see the Altar of Incense, the Menorah, and the Table of Showbread still in use in the Temple shortly after the invasion (*see* 2 Chronicles 13:11)? There is little possibility that these could have been newly constructed; the only items expressly said to have been remade are the shields (this time made of brass—1 Kings 14:27). Because the Ark cannot be remade, it could not reappear later in the text had it been taken by Shishak; yet as late as the time of Josiah, we read that it is still in existence (2 Chronicles 35:3).

For similar reasons, we may reject the theory that the Ark was taken by King Jehoash of Israel in his battle against Judah in 785 B.C. (2 Kings 14:14) or by King Hezekiah of Judah in 729 B.C. as tribute payment to the Assyrians (2 Kings 18:15-16). The purpose of Jehoash's invasion was not to capture the Temple treasure but to teach a lesson to Amaziah, king of Judah (2 Chronicles 25:17-24). While he did take "gold and silver, and all the utensils" from "the house of God," he got them not from the Temple proper but from "the house of Obed-edom," whose family served as gatekeepers (verse 24; cf. 1 Chronicles 26:4-8).

As for Hezekiah, the text makes it clear that the king went "before the LORD . . . enthroned above the cherubim" (that is, to the Temple in which the Ark was housed) to pray for Jerusalem's deliverance from the Assyrian siege (2 Kings 19:14-15). However, it was not possible for a king to enter the Holy of Holies, and certainly not possible for him to snatch the Ark. For instance, when King Uzziah (Hezekiah's great-grandfather) had entered merely the *outer* division of the Temple to burn incense on the Golden Altar, he was struck with leprosy till his death (2 Chronicles 26:16-21).

The Desecration by King Manasseh

Another theory for the Ark's disappearance is that it was removed by the evil Judean king Manasseh when he desecrated the Temple and turned it into a center for pagan shrines (2 Kings 21:7; 2 Chronicles 33:7). Previous kings had placed idols outside the city (1 Kings 11:7; 15:13; 16:32-33) and others had put them inside the city, but always outside the Temple precinct itself (2 Kings 11:18). Manasseh performed the ultimate act of desecration by placing his idols "in the two courts of the house of the LORD" (2 Kings 21:4-5) and even within the house of God itself (verse 7). Some scholars believe that he went so far as to place an image within the Holy of Holies because verse 7 adds the phrase "[the place where] I will put My name forever." The text, however, does not state that this refers specifically to the Holy of Holies but only to "this house" and "Jerusalem."

Menachem Haran is one of those who believe the image of Asherah must have been in the Holy of Holies. He bases his argument on the way pagan worship shrines were arranged in the ancient Near East. Since Manasseh had already placed vessels for Ba'al and Asherah in the outer division of the Temple, the appropriate place for the image of the goddess was within the inner division. Fifty years later, when Josiah removes this image as part of his reforms, the biblical record indicates that the Ark had not been in the Holy of Holies (2 Kings 23:6; 2 Chronicles 35:3). Haran therefore assumes that Manasseh must have destroyed the Ark and other Temple vessels in order to set up images of the goddess and her attendants. While the evidence to the contrary is not as impressive as that against the previous theories we examined, there are some problems that must be considered.

While the biblical text does not say that Manasseh violated the Holy of Holies, it is still possible that he did so. Regardless of whether or not he entered the innermost sanctuary, his act of desecration introduced the first time in history that the Temple ceased to function. For all practical purposes, the function of the Ark was removed, if not the Ark itself. The text does *not* say, however, that Manasseh destroyed any of the Temple vessels; it only tells us that he put others in their place. Manasseh was not attempting to remove God from the Temple but to incorporate Canaanite religion into the traditional religion.

What Manasseh was doing is called *syncretism*—the merging or substitution of the elements of another religion with the original. This is what Jeroboam did when he installed the golden calves at Dan and Bethel. He claimed that he was still true to the Israelite God and that he was merely using different symbols for Him.

Later on in life, Manasseh repented of his ways and brought about reform (2 Chronicles 33:11-16). His return to the Lord came after being captured and tortured by the Babylonians (verse 11). When Manasseh cried out to God in distress, he was released and restored to his throne: "Then Manasseh knew that the LORD was God" (verse 13). Perhaps this can provide some clues about his former conduct with the Temple vessels.

Manasseh's return to the true faith meant he had to dispose of false religion, so he had his idols and cultic implements removed from the Temple and thrown outside the city (verse 15). Notice that Manasseh did not destroy them; he only moved them outside of the city, as was the norm for previous kings who had set up pagan worship centers. That Manasseh did not destroy his own idols is evident from the fact that his son and heir, Amon, restored false worship and "sacrificed to all the carved images which his father Manasseh had made" (2 Chronicles 33:22).

The point is this: If a repentant Manasseh could not destroy his pagan idols, why would we expect him to have destroyed the most sacred and important item in all of Israel, the Ark? I believe Manasseh could not have removed or destroyed the Ark because it had already been put beyond his reach by the Levites. That is implied in 2 Chronicles 35:3, which tells us the priests later returned the Ark to the Temple, which had been purified.

The Babylonian Invasion

The destruction theory commonly accepted by scholars is that the Ark met its end during the Babylonian invasion of Jerusalem between 605–586 B.C. There are two variations of this theory. Some suppose that the Ark was removed along with other Temple vessels when the Babylonians looted the Temple treasuries and carried these items back home (2 Kings 24:13; 25:13-17; 2 Chronicles 36:18; Lamentations 1:10). Others suspect that the Ark was either destroyed with the Temple (2 Chronicles 36:19) or destroyed in Babylon after being stripped of its gold covering. This theory is plausible because the destruction of the Temple implied the destruction or plunder of the Temple vessels as well. Nevertheless, there are formidable difficulties with this thinking.

The Ark Destroyed

The first variation of the Babylonian theory supposes that the Ark was destroyed either before or with the Temple in 586 B.C. In support of such a view, the account in 2 Kings 24:13 says that at the time of Nebuchadnezzar's second invasion the golden Temple items which Solomon had made were cut in pieces. These gold items are listed in 1 Kings 7:48-51 and include an altar, a table of showbread, lampstands, and numerous utensils. Because some of these objects were known to have been within the Holy Place, it is possible that the Ark within the Holy of Holies might have been included.

However, two factors force us to qualify both where and what these vessels must have been. First, the reference to "all the vessels of gold which Solomon king of Israel had made" must be qualified by the dual reference to "all the treasures of the house of the LORD, and the treasures of the king's house" (2 Kings 24:13). These statements point to the Temple treasuries, not the inner sanctuary. This qualification is verified by 1 Kings 7:51, which states that the golden utensils were put in "the treasuries of the house of the LORD." These treasuries contained duplicates of most of the sacred Temple vessels, including the multiple lampstands. This means that the aforementioned items which were destroyed did not come from the inner sanctuary. Also, Isaiah tells us that the Babylonian emissary Merodach-baladan was shown the inventory of these very treasuries by King Hezekiah (Isaiah 39:1-5). When the Babylonians next came calling on Jerusalem, they undoubtedly went straight for this treasury, as the prophet had predicted (verse 6).

Second, at this time in the relations between Judah and Babylon, Nebuchadnezzar was punishing only the Jews' insurrection and lack of tribute payment. His soldiers, like today's repossessors, were making collections on Judah's delinquent account. This resulted in three separate deportations of Jews to Babylon. This was the second deportation; the Temple wasn't destroyed until the third and final act of punishment. Nebuchadnezzar would not yet have violated the Temple at the second stage of his actions. Therefore, "the vessels of gold which Solomon king of Israel had made" and that were broken up by the Babylonians were only votive gifts deposited in the treasuries of the Temple court.

Even if one could argue that the biblical text meant to identify the inner sanctuary, the Ark could not have been included. According to Scripture, the Ark was not of Solomonic origin but had been made by Moses' craftsmen. Also, the Bible records that additional Temple vessels were removed 11 years later and transported to Babylon intact. Therefore, the vessels mentioned in 2 Kings 24:13 must be different from those captured by Nebuzaradan when he destroyed the Temple. Also, if the Ark had indeed been taken, it would not have been cut up for bulk gold to be made into ingots. Because of its connection with Israel's God, it would have been preserved intact as a war trophy in the conquering god's temple, as were other lesser vessels taken from the Temple (*see* Daniel 1:2).

Others have argued that the Ark may have been destroyed in 586 B.C. when Nebuzaradan finally breached the Temple proper and set it on fire. Second Chronicles 36:19 seems to support this when it says the fire "destroyed all its valuable articles." Again, however, we must note that not *all* of these vessels were destroyed; according to Daniel 1:2, some of the vessels were deposited in the Babylonian temple. Therefore, on these counts, it is highly unlikely that the Ark was destroyed by the Babylonians.

The Ark Captured

If the Ark was not destroyed, could it have been captured? The biblical account tells us that Nebuchadnezzar plundered

the Temple before its destruction and carried off all the articles of the Temple treasuries and brought them all to Babylon
(2 Kings 24:13; 25:13-17; 2 Chronicles 36:18). Again, the text
does not specifically indicate any intrusion of the outer or inner
sanctuaries, but the fact that the Temple was burned would
probably have required this. Also, it is unlikely that the soldiers would have destroyed the Temple without first removing
items of value. Again, however, several biblical texts stand
against the probability of the Ark being captured.

First, the lists of captured Temple articles never mention the
Ark (*see* 2 Kings 25:13-17; Jeremiah 52:17-23). In fact, there is
no mention that *any* of the Temple treasures from the inner
sanctuary were captured. Almost every student of the Ark's
disappearance has noted this scriptural silence as a significant
statement against the Ark's capture. It has been suggested that
this omission is due to the Ark's prior destruction; if it had
already been destroyed, obviously it would not be included in a
list of booty. This assumes the Ark was one of the vessels taken
during the second invasion—vessels that were cut in pieces.
But if the Ark had suffered this fate, it is difficult to see why it
would not be mentioned. The omission of the Ark from any list
of spoils would constitute a great contradiction to biblical
history. For example, a previous account of the Philistine
capture of the Ark had warranted *two entire chapters* (1 Samuel
5–6). It seems inconsistent at best—if not impossible—that
the Ark could have been captured or destroyed by the Babylonians without any mention of the fact in Scripture.

Second, it is clear from the lists of vessels taken that all of
these items were later *returned* by the Persians (Ezra 1:7-11).
They had kept an accurate inventory of these items and provided them to the Israelites in Judah for rebuilding the Temple.
Such a careful accounting in the scriptural texts would certainly have mentioned the most famous object of all, the Ark.
Note also that the vessels transported by Nebuchadnezzar *to*
Babylon are apparently the same vessels which Jehoiakim's
contemporaries, after his exile, expected to be miraculously

returned *from* Babylon (Jeremiah 27:16–28:6). They are the same vessels transferred by Cyrus to Sheshbazzar of Judah (Ezra 1:7-11). These vessels, which totaled 5,400 items (or 5,469, according to the LXX), in both name and number do not correspond with any of the Temple treasures of the inner sanctuary.

Third, one of the purposes for capturing the vessels was to take them to Shinar, where the Babylonian temple was located (Daniel 1:2). It is well known that conquerors carried off the statues of the gods of those cities they defeated in order to show the superior power of their own gods. This was what the Philistines had done with the Ark hundreds of years earlier (1 Samuel 5:2). The Ark stood for the imageless God of the Jews, so Nebuchadnezzar, who was no doubt familiar with this object from Daniel and the other deportees, would have wanted to secure it for his temple. The fact that he deposited only the utensils in his temple indicates that he could not obtain the Ark.

Extrabiblical support for the theory that Babylon captured the Ark is provided by the Apocrypha in 2 Esdras 10:21-22 and in the Babylonian Talmud (*Yoma* 53b). Both of these accounts contend that the Ark was taken as a spoil of battle by the Babylonians. The problem with these records is that 2 Esdras was composed at least 600 years after the Babylonian destruction and the Talmud was not completed for another 200 to 600 years after that. This means that the writers were attempting to answer an unknown by speculation. As far as we can tell, there is no historical record or tradition to support their contention. As one Israeli scholar put it concerning the talmudic reference, "this . . . was based on nothing more than midrashic inferences."[5]

Israeli archaeologists have not accepted the Babylonian theories without reservation. For instance, Israeli archaeologist Meir Ben-Dov told me that he thought the Ark was probably destroyed by the Babylonians, although he conceded that the whole question of the Ark's existence was a religious matter. Fellow archaeologist Dan Bahat thinks the Ark probably disappeared during the reign of Hezekiah, well before the Babylonian invasion, because the biblical text (in his opinion) makes no further mention of it and there is no word of it having been destroyed or taken to Babylon. He also told me he believes that the vessels of the Second Temple were taken by the Romans and that some may have survived in Rome or elsewhere. The Ark, he says, must have been destroyed long before, since it did not continue into the Second Temple.

A Possible Solution

The arguments for each of the above views play against one another, leaving none of them viable. Because it is unlikely that the Ark was taken or destroyed by the Babylonians, there is a good possibility that it and the other Temple treasures of the inner sanctuary had already been removed. Perhaps the prophetic warnings of God's irrevocable intention to punish Judah by destroying the Temple (2 Kings 22:17; 23:26-27) induced the Levites to remove the Ark to a hiding place for protection from the threat of enemy discovery and destruction. It could have been moved secretly by the Levites at any time prior to the Babylonian invasion. If this were so, then it would have been relocated at least before the second Babylonian invasion.

Such a removal may have occurred after the first deportation, which took place during the third year of the Judean king Jehoiakim. It was at this time that Daniel and his three friends were taken captive (Daniel 1:1-6). The hiding of the Ark may have occurred before the reign of Manasseh, as 2 Chronicles 35:3 implies. If so, the Levites who were assigned to guard the Ark could have been forewarned by Isaiah's prophecy (*see* Isaiah 37:6-7) or by the actions of the Babylonians themselves. They would have had sufficient time to relocate all the vessels of the inner sanctuary to prepare against certain future invasions.

There is no New Testament or extrabiblical mention of the Ark's presence in the Temple during the Second Temple era, although reference is made to other articles within the Herodian Temple (for example, the Altar of Incense; *see* Luke 1:9-11). If the Ark was hidden, this hiding must have remained a carefully guarded secret. But secrets have a way of being "leaked" through time, and such leakage may have become the basis for strange stories about the Ark during the Second Temple period. With the passage of time and its mysterious disappearance, the Ark eventually attained the status of a legend. Over the centuries, odd tales have been concocted about the Ark's mysterious powers—and in this way, the lost Ark has become further lost in its own legends.

6

Lost in Legends

---

*When the Holy One, blessed be He, in His mercy
will again build His Temple and His Holy Place, He
will restore them* [the Ark, the Menorah, the heavenly fire, and the Urim and Thummim] *to their
position in order to gladden Jerusalem.*

—*Num. Rabbah* 15:10

The Ark of the Covenant has been a source of fascination
and intrigue throughout history. Its supreme sanctity
among holy relics of the past has produced fantastic tales of its
incredible destructive powers. Indeed, the Bible describes in
fearful detail the swift judgment that fell upon any who dared
to desecrate the Ark, whether Gentile or Jew. As we have seen,
when the Ark was captured by the Philistines, it brought death
and plague to whatever village hosted it. After the Ark was
returned to Beth-shemesh, more than 70 Jewish men of that
city lined up to peer into the Ark. For their presumption they
were all destroyed. Even when King David sought to bring the
Ark into the newly won capital of Jerusalem, one of his own
entourage was struck dead for merely touching the Ark.

Conversely, the Ark was heralded as a wondrous source of
divine blessing and protection to Israel. It brought Israel
victory in battle and brought prosperity to the home of

Obed-edom while it remained there. The Ark became not only an object of reverence but also an object of mystery, hidden from the sight of Israel behind a veil of thick curtains sealing off the unapproachable Holy of Holies.

Though the Bible is silent with regard to the fate of the Ark, Jewish tradition has added its own testimony in an endeavor to resolve the mystery. In this chapter we will look at various stories told about the Ark. In each case we will attempt to separate fiction from fact and seek to discover the true Ark lost within the legends.

Holy Powers of the Ark

The biblical accounts of the Ark's use on the battlefield spawned extrabiblical embellishments of its legendary accomplishments. These powers were depicted as a supernatural force that repelled foreign invaders. The Ark was also believed to be capable of flight. This supposedly demonstrated the presence of God.

A Superweapon

In one tradition, the Ark was described as a mighty and inconquerable weapon of warfare. Two fiery jets were said to issue from between the cherubim above the Ark, burning up snakes, scorpions, thorns, and enemies in the Israelites' path.[1]

The Conjecture

That such legendary attributes were ascribed to the Ark may indicate that it was thought to have an independent power apart from God. This kind of thinking is popular today largely due to the influence of nonreligious sensationalists and the Hollywood film industry. An example of the first category is the Erich Von Daniken series of proto-New Age books and television specials, which caused a sensation two decades ago. Von Daniken believed that God was an ancient astronaut and that the earth had originally been colonized by extraterrestrials. He tried to prove that the Bible, as well as other ancient records, cryptically referred to these aliens and their advanced technology. In his book *Chariots of the Gods?* he explains his beliefs about the Ark of the Covenant:

> Undoubtedly the Ark was electrically charged! If we reconstruct it today according to the instructions handed down by Moses, an electric conductor of several hundred volts is produced. The border and golden crown would have served to charge the condenser which was formed by the gold plates and a positive and negative conductor. If, in addition, one of the two cherubim on the mercy seat acted as a magnet, the loudspeaker—perhaps even a kind of set for communication between Moses and the spaceship—was perfect.[2]

This kind of antisupernaturalistic imagination requires no refutation because it offers no evidence to refute. Still, it should be noted that replicas of the Ark have been made according to the biblical specifications without any such conductivity resulting. In addition, there exist a great many Egyptian relics in mint condition which duplicate the Ark's design and serve to prove only that this style (and technology) was typical of the period in which it was built.

Even so, Hollywood has perpetuated this concept, principally through New Ager Steven Spielberg and George Lucas in their film *Raiders of the Lost Ark*. In the opening sequences of the movie, Indiana Jones shows U.S. intelligence officials the coverleaf of an old Bible, which features an illustration of the Ark going into battle while emitting rays that destroy the enemy. In the film a museum curator, Indy's usual sponsor and patron, said, "The Bible says that the Ark could level mountains and destroy whole regions." Following this premise, the whole plot of the movie is built upon the idea that the Nazis want to find this superweapon and use it against the Allies. In the final sequence, which combines the electromagnetic theory with the end-time plague described in Zechariah 14:12, the producers portrayed the empty Ark as an occultic device that channeled powerful spirits and consumed those who looked at it.

The Refutation

The Bible condemns this kind of superstitious thinking about the Ark. First Samuel 4 reveals that instead of having an innate power as a superweapon, the Ark was powerless to prevent its own capture by the enemy. After the Israelites recoil from losing 4,000 men in battle, their elders conclude that "the LORD [has] defeated us today before the Philistines" (verse 3) and seek somehow to circumvent the Lord in the next engagement. They decide, "Let us take to ourselves from Shiloh the ark of the covenant of the LORD, that it may come among us and deliver us from the power of our enemies."

Did the Israelites really believe that the *Ark* of the Lord could do for them what the *Lord* of the Ark would not? Maybe they thought that God would be forced to deliver them if His Ark was on the battlefield. What's ironic is that the Philistines apparently had a correct understanding of the Ark. When it was brought into the Israelite camp, they said, "God has come into the camp," and "Woe to us! Who shall deliver us from the hand of these mighty gods? These are the gods who smote the Egyptians" (verses 7-8). Whatever the Israelites' twisted reasoning, the end result shows how badly their faith was misplaced. Not only did 30,000 more Israelites die—including the high priest and his sons—but the Ark itself was taken by the enemy (verses 10-18).

We can know with certainty that the Ark did not possess its own power. God Himself was the true power of the Ark. When God's presence was with the Ark and the Israelites, they knew victory. God's presence is said to have gone out from it to dispel the enemy and then return (Numbers 10:35-36; cf. Psalm 68:2). But when He was not present with the Ark, it was as powerless as any other manmade object. The Bible reminds us that "without faith it is impossible to please Him" (Hebrews 11:6); God's displeasure was shown to faithless Israel by withdrawing His presence from the Ark.

Today, as then, the real tragedy is that people who profess faith still go out to do battle with God's enemies without realizing that He is gone. They charge forth in their own strength, sometimes with superweapons of their own invention, but return defeated. Much of what Christians do these days is in the energy of the flesh. I sometimes wonder what would happen if God were to withdraw His Spirit from the world. Would church programs and missionary endeavors continue right on without people ever noticing that something had changed? Let us learn from the Ark to separate fiction from faith and find our deliverance in the Lord alone.

A Flying Machine

The Conjecture

Jewish legend has pictured the Ark as a flying device that hovered vertically and moved horizontally through the air. The biblical account of the Ark "going before" the Israelites in their march through the wilderness has been embellished to explain how the Ark's flight convinced the Jews of God's presence. Because the Shekinah supposedly was not visible to all the camp, it was thought that the Ark took to the air to demonstrate God's presence. This odd interpretation comes from a misreading of Moses' prayer in Numbers 10:35-36 and calls for a literal demonstration of supernatural power:

> Do what the Shekinah bids you do [i.e., break
> camp and move]. But they would not believe Moses
> that the Shekinah dwelt among them unless he
> spoke the words: "Rise up, Lord, and let Thine
> enemies be scattered; and let them that hate Thee
> flee before Thee," whereupon the Ark would begin
> to move, and they were convinced of the presence of
> the Shekinah.[3]

This movement was described in detail. The Ark was said to
have given the signal for breaking camp by soaring up high and
then moving rapidly before the Israelites for a distance of three
miles until it found the next proper place for the camp.[4]

A similar legend is preserved in the Ethiopian royal chronicles, called the *Kebra Nagast* ("The Glory of Kings"). Here
not only does the Ark possess antigravity powers, but it is also
able to make men, animals, and equipment soar with it above
the ground. In the story of the transport of the Ark, the entire
company escorting it toward Ethiopia is said to have been
miraculously lifted up anywhere from a foot and a half to five
and a half feet into the air:

> They loaded the wagons and the horses and the
> mules in order to depart. . . . And as for the wagons,
> no man hauled his wagon: and whether it was men,
> or horses or mules or loaded camels, each was
> raised above the ground to the height of a cubit; and
> all those who rode upon beasts were lifted up above
> their backs to the height of one span of a man, and
> all the various kinds of baggage which were loaded
> on the beasts, as well as those who were mounted
> on them, were raised up to the height of a man, and
> the beasts were lifted up to the height of one span of
> a man. And everyone traveled in the wagons . . . like
> an eagle when his body glides above the wind.[5]

The Refutation

Flying, or being mystically transported from place to place, is a common theme in many legends of the Near East (especially Muslim). The idea was to symbolize the supernatural element in the story, although the storytellers probably did mean for it to be accepted literally. In the Bible there are similar accounts of the Spirit supernaturally moving someone from one place to another (*see* Ezekiel 3:12-14; 11:1; Acts 8:39); but these are usually visionary (as Ezekiel 8:3 states) or meant to be a means of divine guidance. One exception is Elijah's translation (2 Kings 2:11) which was performed by a heavenly chariot.

The Ark was perhaps symbolic of God's heavenly chariot by which He moved from place to place (Psalm 68:17; Isaiah 66:15; Ezekiel 1; 10:6-22); nowhere, however, is this said to be a literal means of aerial conveyance. It was an angel of God who accompanied the glory-cloud that lifted up and moved before the Israelites (Exodus 14:19; 23:20-23; 32:34). And it was this same glory-cloud or Shekinah, accompanied by heavenly cherubim, which departed in flight over the Mount of Olives (Ezekiel 11:23). The biblical evidence shows that legitimate cases of flight are connected with angelic beings and have no direct connection with the Ark.

Hiding Places of the Ark

Various traditions place the Ark in a number of hiding places. All of these are considered secret locations, although it is generally agreed that the Ark will be revealed in the last days.

One especially curious legend has the Ark taken to the Irish isles by Ollam Fodhla ("holy prophet") and a small band in 584 B.C.[6] According to this account the group landed near Ulster, where the descendants of the Tribe of Dan lived. The "holy prophet" who had brought the Ark was the prophet Jeremiah, and he subsequently buried it under a hill known today as Ollam Fodhla's Cairn ("Jeremiah's Cave"). He also brought the stone that Jacob used as a pillow (see Genesis 28:11). This is claimed to be the coronation stone that sits under the throne-chair in Britain. This legend has no historical support, but I include it because British-Israelitism seems to be making a return among anti-Semitic groups in America and abroad.

Let us now consider in detail other hiding places, each with its own historical tradition, and seek to evaluate whether there is any real substance to their claims. These hiding places are said to be within the crypts of the Catholic church or the chambers of the Temple Mount.

In the Church Crypts

Some believe that if the Ark were hidden, it would have been discovered and removed by the Romans in A.D. 70. While no historical evidence exists to verify that the Ark was among the Temple treasures taken by the Romans, those who trace the exodus of these vessels have suggested that the Ark, if it is anywhere, must be with these items. In following the trail of these treasures, we find that two separate locations are said to house the relics: the vaults of the Vatican in Rome and the vaults under the remains of the ancient Nea Church in Jerusalem.

At the Vatican

It is clear from the Arch of Titus that the items captured from the Temple were taken to Rome. Rome's history from that point onward was quite turbulent, however, and once Christianity became the dominant religion of the empire, these treasures fell into the hands of the Catholic church. Historical records reveal that these treasures (and some records include the Ark) were in the possession of Pope Vitalian in

A.D. 657. I have personally heard rumors of special visitors to the Vatican who claim to have seen Temple treasures still preserved in closed rooms. Author J.R. Church once published the claims of such an eyewitness, identified as Nelson Canode of Amarillo, Texas.[7] Mr. Canode testified that he once served as a Benedictine monk at the monastery at Subiaco, Italy, located 30 miles from Rome. While there, Canode says that he was taken to a room in a cave about four stories under the monastery. Here in this room were deposited ancient artifacts that he helped to move back and forth between Subiaco and the underground vaults of the Vatican. When he asked his superiors what these items were, he was told they included the disassembled Tabernacle and the Ark.

It is not doubted that articles from the Second Temple were deposited in Rome. Josephus records that the emperor Vespasian put some of the captured Temple treasures in a specially built "peace sanctuary" that he erected after the Jewish War to commemorate the Temple's destruction (*Wars of the Jews* 7:148-150). It *is* doubtful, however, that any of these items dated from the First Temple. The portrayal of a menorah and table of showbread on the Arch of Titus do not necessarily prove they were from the First Temple; remember, there were many duplicates of these objects kept in storage in the Temple treasuries in case the vessels in use were defiled (*see* Talmud, *Hag.* 26b, 27a). One reason many Jewish scholars do not believe that the menorah depicted on the Arch is the original is because the menorah's octagonal base is shown to have engraved images. Archaeological evidence of the earliest form of the Menorah reveals a *three-legged stand*, not an octagonal base. The three-legged menorahs undoubtedly are patterned after the Mosaic model. Furthermore, no Jewish menorah ever possessed images because they were considered a form of idolatry (*see* Exodus 20:4; Deuteronomy 4:16-25; 5:8). It is suspected that the menorah on the Arch was a non-Jewish creation made by Herod's craftsmen as a gift to Rome.

In support of this is Josephus' statement that priests gave to Titus "two lampstands similar to those deposited in the Temple" (*Wars of the Jews* 6.388). It is highly unlikely that any priest would have handed over the holy Menorah. And if that were true of the Menorah, how much more would it have been true of the untouchable Ark! Nelson Canode's story may be true, but the priest who identified these articles for him may have merely passed on a tradition or rumor.[8] At any rate, there is no substantive evidence to support a hiding of the Ark in the vaults in Rome.

At the New Church

Some believe the Ark and other Temple treasures are in the underground vaults of the ancient Nea ("New") Church that has been excavated in Jerusalem's Jewish Quarter. This vast church was built in the sixth century A.D. by the emperor Justinian and was consecrated to the Virgin Mary. It was destroyed a few decades after its dedication and records of its existence were preserved only in Christian sources until its discovery a few years ago. Even today the publication of the excavation report is pending.

The church's connection to the Temple treasures and the Ark comes by way of the sixth-century Byzantine historian Procopius of Caesarea in the introduction to his history of the Gothic War. He reported that the "treasures of the Jews" were carried in Belisarius' triumphal procession in Constantinople (Byzantium) after his victory over the Vandals, who had sacked Rome and taken these vessels to Carthage in A.D. 455. Medieval sources confirm that Temple treasures were deposited there in the palace library of Emperor Julian.[9] Procopius goes on to tell how a Jew warned a high official on Justinian's court not to keep the vessels in Byzantium because they had brought defeat to the Romans and Carthaginians. Therefore, Procopius says, Justinian sent a military mission to retrieve all the vessels and restore them to Jerusalem, "placing them in one of the churches there." Because the Nea Church was built at precisely this time, it was the logical place to store such treasures for safekeeping.

Archaeologist Meir Ben-Dov, however, believes that story was part of an elaborate government disinformation program.[10] He suggests the real reason that the treasures were stored in the Nea Church was because it had been constructed, in part, from stoa pillars stolen from the Second Temple's remains. He proposes this desecration of the Temple Mount as the reason that Jews destroyed the Nea Church after the Persian conquest of A.D. 614. He argues that an earlier story of Procopius, which stated that the pillars had been especially made for the emperor by God and were revealed standing on a hill just opposite the Nea Church, was connected to this later story of the Temple treasures. Ben-Dov says the pillar story was fabricated to cover up the theft of Temple Mount remains, and he believes the same is true about the story of the Temple treasures. He imagines that at the time when the pillars were removed and rumors were spread that valuables from the Temple Mount were being taken to the Nea Church, Procopius concocted the story about the Temple treasures transported from North Africa as a cover-up for the theft of the pillars. If Ben-Dov is correct, then Procopius' story is but another of the legends of the Temple treasures (which, even so, do not mention the Ark).

Whether the story is fiction or fact, archaeological excavations at the site have produced no trace of Temple treasures. Israeli archaeologist Dan Bahat confirmed this:

> The possibility of finding any [of the Temple treasures] here in Jerusalem is almost nil. If there is any chance of finding anything, it will be in the Jewish Quarter where the Nea Church was. Maybe there is a foundation, a treasury, or something, but we never found them, although we know precisely the location of that church.[11]

In the Temple Mount Chambers

Jewish tradition says that the Ark continued in existence and that it will be rediscovered and restored to Israel when the Messiah appears. Contrary to apocryphal sources that say the Ark is hidden at Mount Sinai or Mount Nebo, the Ark has always been hidden under the Temple Mount. According to the Mishnah (*Sotah* 9a), the Tabernacle was stored under the Temple Mount in a subterranean chamber:

> With regard to Moses the Master said: "After the First Temple was erected, the Tent of Meeting was stored away, its boards, hooks, bars, pillars, and sockets." Where [were they stored]? Rabbi Hisda said in the name of Abimi: "Beneath the crypts of the Temple."

Along with the Tabernacle, Jewish tradition says that the Ark, the Altar of Incense, Aaron's rod, the pot of manna, and the tablets of the Law are all hidden within a secret compartment beneath the Pen of Wood or Woodshed on the west side of the Temple, close to where the Holy of Holies stood.[12] This spot on the Temple Mount was considered so sacred that it affected the normal pattern of worship for those who knew its secret. It was the regular custom of the priests to bow at 13 stations in the Temple. It is said, however, that members of the house of Rabbi Gamaliel and of the deputy high priest, Rabbi Hananiah, used to bow at 14. This additional place faced the woodshed. Sources say that they did this because they had inherited from their ancestors the secret that this was the place where the Ark was hidden.[13] All others who did not know of this secret believed that the Ark had been taken to Babylon; consequently they observed only 13 locations.[14]

Because certain vessels were kept with the Ark in the Temple, when the Ark disappeared, so did these other vessels. This, at least, is consistent with the historical record. But what about this tradition of a hidden Ark? Let us consider whether any basis for this tradition exists.

The Historical Evidence

It is said that when King Solomon built the Temple, he foresaw its eventual destruction and built a secret chamber deep within the Temple Mount to conceal the Ark at such a time of danger. The biblical text records that such a threat was present, for the Temple treasury was pillaged soon after Solomon's death by Pharaoh Shishak (1 Kings 14:25-26). Later, during the dark days of the kings Manasseh and Amon, who desecrated the Temple with abominable images, the Ark as well as the other primary Temple treasures may have been moved to this secret chamber for safekeeping. Manasseh's pollution of the Temple and the corresponding cessation of the Temple ritual would have demanded that the Temple priests and Levites go into hiding. That they neglect to take with them the holy Ark that was committed to their care would be unthinkable.

Jewish rabbis have concluded that the apostasy in Israel which began during Manasseh's reign and continued through Amon's reign was too deep-seated to have been completely reversed by Josiah's reforms. Consequently, when Josiah died, the nation returned to its sin and merited divine punishment. The rabbis said that when Josiah made extensive repairs to the Temple (2 Kings 22:5-6), he decided to hide the Ark for safekeeping because he believed the prophecies of destruction were true and would shortly come to pass. It is recorded that as part of his religious reforms he reinstituted the priestly service and commanded the Ark to be returned to the Temple: "Put the holy ark in the house which Solomon the son of David king of Israel built; it will be a burden on your shoulders no longer" (2 Chronicles 35:3).

In their commentaries, the rabbis disputed the meaning of the last part of this verse—"it will be a burden on your shoulders no longer." Some argued that this implied that the Ark was hidden in a secret chamber not only in the days of Manasseh and Amon but also during the Babylonian invasion and thus was preserved (*Yoma* 52b). What else could this verse mean but that the Ark had been deposited in a subterranean chamber of the Temple? Where else could the Ark have been during the years in between? How else could the Ark have remained free from defilement in the presence of a defiled Temple?

Other rabbis, however, interpreted the command of Josiah to mean that the Levites were to put the Ark *back* in the subterranean chamber. They argued that the Ark had *always* been in the Temple, so how could it be put back into the Temple? Yet, if that were what Josiah meant, why did he say the Ark should be taken *to* the "house which Solomon built"? The rabbis had an answer for this. They said the Temple to which the Ark was taken was a *different* temple from where it had been. They explained that the Ark had to have been removed from the First Temple to fulfill God's prophecy about the Temple's destruction by the Babylonians. As long as the Ark remained, they saw the Temple as invulnerable to attack; but once it was removed to the underground labyrinth below the Temple, the upper part of the Temple became merely an outer shell devoid of sanctity. Thus, it could be destroyed. This meant that the true "house of Solomon" now existed in the vaulted region beneath the Temple. Therefore the command to return the Ark to the "*house* which Solomon built" meant this subterranean "house." Much elaborate argumentation exists among the rabbis in support of this view.[15]

According to Jewish thought, the Ark remained beneath the Temple Mount during the Second Temple era and from that time onward. The fifth division of the tractate *Mo'ed* in the Mishnah, called *Yoma*, confirms the Ark's absence from the Second Temple when it explains that the high priest made his offering not at the Ark but upon an ancient rock that protruded through the floor within the Holy of Holies called the "Foundation Stone" (Hebrew, *'Even Hashtiyah*). It was around this stone, the highest point of Mount Moriah, that Abraham had offered Isaac. It was there also that King David had seen the angelic destroyer of Jerusalem on the threshing floor of Araunah the Jebusite. And it was upon this stone that the Ark had once stood.

The reason the Ark could *not* have been returned to the Second Temple when it was constructed by Zerubbabel may be understood from a review of the historical and religious context in which this Temple existed. During the time of Zerubbabel, Judah was under the authority of Persia; under Herod it was occupied by Rome. During both periods, the Temple was never free from the threat of attack. In fact, during the latter era the Roman eagle insignia had been placed above the eastern gate of the Temple and various attempts were made to set standards bearing images of the emperor in the Temple precincts. In addition, many Jewish sects felt that a non-Zadokite priesthood and the political corruption of the high priesthood had desecrated the Herodian Temple. There was even a popular opinion that the Second Temple would soon be destroyed to make room for God's final and purified Restoration Temple. Under these political conditions, no Levite who knew the secret location of the Ark would have revealed it, nor would he have considered returning the Ark to its Foundation Stone platform within the Holy of Holies.

The Ark certainly had not been returned to the Second Temple; when the Roman general Pompey invaded Jerusalem in A.D. 63, he entered the Holy of Holies and found it empty.[16] He was surprised; he thought the Jewish Temple would house great treasure because the Jews protested his entrance at the offer of their own lives. If they believed the Ark was hidden beneath the Holy of Holies, however, the Temple would have continued to retain its sanctity and been worthy of their sacrifice. Such a regard for the Temple Mount still persists among

Jews, based on this same thinking. Rabbi Aryeh Kaplan explains:

> Even today, it is possible to experience this feeling of proximity. These most sacred objects still remain hidden in Jerusalem, buried deep in a vault under the Temple Mount. Here they will remain until the time when we are worthy to uncover them once again. And even though we may not actually be aware of these sacred objects, the very fact of their proximity is sure to make a most profound impression on our souls.[17]

An account in the Mishnah revealed the secret of where the Ark was hidden while at the same time indirectly giving a warning to those who might seek for it. In tractate *Shekalim* 6:1-2 (cf. *Yoma* 52a-54a) it is recorded that a priest during Second Temple times was in the "wood store," separating the good wood from the bad (wormy) for the sacrificial altar. As he was working, he noticed that some of the stones in the floor of the room were different from the others. This was interpreted by the rabbis to mean that a certain flagstone was higher than the rest and that the priest surmised this stone had once been removed and then replaced to hide the Ark. The account says that when the worker went to tell his fellow priest that he had discovered the Ark's secret chamber (which apparently was entered from the "wood store"), he was struck dead in mid-sentence, thus confirming that the place was indeed the repository of the Ark. Rabbi Rivevan explained that the priest was struck down because if the secret were known, Gentiles (that is, the Romans) might learn this information and seize the Ark.

The Archaeological Evidence

Talmud *Yoma* 54a argues on the basis of this "wood store" story in *Shekalim* that Nebuchadnezzar had left the foundation intact when he destroyed the Temple. Although the Temple Mount has been inaccessible for excavation because of almost 2,000 years of foreign occupation, such accounts preserved in the Mishnah have kept orthodox rabbis confident of the Ark's existence beneath the Temple platform. Since the return of East Jerusalem and the Temple Mount to Jewish control, some limited (and secret) exploration has been able to confirm that indeed this foundation was left intact. It may even be known where the "wood store" and its hidden chamber are located.

Evidence of the Temple Mount's subterranean passageways was originally gathered from early British exploratory maps. There were also some hasty surveys conducted after the Israeli capture of the Temple Mount in the Six-Day War of 1967. The group was led by a team of army engineers under the authority of then Israel Defense Forces Chaplain Rabbi Shlomo Goren. In addition, excavations in the Western Wall Tunnels over the past 15 years have confirmed the presence of this foundation pavement and have uncovered one of the original ancient entrances to the Temple Mount, now known as Warren's Gate. Other excavations from this gate in the direction of the Holy of Holies are believed to have discovered a tunnel leading to a chamber 48 feet below the present surface. This tunnel (according to some sources) leads to the secret repository of the Ark. The area where this chamber is located is called the *Gear Ha'Etzem* ("Chalk of the Bone") and has now been confirmed by excavators. We will leave the details of this excavation to chapter 10.

On the basis of our survey in this chapter, we can say that the Ark remains lost in legends. Is it possible, however, that one legend—that of the Ark hidden under the Temple Mount—may offer some substantial leads as to the present location of the Ark? Before we move on to address that question directly, let us consider the most popular belief Christians hold in regard to the Ark.

7

Do All Arks
Go to Heaven?

It seems impossible that God would have allowed the ark to be destroyed. . . . People have rumored it is preserved somewhere in a cave in Ethiopia, or in the Arabian desert, or somewhere else. But there is no mystery as to where it is. God showed John, when He revealed to him the Apocalypse, that it was safely stored in the heavenly temple. No doubt the Ten Commandments are there as well. If God could translate Enoch and Elijah to heaven, and if the resurrected Christ could ascend to heaven, He would be quite able to have an angel remove the ark from Jerusalem before Nebuchadnezzar's armies sacked the temple, and then have him carry it safely to the true tabernacle in the New Jerusalem under construction in heaven.[1]

—Henry Morris

Some time ago a feature-length cartoon entitled *All Dogs Go to Heaven* was released here in America. When the movie appeared in Israel, the translators had trouble rendering the title into Hebrew and so it appeared as *Gan Eden l' Kelaphim (Heaven Is for Dogs).* This left Israelis wondering whether

Americans thought their dogs went to heaven or maybe heaven had gone to the dogs!

In the same way, a popular explanation among Christians for the disappearance of the Ark is that it went to heaven. In radio interviews during which I have spoken about the Ark, callers invariably protest that the Ark of the Covenant cannot be found on earth because the Bible says it was taken to heaven just before the ascension of Jesus. The callers, however, cannot give a biblical passage in support of their position. Nor can they explain how the Ark got to heaven or why it should be there. I admit that the Bible does indeed reveal an Ark in heaven, but we must carefully consider whether this is the same Ark as that which existed on earth. In other words (taking our cue from the title of the cartoon movie), Do all Arks go to heaven?

Two New Testament texts do mention the presence of an Ark in heaven. Let us examine each of these passages to see whether they support the "rapture" of the earthly Ark.

An Ark Seen in Heaven

In Revelation 11:19 the apostle John declares that he saw an Ark revealed in the heavenly realm: "The Temple of God which is in heaven was opened; and the ark of His covenant appeared in His temple." Many excellent commentators, eager to reconcile the disappearance of the Ark in the past with this appearance in the future, have quickly identified this as the lost Ark. Characteristic of such reasoning is the following:

> Just as Yahweh is said to have personally buried
> Moses with his own hand (Deuteronomy 34:5-6)—
> lest the body of Moses become an object of national
> veneration, as is the case with the body of Lenin in
> Moscow—so the testimony of the Apocalypse is

that God returned the Ark of the Covenant to Himself. There it remains to be revealed at the final theophany on the last day (Apocalypse 11:19).[2]

On the surface, this view does offer an attractive solution to the problem of the Ark because it seeks to perpetuate the existence and sanctified purpose of the Ark without historical interruption—albeit in the heavenly realm. On closer examination, however, the preservation of the earthly Ark in heaven forces the question of other Temple vessels which also appear in heaven in the book of Revelation (for example, the Golden Altar, incense, censers, harps, bowls, trumpets, ephods—Revelation 5:8; 7:9, 14-15; 8:2-5; 15:2, 5-7). And what of the heavenly appearance of the Tabernacle, Tent, and Temple?

If we assume that the Ark was translated to heaven, should we not assume that all of these—equally a part of the Temple worship system—were also translated? After all, no physical trace of the earthly Temple has ever been discovered. Perhaps the report of its destruction by the Romans, being extrabiblical, was a legend, and instead it was carried to heaven to become the Temple which John saw. Some rabbis have said that the entire Temple was supernaturally removed to heaven and will remain there until the last days. But they held that view because they could not conceive of the Holy Place as having been destroyed. As far as I know, no Christian interpreter who holds the heavenly translation view of the Ark shares this mystical theory.

The Temple Seen in Heaven

How, then, do we account for John's clear statements that he saw the Ark and the Temple in heaven? The answer is that John saw the *heavenly* Ark that has *always* existed in the *heavenly* Temple with God. This Temple, complete with its vessels, appears at crucial intervals in Revelation. This heavenly Temple is not the same as the earthly Temple. John makes this

clear when he measures the Tribulation Temple and omits the
outer court, which will be trodden down by the Gentiles
(Revelation 11:1-2). Because the Tribulation Temple exists *at*
the same time as the Temple in heaven, they cannot be the same
structure. Therefore, it was the heavenly Temple and Ark,
existing long before any earthly replica, which John saw and
described in Revelation 11:19.

One reason for the confusion about the earthly and heavenly
Temples is because many Christians are unfamiliar with the
concept that the heavenly structures served as the models for
the Tabernacle, the Temple, and their primary vessels. Let's
briefly survey the teaching of the Old and New Testaments on
this truth.

Heaven's Temple Seen in the Old Testament

Many references in the Old Testament indicate the existence
of a heavenly Temple where God dwells.[3] In the Psalms, God is
depicted as in His holy Temple (or holy mountain, Psalm 3:4;
46:4) looking down upon men to test them (Psalm 11:4) and
positioned to hear their cries of distress or prayers of worship
(Psalm 18:6; 102:18-19; cf. 1 Kings 8:29-52). The prophet
Isaiah beheld the glory of the God of Israel in this Temple
(6:1-7), and Micah (1:2), like John in Revelation, declared that
from this Temple God would one day descend to judge the
earth.

As God's people were on their way to the Promised Land,
further details of the earthly sanctuary were revealed so that
God's presence might dwell with them. Orders were first given
to Moses to construct for God a "sanctuary" (literally, "dwelling place"). Such a supernatural structure had to have a spiritual design that would permit God's holiness to exist among
sinful men without destroying them, yet at the same time be of
earthly construction to physically accommodate those who
would daily manage the routine of worship.

The Heavenly Pattern
for the Earthly Ark

In the Pentateuch (Exodus 25:8-9, 40; 26:30; 27:8; Numbers 8:4) as well as in the historical books (1 Chronicles 28:11-19), we are told that God showed Moses—and later David—some sort of model or pattern by which they could construct the Tabernacle, the Temple, and especially the Ark. Let's compare two of these accounts:

> Let them construct a sanctuary for Me, that I may dwell among them. According to all that I am going to show you, as the *pattern* of the tabernacle and the *pattern* of all its furniture, just so you shall construct it. . . . you shall make a mercy seat of pure gold. . . . you shall make two cherubim of gold. . . . the cherubim shall have their wings spread upward, covering the mercy seat. . . . And see that you make them after the *pattern* for them, which was shown to you on the mountain (Exodus 25:8-9, 17-18, 20, 40, emphasis added).

> David gave to his son Solomon the *plan* of the porch of the temple, its buildings, its storehouses, its upper rooms, its inner rooms, and the room for the mercy seat. . . . and gold for the model of the chariot, even the cherubim, that spread out their wings, and covered the ark of the covenant of the LORD. "All this," said David, "the LORD made me understand in writing by His hand upon me, all the details of this *pattern*" (1 Chronicles 28:11, 18-19, emphasis added).

In each of these accounts, the word translated "plan" or "pattern" is the Hebrew term *tabnit*, which may indicate something like an architect's plan, denoting either the original from which a replica is made or the replica itself.[4] While both Moses and David passed on written blueprints to their design engineers, what they beheld was probably not a replica or miniature model[5] (as the Jewish commentators Rashi and Ramban thought) but the actual, heavenly original. This appears probable because most of the references to the heavenly original in the Old Testament seem to indicate a solid object.[6] It is also supported by the almost universal concept in the ancient Near East of a heavenly or cosmic mountain as the model for temples, cult objects, and laws.[7] As with most all biblical parallels from the ancient Near East, the common source was probably an original, uncorrupted, oral account from a time before the division of mankind at the Tower of Babel. In addition, Exodus 24:9-11 tells us that when Moses and the elders of Israel sat in God's presence on Mount Sinai, eating and drinking, they actually saw some sort of celestial pavement beneath the throne of God (compare a similar incident in Ezekiel 1:26-28).[8] It was from this mountain that Moses received the "pattern" for the Tabernacle and the Ark (Exodus 25). Professor Noel David Freedman affirms this identity when he concludes:

> It was on this mountain that Yahweh's palace stood, a palace made by Yahweh for himself with its throne room and throne, on which he is seated, king forever (v. 18). . . . This heavenly temple or sanctuary with its throne room or holy of holies where the deity was seated on his cherubim throne constituted the *tabnit* or structure seen by Moses during his sojourn on that same mountain.[9]

Therefore, we may understand that the Temple with its Ark of the Covenant in heaven is none other than the true and original Temple and Ark—the pattern from which the earthly copy was made. In Revelation, the frequent appearances of the Tabernacle, Temple, and vessels[10] may serve as a means of assurance that God's Holy Place is beyond the reach of the Antichrist's defilement and that the restoration of holiness on earth, which will include the restoration of the Temple and its vessels, is imminent.

Christ's Blood and the Ark in Heaven

Those who say that the earthly Ark was transported to heaven use Hebrews 9:11-12 to teach that the earthly Ark was present in heaven to receive the literal blood of Christ.[11] This view maintains that Christ, in accordance with the Old Testament type, entered as a High Priest into the heavenly Holy of Holies *with* His sacrificial blood. They further point to verses 21-24, which compare the ministry of the earthly high priest in the earthly Tabernacle with that of Christ in the heavenly Tabernacle:

> In the same way he [the earthly high priest] sprinkled both the tabernacle and all the vessels of the ministry with the blood. And according to the Law, one may almost say, all things are cleansed with blood, and without shedding of blood there is no forgiveness. Therefore it was necessary for the copies of the things in the heavens to be cleansed with these, but the heavenly things themselves with better sacrifices than these (verses 21-23).

These verses are interpreted to teach that Christ took His literal blood to heaven and sprinkled it on the mercy seat of the Ark. If Jesus' literal blood was transported to heaven, would this not imply that the literal Ark must also have been transported to heaven to receive this blood? Because the earthly high priest had offered animal blood on the earthly Ark, would it not be in keeping with the literal correspondence if Christ, as a superior High Priest, likewise offered His own blood there?

I agree that a literal, rather than a figurative, interpretation of Christ's priestly ministry is in view; however, the text does not state that Christ's literal blood was taken to heaven. Those who make this claim translate the Greek preposition *dia* in verse 12 as "with," giving the translation "but *with* His own blood, He entered the holy place." This preposition here is better understood in an instrumental sense, which gives the translation "but *by means of* His own blood, He entered the holy place." In other words, Christ did not come into the heavenly Tabernacle carrying His blood to obtain forgiveness. Rather, He came by virtue of the fact that He had already shed His blood and obtained forgiveness. The completion of redemption before Christ entered into heaven is emphasized at the end of Hebrews 9:12 by the use of the aorist participle: "He entered the holy place once for all, *having obtained* eternal redemption" (emphasis added)—that is, *after* He had secured eternal redemption. The tearing of the veil in the earthly Temple from top (heaven) to bottom (earth) was evidence that the way of spiritual approach to God had been divinely accomplished at the cross (Matthew 27:51; Mark 15:38; Luke 23:45). We must also ask *when* Christ could have taken His blood to heaven, since there is no scriptural evidence of such a presentation after the resurrection or at the ascension (Acts 1).

Furthermore, those who argue that the analogy of the earthly high priest on the Day of Atonement demands this literal correspondence should observe that the priest entered the Holy Place with his own blood *still within his body*. And contrary to popular belief, no biblical passage teaches that Christ's resurrection body was bloodless. The statement in Luke 24:39 describing Christ's resurrection body as "flesh and bones" does not mean His body was bloodless any more than the failure to mention skin meant that it was skinless! Neither does the statement that "flesh and blood cannot inherit the kingdom of God" (1 Corinthians 15:50) exclude blood from the resurrection body, since the text excludes *flesh*—and Luke 24:39 states that Jesus' resurrection body includes flesh. In the

Corinthian passage, Paul was simply saying that mortal flesh—unglorified bodies—cannot inherit the eternal kingdom.

Keep in mind that a literal correspondence between the earthly and heavenly Tabernacles does not require *identical* correspondence in every detail. In fact, we see in the book of Hebrews that the Old Testament sacrificial system features as many *contrasts* as *similarities*. The point of comparison between the earthly high priest and Christ is one of reference, involving two different levels and purposes of sacrifice. The ministry of the earthly priesthood was limited to the earth, whereas Christ's ministry reaches to the heavens. Although His death on the cross transpired on earth, it was an event in the spiritual realm intersecting time and eternity. Consequently, there was no need to translate the earthly Ark to heaven because its function was relegated to Israel's geographical worship in the Temple past and future.

This text in Hebrews teaches that the heavenly Tabernacle, possibly defiled through Satan's presence in the heavenlies (Zechariah 3:1; Colossians 1:20; 1 John 2:1; Revelation 12:10) and affected in some manner by the sin of man (Romans 8:21; Revelation 21:1), was spiritually purified by the heavenly oriented sacrifice of Christ on earth. In contrast to the Israelite priest who had to *leave* the earthly Ark (that is, the presence of God) when his work was finished, Christ the Great High Priest *abides* before the heavenly Ark eternally in the presence of the Father.

Where, Then, Is the Ark?

My conclusion from the biblical accounts is that the Ark did not go to heaven. Because the heavenly Ark always has been in heaven, the earthly Ark had no reason to be transported there.

This leaves us with our previous options that the Ark either must have been destroyed or still remains in existence. Since in earlier chapters we concluded that it is highly improbable that the Ark could have been destroyed without some biblical comment to this effect, and that the New Testament continues to affirm the importance of the earthly Ark by reference to its heavenly prototype, we may have good reason to suggest that the Ark yet has a future role to play in the divine purpose. Therefore, the Ark is most likely hidden in some secret location, awaiting the proper time on God's calendar to make its reappearance.

PART TWO

The Search Continues

8

The Great Treasure Hunt Outside Israel

Ever since the premiere of the popular movie
Raiders of the Lost Ark, *hardly a year passes with-
out someone claiming to have found the Ark of the
Covenant.*[1]

—Dr. Ephraim Isaac, Director,
Institute of Semitic Studies,
Princeton

We did not bring home the Ark," wrote Claude Conder
of the first publicly supported archaeological expedition to Israel, known as the Palestine Exploration Fund. In
those early days of adventurers in the Holy Land, archaeology
was still a romantic pursuit. The remnants of civilizations
past—Assyria, Babylon, Greece, and Egypt—had already
whetted the appetites of the people who lived in the empire
"upon which the sun never set." The British populace wanted
biblical treasures to emerge from Israel on a scale with the
Egyptian pyramids and Grecian temples. As Jerusalem author
Naomi Shepherd put it, "Evangelicals [Christians in Britain]
wanted the Ark of the Covenant to be found, as Lord Shaftesb-
ury said, 'as evidence in a day of trouble, of rebuke, and of
blasphemy.' "[2]

Anxious Without Access

With so much to gain, much was ventured in the early quest for the Ark. Behind the recorded accounts of tortuous descents into wells and subterranean vaults near or on the Temple Mount—often at night in the dead of winter and without lights—was the exciting dream of discovering the Ark. Since that era the technology for exploration has improved, but the opportunities to explore have not. Even though the Temple Mount has been a part of Israel since 1967, control of the area has remained exclusively with Muslim authorities, who permit no entrance to the structures beneath the site.

Rabbi Shlomo Goren, chaplain of the Israel Defense Forces and later Chief Rabbi of Israel, was in complete control of the Temple Mount for one brief month (June 7–July 7, 1967) following the Six-Day War. He sent an army corps of engineers to survey the Mount for two weeks, yet regretted that he was not able to conduct explorations beneath the Mount. He explained:

> They didn't do it [explore the subterranean structures]. I didn't have enough orientation to tell them what to do. We were all so excited and so rushed. I put them inside the Temple Mount the first day after the liberation, but I didn't know what to look for! We could enter the Dome of the Rock to investigate beneath the rock itself; we could go everywhere, but we didn't![3]

The inaccessibility of the Temple Mount only sent explorers looking in other directions for the Ark, even though some, like Rabbi Goren, continued to pursue matters beneath the Mount (as we will see in chapter 10).

Let's turn our attention now to some early and recent attempts to find the Ark. While peculiar views abound (such as Iris Love, who believes the Ark is now among Babylonian antiquities stored in a museum basement[4]), most explorers and researchers believe the Ark is "out there somewhere."

The Earliest Recorded Hunt

One first-century religious group, the Samaritans, actually tried to make its legend live. They taught that the Temple treasures were hidden on Mount Gerizim and that at a future "ingathering" they would be revealed. A short time after Jesus' death and resurrection, the Samaritan community apparently interpreted "ingathering" to refer to those who would dare to assemble together and ascend the mountain as a group. Upon doing so, they believed, the vessels would be revealed to them. Therefore, a group actually gathered, went up the mountain, and awaited the fulfillment of the prophecy. However, any hope of recovering the Ark and other Temple vessels was interrupted when the Roman governor Pontius Pilate heard about the multitude gathering on Mount Gerizim. He sent troops to quell what he thought was a revolt against the empire. Pilate interpreted a word in the Samaritan text (which the Samaritans interpreted as "refugees") describing this "ingathering" to mean "rebels," and so deployed his troops. Pilate's brutal tactics were later described to Rome by the Samaritans and the governor was soon removed from office.

Searches of the Past Century

The Middle East was opened to the West by a constant stream of foreign explorers who wanted to survey, map, and identify biblical remains, including the Temple treasures. While the stories of these men's adventures are legion, I will offer here only the most famous of the searches that centered on the Ark.[5] Dr. Dan Bahat, a professional Israeli archaeologist, made reference to this story, which he implied had its origin in fortune-hunting adventurers of the past:

The story [of treasures beneath the Temple Mount] started in the previous century. Gentiles, mostly British, believed that they knew where the secrets of the Temple were. The most famous of all was a man named Montigue Parker who was [in Jerusalem] in 1911. He looked for the [Temple] treasures, but what he really found were tombs that dated from the Early Bronze age, thousands of years before the Temple was constructed.[6]

From the outset, Lieutenant Parker's expedition was mounted to discover and retrieve the Ark. His lead had come from Finnish mystic Valter Juvelius, who at Swedish University in 1906 had delivered a paper that claimed to provide reliable information as to the hiding place of the Ark. This information, Parker learned, was based on Juvelius' discovery of a cryptogram or cypher hidden within the writings of Jeremiah. This coded message supposedly told how Jeremiah had rescued the Ark and hidden it in an underground passage leading to a secret chamber beneath the Temple. It also contained detailed guidance as to where this passage and chamber lay and how access to them could be obtained.

With this information and sufficient funding, Parker began his search for the secret passage at what was called the Virgin's Fountain, so named because it was believed that the Virgin Mary had once drawn water there (this was actually the northern entrance to Hezekiah's Water Tunnel). Parker believed that from this area access could be had to a subterranean passageway connected with a secret chamber whose northern entrance was beneath the sacred area adjacent to the Al-Aqsa mosque. One story of Parker's attempt to explore this area says he found the chamber and penetrated all the way to the north and emerged under the Dome of the Rock—yet without finding the Ark.[7]

More reliable accounts[8] say that he bribed the Turkish Pasha of Jerusalem, Amzey Bey, and the guardian of the Dome of the Rock, Sheikh Khalil, to secretly dig at night beneath the "Well of the Souls" located below the cave floor of the great stone in the Dome. His work continued undiscovered for a week. But on the morning of the eighth day a Muslim priest saw the workers dumping baskets of rubble near the Dome and alerted the Muslim populace. Parker and his team immediately fled for their lives and left the country via their yacht anchored at the port of Jaffa.

The events of Parker's expedition make for fascinating reading. William le Queux turned the factual tale into sensationalized fiction in his novel *The Treasure of Israel*, while an earlier, more scholarly work, *Jerusalem Underground: Discoveries on the Hill of Ophel, 1909–1911*, chronicled Parker's attempts until his hasty departure.

Searches of the Present Century

The past decade has witnessed a growing excitement over the possibility of recovering the lost Ark of the Covenant. The international success of the film *Raiders of the Lost Ark* most likely ignited this new wave of Ark fever. During this period of time, competing claims to the discovery of the Ark both in and outside of Israel have appeared. Let's look at two of the most popularized recent reports outside of Israel.

The Search in Jordan

About the same time that movie screens showed Indiana Jones searching for the Ark in Egypt, American Tom Crotser made international headlines with an announced discovery of the Ark under Mount Pisgah (the highest point in the Mount Nebo range) in Jordan at 2:00 A.M. on October 31, 1981. In stating his motivation for seeking the Ark, he said:

> I believe God allowed me and my three companions to locate the Ark in Mount Nebo in Jordan

because the time has come for Israel to begin their sacrificial system and that announces the soon return of Jesus Christ.[9]

Crotser had obtained a map[10] made by American explorer Antonio Frederick Futterer, who in the 1920s had himself searched for the Ark in Jordan. Futterer had made his expedition after the British General Allenby had taken Palestine from the Turks and while Jordan was still Transjordan and a part of the captured territory. While he did not find the Ark, he believed he had located a secret passageway under Mount Nebo leading to the Ark and other Temple treasures.[11]

Futterer had depended on the accuracy of the apocryphal account in 2 Maccabees 2:1-8, which said Jeremiah hid the Ark on "the mountain where Moses saw God's inheritance." While this has been identified with both Mount Sinai and Mount Nebo, Futterer chose the latter as more historically feasible. Futterer claimed to have found an ancient inscription on the sealed entrance of a passageway he discovered near Mount Nebo. Crotser says Futterer had a copy of this inscription translated by an unidentified scholar at Hebrew University in Jerusalem, and it supposedly read, "Herein lies the golden Ark of the Covenant." According to Futterer's own report, the inscription was in "hieroglyphics" and was deciphered "numerically" in Hebrew letters to yield a value of 1927, thought by Futterer to confirm his eventual discovery of the Ark itself on that date.[12] For the record, Futterer was never able to produce any copy of this alleged inscription.

Based on this information, Crotser took three companions and conducted an unauthorized excavation for the Ark.[13] The team was in the Mount Nebo region for four days. They claim that they managed to locate on neighboring Mount Pisgah what they believed was Futterer's passageway, a natural cave opening leading to a 600-foot-long tunnel with two blocked entrances along the course. Inside the farthermost point of the tunnel, the team members say they found a room measuring 10 feet by 12 feet. In one corner, says Crotser, was an object covered with a blue cloth; lying to the side of it was another wrapped bundle. Crotser removed the cover and took pictures of a golden-hued metal box, which he afterward measured (without touching it) and found to be 62 inches long, 37 inches high, and 37 inches deep. When Crotser crossed the border into Israel with his story, he was not believed. Still, the *Jerusalem Post* did a news brief about his claim. As a result, his story went through the UPI wire service and received international coverage, accompanied by a mistaken rumor that Israeli authorities had verified the claim.

Verifying the Claim

Because of this attention, the Biblical Archaeology Society asked the respected archaeologist Siegfried Horn, whose own expedition to Tel Jalul had been cancelled as a result of Crotser's activities, to investigate Crotser's evidence and personally inspect his photographs. Dr. Horn's conclusion, published in the May/June 1983 issue of *Biblical Archaeology Review*, stated that only one slide was legible. While it pictured an unknown object, it was not an ancient artifact but rather a modern fabrication, since it appeared to bear the markings of a machine-tooled design.[14] The object pictured is of simple construction with attached plates bearing a filigree pattern.

This photo is a far cry from the description given by Jim Bolinger, one of the four team members, to a *Dallas Morning News* reporter shortly after his return from Jordan. At that time he described the Ark as "a gold-covered chest four feet wide, five feet long, and four feet high, with two nine-foot golden wings of cherubim on either side of the mercy seat. . . . a two- or three-foot apron was on top with dried skins covering the ends."[15] Whether Bolinger was describing the "Ark" his team discovered or the Ark in the Bible, by either comparison, something is terribly out of sync.

Crotser has since published his own book on the alleged discovery.[16] At his organization's compound he displays a papier-mâché facsimile of the "cave" with his "Ark" slide-projected from the rear. Thus far, no professional archaeologist has substantiated Crotser's claim, although the Nazareth-born, Christian-Arab evangelist Dr. Anis Shorrosh published a book on the Ark (which initially sold more than 25,000 copies)[17] that accepted and promoted Crotser's claim as genuine.[18]

Doubtful Details

I first came into contact with Crotser while in seminary in 1974 when I corresponded with him concerning his then-controversial claim to have found and photographed Noah's Ark.[19] Rather than respond specifically to my letter, he sought to recruit me to his religious commune, the Holy Ground Mission, which he then managed in Frankston, Texas. In addition to his "discovery" of Noah's Ark, he also has claimed to have found the Tower of Babel, the City of Adam, and the stone of Abel.

The heads of several Christian research organizations who have spoken with Crotser in the past have told me that they consider his claims highly doubtful. In relation to the Ark of the Covenant, several details about his account of the discovery are questionable.

First, he reported that the "cave" entrance was covered by a tin sheet, that the blocked entrances were easily opened, and that the last 300 feet of the tunnel were lined on the sides by "ancient tombs that resembled catacombs." These features indicate that the site may have been a necropolis (burial spot)—probably for monks, since Crotser's map placed the site in close proximity to the Church of the Franciscan Fathers of Terra Santa. If this is so, the flimsy coverings would have been designed for easy entrance to make new intermits. Crotser explained these catacombs by saying he believes the area houses Moses' tomb.

What is even more disturbing is that his map reveals that the room where the "Ark" was discovered is directly beneath a building that preserves the remains of an ancient Byzantine church. It is likely that this room is related to the museum storerooms located nearby.

These details affirm that the monks were familiar with this site; it was not some secret cave sealed from the time of Jeremiah. Crotser recognized this and took it as proof of the monks' conspiracy to keep the Ark hidden from the outside world: "There's a shaft that leads right up next to the church's baptismal. You've got to believe they've known about it."[20]

In addition, Crotser's claim to have removed the blue cover from the box but not to have investigated the wrapped bundle beside it (which he speculated held the mercy seat with the cherubim, legs, and transport poles of the Ark) is suspicious. Why examine the one and not the other? He could have unwrapped the bundle without touching what was inside, if this was indeed his concern. Later, when interviewed by Dr. Shorrosh, Crotser declared that the mercy seat had probably been taken by Jeremiah to Ireland along with King Zedekiah's daughter when Jerusalem fell![21]

Third, since Crotser's objective was to find the Ark, why didn't he take better photographic or documentary equipment? This is especially curious in view of doubts concerning his poorly documented searches for other lost biblical artifacts. When reporters asked Crotser for his photographs of the "Ark," he stated that the only person he would release them to was London banker David Rothschild, whom he believed to be a direct descendant of Jesus and who had the financial resources to rebuild the Jewish Temple.

In my opinion, both Crotser's account and his evidence are doubtful. Apparently this opinion is shared by others, because more than a decade has gone by and still no one has seriously pursued Crotser's claim. Perhaps for now it is best to agree with the official verdict of Adnan Hadidi, director of the Jordanian Department of Antiquities: "The whole story, as far as we are concerned, is nonsense. This is an irresponsible group."[22]

The Search in Ethiopia

A Modern Theory

One of the most interesting theories published in the past few years argues that the Ark has been hidden for centuries in the sanctuary chapel of Saint Mary of Zion Church in Axum, Ethiopia. The legend that the Ark is in Ethiopia is ancient, but in recent years the theory has been popularized in the writings of Canadian Christian researcher Grant Jeffrey and advanced by British journalist Graham Hancock. The latter published the largest recent volume on the Ark, titled *The Sign and the Seal: The Quest for the Lost Ark of the Covenant.* In this nearly 600-page book, which reads much like a novel, Hancock traces the legend of the Ark through modern times and traditions, connecting it with the Knights Templar and their search for the Holy Grail. His journey takes him to Axum to witness the once-a-year ceremony known as the *Timkat*, at which the *Tabot* (supposedly the Ark) is brought out in public view.

A reserved yet favorable evaluation of Hancock's book was made by Ephraim Isaac, director of the Institute of Semitic Studies, Princeton, New Jersey.[23] While admitting that some of Hancock's theories were controversial, he observed that "it is evident to anyone knowledgeable in the literature and history of Ethiopian Christianity that this claim contains little that is new."[24] In fact, several Christian books either devoted to or contributing to this topic well preceded Hancock's volume.[25] Nevertheless, Hancock's book announces, "The subject of this book could constitute the single most shattering secret of the last three thousand years."

Yet Hancock produces no evidence for the existence of the Ark in Ethiopia except the testimony of Ethiopian legends[26] and Christian mystics of the Middle Ages (who may have identified the Ark with the Holy Grail). Ethiopian Christian monks who were interviewed by Hancock refused to answer his questions and provided only an indirect argument from silence. Hancock did see a rectangular object, covered with a heavy blue cloth bearing an emblem of a dove, carried about by priests at the Timkat ceremony. This object has been paraded for centuries in this annual ceremony, and pictures of it have long been published in standard works on Ethiopia.[27] However, Hancock was forced to conclude that it was only a replica of the true Ark.

Hancock contends that the true Ark remained guarded in its secret chamber within the innermost recesses of the church during this ceremony because he never saw the "guardian" monk Gebra Mikhail leave the sanctuary chapel. But this only adds speculation to unfounded theory. He provides no material evidence that it is the true Ark (and not an ancient Christian relic) that is guarded within the church. Neither does he provide any eyewitness accounts verifying the true Ark's presence in Axum except one historical account—that of the thirteenth-century geographer Abu Salih, who described an object that he was told or thought to be the Ark. This paucity of proof gives us no reason to consider Hancock's theory over competing Ark theories.

An Ancient Account

The Ethiopian Ark account comes from a tradition recorded in the Ethiopian royal chronicles called the *Kebra Nagast* ("Glory of the Kings"). This work says the original Ark was transferred from Jerusalem to Ethiopia by Menelik I, the alleged son of the Queen of Sheba (an Ethiopian ruler) and King Solomon. A Zadokite priest who left with Menelik I took the original Ark from the Holy of Holies in Solomon's Temple and left a replica in its place. When Menelik I discovered that his entourage possessed the Ark, he surmised that they must have had divine approval, since God certainly would have prevented the removal of the Ark had He not willed it.

The account further states that the Ark was taken from Jerusalem to protect it from Manasseh, who would later defile the Temple with idolatrous images. Other traditions say that the Ark was taken first to a local temple in Elephantine, an island in Upper Egypt that had a Jewish community.

Proponents of this theory have been asked to explain why the Jews in exile would build a temple at Elephantine and not in Babylon. One answer is that the Ark had been brought to Elephantine. Another answer is that in Elephantine the Jewish settlement had freedom of worship, whereas in Babylon the exiles were subject to a pagan political and religious system. The problem with both answers is that it was considered illegitimate to construct a Jewish temple in a foreign land. To take the Ark to a foreign temple would have been an act of desecration.

The fact that Jewish traditions have been preserved among Ethiopian Jews from antiquity may argue for a historical basis to the Ark's presence in Ethiopia. On the other hand, Judaism's entrance into Ethiopia may be much later than the *Kebra Nagast* claims. A number of scholars have said that Judaism entered Ethiopia through Egypt after the Babylonian invasion of 587–586 B.C. But Dr. Steven Kaplan, chairman of Hebrew University's African Studies department, claims in his book *The Beta Israel in Ethiopia* that Ethiopian Jewry can be traced back only 600 years to sometime between the fourteenth and sixteenth centuries.[28] In addition, historians have almost universally agreed that Ethiopia could not have been connected with the Queen of Sheba because of geographical and demographical difficulties. The land over which the Queen of Sheba ruled was probably Yemen, and in the time of Solomon (about 960 B.C.), Ethiopian settlements were too small to support an empire.

Harry Atkins, who researched Ethiopian history as a lecturer for the Ethiopian government at the Menelik II School in

Addis Ababa, contends that there was no record of the Ark being in Ethiopia until the end of the thirteenth century. He writes:

> At that time there was a dispute over who should be king. One of the claimants to the throne said he was a descendant of King Solomon and the Queen of Sheba. When Ykuna Amlak became king (1274–1285 A.D.), the legend of the Ark being in Ethiopia entered Ethiopian history.[29]

This evidence accords with the earliest attested source for this theory, which is the medieval Armenian writer Abu Salih (thirteenth century), whose description of an Ethiopian Christian mass appears accurate. Even though he recorded that "the Abyssinians possess also the Ark of the Covenant," he described it as "overlaid with gold; and upon its upper cover there are crosses of gold; and there are five precious stones upon it, one at each of the four corners, and one in the middle."[30] While Abu Salih assumed (or was told) this was the biblical Ark, what he described is more likely a Christian relic—unless, of course, the Ark was radically altered for Christian worship. But this would present problems that question the Ark's sanctity and the Ethiopians' respect for that sanctity.

Perhaps the most dubious aspect of the account in the Ethiopian royal chronicles is how the Ark could have been secreted out of the Holy of Holies and removed from Jerusalem. Rabbi Goren contends that it was impossible for anyone—even for the legitimate Zadokite priests—to have unguarded access to the Ark:

> Nobody could make switches and nobody had free access to the Ark. Whatever time [of day or night] it was—even on Yom Kippur when [the high priest] had just a few minutes inside—they wouldn't let anyone go inside, they would kill them![31]

To appreciate just how impossible it would have been for even a priest to have snatched the Ark, consider this record of how carefully the entrance to the Temple was guarded:

> As the "family" whose daily "ministration was accomplished" left the Temple, the massive gates were closed by priests or Levites, some requiring the united strength of twenty men. Then the Temple keys were hung up . . . [in] the chief guard-room of the priests. Already the night watches had been set in the Temple. By day and night it was the duty of the Levites to guard the gates, to prevent, so far as possible, the unclean from entering. . . . At night guards were placed in twenty-four stations about the gates and courts. Of these, twenty-one were occupied by Levites alone; the other innermost three, jointly by priests and Levites. Each guard consisted of ten men; so that in all two hundred and forty Levites and thirty priests were on duty every night. The Temple guards were relieved by day, but not during the night, which the Romans divided into four, but the Jews, properly, into three watches, the fourth being really the morning watch. During the night the "captain of the Temple" made his rounds. On his approach the guards had to rise and salute him in a particular manner. Any guard found asleep when on duty was beaten, or his garments were set on fire—a punishment, as we know, actually awarded. But, there could have been little inclination to sleep within the Temple, even had the deep emotions natural in the circumstances allowed it . . . [because] the preparations for the service of the morning required each to be early astir. The priest whose duty it was to superintend might any moment knock at the door and unexpectedly, no one

> knew when. . . . Those who were prepared now fol-
> lowed the superintending priest. . . . One company
> passed eastwards, the other westwards, till, having
> made their circuit of inspection, they met at the
> chamber where the high priest's daily meat-offering
> was prepared, and reported, "It is well! All is
> well."[32]

A final and (I think) insurmountable problem is the biblical statement in 2 Chronicles 35:3 that the Ark was still in the Temple during the time of King Josiah (622 B.C.). Hancock believes that this passage teaches the opposite—that the Ark was not in the Temple at this time.[33] His only support for this is his supposition that the Levites did not appear to obey Josiah's request to bring the Ark back to the Temple, since no installation service is recorded. Hancock also connects this with Jeremiah's prophecy concerning the Ark (Jeremiah 3:16), which he believes announces the disappearance of the Ark. Hancock thus contends that the reason the Levites could not obey Josiah's request because the Ark had already been taken to Ethiopia.

Yet there is no reason to assume that the Levites did not obey Josiah's command. If there were no Ark to move, a fact that the Levites would have known, why would the king have issued the order? Furthermore, 2 Chronicles 35 includes Temple reform as one of Josiah's religious successes. It seems incredible that the Chronicler would record an embarrassing failure to restore the most significant item of Temple worship. This is inconsistent with the Chronicler's pattern of promoting a positive image of the Temple and the Ark.[34] Also, many commentators agree that Jeremiah's prophecy cannot be used to imply that the Ark was no longer in existence when Jeremiah wrote this verse toward the end of the monarchy. Conversely, it may be a text that asserts the promise of the Ark's preservation and restoration in Judah (*see* chapter 15).

What Is in Ethiopia?

One member of the Ethiopian community I interviewed in Israel, Fantahune Melaku, formerly from the Gondar region, was familiar with a tradition that claimed the Axum church contained the *Torat Moshe:*

> There are guardians of the church [of Saint Mary of Zion in Axum] who will not allow Jews to enter. However, it has been said that once a man named Ademas received permission and was allowed even to enter into the cement vaults below the church, if he promised not to talk about what he saw. What he said that he saw were [columns with] titles written in Hebrew letters.[35]

It was difficult to get clarification beyond this description, but the impression Mr. Melaku got was that this referred to the *Torat Moshe*, the original composition of the Pentateuch made in the wilderness and once deposited alongside the Ark. (I must repeat that Mr. Melaku, as well as others, had not heard that the Ark itself was there.)

Jewish tradition holds that the *Torat Moshe* was later put within the Ark; but the Old Testament tells us that at the time of the First Temple, when the Ark was last seen, it contained only the stone tablets of the Ten Commandments (1 Kings 8:9; 2 Chronicles 5:10). If the "book of the law" discovered during repairs to the Temple in the time of Josiah was the *Torat Moshe* (2 Chronicles 34:14-15), we have evidence of its separation from the Ark. However, this does not warrant the supposition that it might have been removed at this time to Ethiopia. First, there is no historical evidence of Ethiopian contact (in that era) that would have permitted such a transfer. Second, the *Torat Moshe* sparked a significant revival when it was discovered (2 Chronicles 34:18-33). Consequently, it would have been guarded as a national and spiritual treasure. And third, it appears that this same "book of the law" was still with Israel after the return from exile and rebuilding of the Temple; when Ezra read it before the people, a similar spiritual response took place (*see* Nehemiah 8:1–9:38).

Some proponents of the Ethiopian theory suggest that originally there were two Israelite Arks. This is based on an account in the *Aggadah* (Jewish legends) that claimed there was a wooden Ark containing the fragments of the first tablets of the Law and a second gold Ark housing the second set of tablets and the *Torat Moshe* (or Torah). According to this view, the First Ark was taken into battle, while the second was taken out by the Israelites only on special occasions. Some believe it was this Ark that was taken to Ethiopia.

This, however, does not satisfy the statement in the Ethiopian royal chronicles that a replica replaced the true Ark; the *Aggadah* legends say both Arks were true Arks. Even so, Jewish tradition contends that these two were later combined as one by Solomon and placed within the Temple. The Talmud may support this idea when it states that *both* the whole and the broken tablets were contained in one single Ark (*Berakot* 8b; *Baba Bathra* 14b).[36] At any rate, if two separate Ark-boxes ever existed, they were made inseparable before the time of Menelik's birth (according to the Ethiopian legend).

The object known as the Tabot was said to be a Christian document written on wood and housed within a box, replicas of which are contained in every church. Hancock was shown examples of tabatot that were in the possession of the British Museum. They had been taken from Ethiopia during the Napier expedition to Abyssinia (1867–1868) and are presently housed in the ethnographic store in Hackney as part of the Holmes collection. These tabatot were square and rectangular wooden objects about 18 inches in length and width and three inches thick. They were written upon in *Geéz*, a liturgical language, and inscribed with crosses and other devices.[37] Hancock believes these were actual representations of the true Ark that supposedly resides in Axum.

Again, no one with whom I spoke had heard that the Ark of the Covenant was at Axum—only that the ancient Torah scroll which had once accompanied the Ark was there. Even this, however, is probably a matter of mistaken identification by orthodox priests of the past. While Axúm probably houses an ancient Christian artifact (and one cannot yet rule out even an ancient Semitic artifact), there is no evidence—except popular Ethiopian tradition based on the Ethiopian royal chronicles— to support the claim that this is related to the Ark. An Ethiopian in Ashdod named Abebe Brhane has been researching this issue for years and is planning to publish his findings. Perhaps when this information is made available we will have a clearer picture of the object in Axum.

Even so, the theory that the Ark may be in Ethiopia is rejected by the rabbis with the most direct control over and knowledge of the search for the Ark. They say that such a story is patently absurd. For example, Rabbi Shlomo Goren replied to the Ethiopian question in general by saying:

> I have heard this and it is a foolish suggestion! It is a joke! The same people even say that Noah's Ark was taken to Ethiopia! The ten tribes didn't even take the Ark with them when they were exiled from Israel because they didn't govern [control] the place of the Ark. They were in Samaria and the Ark was in Jerusalem, so they couldn't get to it. So how could the Ethiopians?[38]

Was the Ark Moved?

Author Grant Jeffrey says that members of Ethiopia's royal family told him that they have held the Ark in safekeeping for generations so that it could one day be returned to a restored Israel and placed in the rebuilt Temple. In a recent conversation, Grant told me that he believes the Ark was returned to Israel with the last Ethiopian exodus (Operation Solomon) in

1992 and is being held by orthodox rabbis in a guarded location in Jerusalem.[39] If this is so, then we need only await a newsbreak telling the world that the Ark has been recovered.

However, my sources in the Ethiopian *(Falasha)* community in Jerusalem, including one of the Ethiopian priests, denied that any such event could have occurred because the object in Axum is highly guarded by Christian monks who have no reason to negotiate with Jews or the State of Israel over what they consider a sacred Christian possession. These sources said their connections with the government and religious leaders were such that if any such transaction took place, they were in a position to know. They thought this rumor may have originated from a radio broadcast that said a torah scroll was discovered on the small island of Bahada in the northern part of Ethiopia and brought to Israel. It was believed that former Ethiopian monarch Haile Selassie hid it there and that it was recovered during Operation Solomon. On the basis of their testimony, if ever such an ancient treasure were in Axum, it is in Axum still.

The identity of this treasure, however, is still subject to debate. Ethiopian tradition, which lacks any corroborating scriptural support, does not offer convincing testimony that the treasure is the original Ark. More likely, the object at Axum is entirely of later Christian origin, possibly a portable shrine (called a *feretory*) which housed the relics of saints.

The quest for the Ark outside of Israel is exceeded only by the search within Israel itself. It is to this search that we now turn.

9

The Great Treasure Hunt Inside Israel

I know many among us who live in this country that believe they know the secrets to the Treasures [of the Temple].[1]

—Dr. Dan Bahat, former official archaeologist for the City of Jerusalem

While the hunt for the Ark outside the land of Israel has had strong supporters, by far the most popular search sites have been within the borders of the modern Israeli state. Ancient relics hidden in the Holy Land do not preserve well; only those things buried within moisture-resistant subterranean vaults or sequestered in sand or concealed in the caves of the Judean desert can be expected to survive. For this reason, theories most often point to crypts in Jerusalem and the Dead Sea region as the most likely sites for the recovery of Temple treasure. Since in biblical terms one always goes "up" to Jerusalem, let us begin with the lowest of levels (in fact, the lowest on earth)—the area of the Dead Sea.

The Search at Ein-Gedi

The principal character in this story was an American by

the name of Larry Blaser. In reading the works of Ellen G. White (founder of the Seventh-Day Adventists), Blaser came across White's conjecture that the Ark had been hidden in a cave before the Babylonian destruction of Jerusalem. Rejecting all other historical evidence, Blaser imagined that the best place to have hidden the Ark would have been at Ein-Gedi, because David, Israel's national hero, once hid there. While it is not impossible that artifacts and even treasure may be hidden at Ein-Gedi (since a rare aromatic balsam oil was harvested for the Temple service from trees that grew only at this site), Blaser's convictions were not based on such empirical data.

Mounting an expedition with professional miners—experts at locating underground anomalies—Blaser arrived at a rocky hill at Ein-Gedi that he identified as the Rock of the Wild Goats, in which he supposed was the cave of David. Preliminary soundings seemed to indicate the presence of a manmade wall blocking the entrance to a cave. With this information, Blaser was able to secure an excavation permit from the Israeli Department of Antiquities. When his team began work at the site, however, they soon discovered that the "artificial wall" was simply a natural bedrock seal and that the "cave" was just a natural cavity that had never been entered.[2] Blaser, therefore, returned home with only his vision and without further intentions to continue his search.

The Search at the Wadi Jafet Zaben

In March of 1994, the National Geographic Explorer series aired a segment entitled "The Search for the Lost Ark." This presentation featured a search undertaken in the Dead Sea region by Texas resident (and Israeli citizen) Vendyl Jones. Jones last made international news in April of 1992 when he announced he was "on the verge of recovering the lost Ark." His archaeological dig had reportedly unearthed an estimated 900 pounds of a reddish substance at the entrance to a newly excavated cave adjacent to his earlier-worked "Cave of the Column" located north of Qumran at the Wadi Jafet Zaben. Jones claimed that the substance had been identified by chemical analysis at the Weizman Institute of Science as the *pitum haketoret*, a specially mixed incense used in the ancient Temple service.[3] Jones claimed his discovery was significant because this kind of incense was allegedly listed among the items supposedly removed from the Second Temple and hidden in the Judean desert before the Roman destruction of Jerusalem.

Buried Treasure

Jones believes the location of the Temple treasure was preserved in the Copper Scrolls, one of which was found at Qumran in Cave III in 1952, next to his site. (In fact, Jones chose this site because he believed that a second Copper Scroll [mentioned in the first] may be located nearby.) Inscribed on this metallic scroll are directions for retrieving Temple treasure and other items buried in 64 separate and secret places throughout the desert region. Jones believes that his "Cave of the Column" is the one indicated in this scroll.

Jones began digging in the Judean desert in 1977. One of his initial, and continuing, motivations has been his impression that he is destined to uncover the Temple treasures. This belief stems from his discovery of the text on a fifteenth-century A.D. woodcut of the red heifer ceremony, which he translated as saying, "There is a Gentile, who is not an idol worshiper, a Gentile who believes in the one God, and he will find the ashes. . . . And they will sweep every corner until they have found her." Jones, of course, applies this text to himself, and has frequently quoted Rabbi Shlomo Goren's statement that Gentiles will assist in the discovery of the Temple vessels and the restoration of Temple worship (a conclusion based on Zechariah 6:15).

In 1988 Joseph Patrich, an archaeologist with Hebrew University, was excavating at a cave adjacent to the one in which

Jones claims he found the incense. One of Patrich's workers, Benny Ayers, found an ancient juglet holding a liquid that Jones has identified as the anointing oil used in the Temple ritual. This, he believes, "matches the description" in the Copper scroll, and along with the "Temple incense," has convinced him that he is on a predestined path. He says:

> We hope to find [in the new cave] a burial stone that closes the mouth of a second chamber and 40 steps that lead to a massive underground chamber. That's where everything is hidden. The incense and the anointing oil were deposited in this area to encourage you to say, "You are on the right trail."[4]

However, Joseph Patrich does not connect the juglet with the Temple or its service. He says, "What does the anointing oil have to do with the temple artifacts? He's [Jones] just wasting money and wasting time and wasting the goodwill of people because of the place he insists on excavating."[5]

A similar denunciation of the "Temple incense" has been made by Temple Institute Public Relations Director Chaim Richman, who contends that if it is "Temple incense," it must have been rejected as improperly mixed because it was found scattered on a floor and not contained in a stone vessel as required by Jewish law. In addition, Dr. Gary Collett, who is also excavating at Qumran, has said he heard that the Weisman Institute die *not* perform a chemical analysis on the "incense" and that the story was concocted by Jones.

Whether or not this is true, shortly after the discovery of the "incense," the Israeli Antiquities Authority closed down the dig—just as, Jones says, he was on the verge of locating the Ark. Antiquities Authority spokesman Efrat Orbach explained that Jones could not be granted an official excavation permit (although he has received temporary permits because of the volunteers he brings) because he is not a full-time archaeologist nor is he connected with any acceptable sponsoring institution such as a university. Nevertheless, Jones returned to his site in 1994 with about 40 volunteers to renew his dig and to employ remote sensing equipment designed to locate his cave's supposed hidden chamber.

The Ark Connection

Jones's specific quest for years has been the ashes of the red heifer, which he argues are necessary to convince the Muslim world of Israeli superiority, purify the Jewish priesthood, and permit the rebuilding of the Third Temple. Originally he also talked about the Ark, but only as secondary to the ashes of the red heifer. Since the *Raiders of the Lost Ark* film, however— whose character of Indiana Jones he claims to have inspired, a claim denied by the film's producers, Steven Spielberg and George Lucas—Jones has put the Ark to the fore, announcing in all his interviews that he believes he will find not only the Ark but also the Tabernacle at his site.

I believe Jones's early lack of emphasis on the Ark may be explained on the following counts. First, he was then associated with the late Pesach Bar-Adon, a respected Israeli archaeologist whose own finds in the Judean desert were renowned. Pesach, whose brother Aaron is also a scholar on the Dead Sea Scrolls and was my professor during my doctoral work at the University of Texas, believes his brother would not have served such a sensationalist goal. Second, the Copper Scroll does not mention the Ark, and Jones sought verification for his work on the basis of the scroll. (In addition, Jones has contended that the Ark's powers can be restored only after it has been purified by the ashes of the red heifer.)[6] Third, while the search for the Ark has always generated interest, the Hollywood film and Jones's boast on the theme assured him of endless volunteers (if not increased financial support), so he capitalized on the Ark's new attraction.[7] At any rate, Jones says he is confident that he will uncover the ashes of the red heifer in 1994 and he plans to continue until he has found all the Temple treasures.

Who Is Vendyl Jones?

Vendyl Jones, who once served Baptist pastorates, has renounced his Christian faith (though he continues to minister!). He believes that the New Testament is a fraud contrived by the Catholic church in the fourth century from collections of apostolic writings with the intention of replacing Judaism. After moving for a time to Israel, divorcing his wife (leaving five children), and taking a younger Israeli wife, he started the *B'nai Noach* ("Children of Noah") movement.[8] This group seeks ostensibly to teach Torah to Gentile Christians but in fact has disrupted local churches and attempted to make church members convert to Judaism. I spoke directly with Jones about his theology when our groups met on tour in Israel. He stated that the New Testament, Jesus, and the idea of the Triunity of God are all false. He maintains that "Jews are saved through the Abrahamic covenant, not Jesus!"[9]

While Jones may live however he wishes and believe whatever he wants, I am concerned because he still makes the circuit of Christian churches and radio programs and is joined by many Christians on his digs. Apparently people are unaware of his beliefs or they have insufficient background to distinguish his teachings from those of orthodox Christianity. Evangelical Christians in particular are attracted by his support for Israel and his views about Israel's prophetic future. They assume his theology is consistent with similar views espoused by evangelical teachers, or simply disregard his "theological eccentricities" in favor of the "archaeological" contribution they imagine he is making. If Christians desire to join with him in his work, they should first understand what they are supporting.

The Search at Qumran

The Claim

Jones's site is not the only one in the Dead Sea area claimed to contain the treasure described in the Copper Scroll. At one time O'Neil Carmen sought for the treasure about half a mile from Jones's site. The most recent competitive claim, however, is that of Dr. Gary Collett. He has concluded that Jones is digging in the wrong place because Jones mistakenly believes his site is the Wadi Ha-Kippah mentioned in the Copper Scroll; Collett believes the correct site is Qumran. He has submitted the evidence for this identification to the Israeli Department of Antiquities. *Kippah* (the Hebrew word used for the Jewish skullcap) can mean "vault," "arch," or "doorway," and Collett argues that it comes through the Aramaic language in its nominative form as *qimron.* This was the first-century name of the present Wadi Qumran and of Khirbet Qumran (supposed home of the Essene community) and the caves of the Dead Sea Scrolls.[10] Collett also believes that Cave IV bears resemblances to the First and Second Temples and that its lower level may have at one time housed the Ark during the time of Jeremiah. He bases this on an account in 2 Maccabees that he interprets to refer to Qumran rather than Mount Nebo.[11] Collett's purpose is similar to that of others searching for Temple treasure; in a recent newsletter from his supporting organization the following was stated:

> If we should find the ashes of the red heifer (Numbers 19) and also the Tabernacle of David (Acts 15:16) and (Amos 9:11) how long would it take to set up Temple worship?[12]

Collett believes he or others from his organization may be destined to find the Temple treasures because of predicted Gentile involvement in the last days. Paul Synder, who directs the organization stateside, has voiced just this conviction in a letter to supporters:

> As we have said before, Rabbi Goren, formerly chief Rabbi of Israel, an elderly man that we have much respect for, has told us that the ashes of the red heifer must be found by Gentiles from a far country that loves Israel.[13]

Dr. Collett believes that his work is part of the prophetic plan that will usher in the days of messianic glory for Israel. While he believes that the Ark is most likely under the Temple Mount in Jerusalem, he is convinced his site contains the necessary items, particularly the ashes of the red heifer, that will permit the reinstitution of the sacrificial system and enable the Ark to be restored to a rebuilt Third Temple.

The Evidence

Geophysical investigation of the Qumran plateau overlooking Cave IV (thought to be the site of the Wadi Ha-Kippah) using ground-penetrating radar and seismic-reflection profiles was conducted by two scientists from Tel-Aviv University's Department of Geophysics and Planetary Sciences in 1992.[14] Their published report revealed anomalies that were interpreted by Collett and his associate Aubrey Richardson as tunnels and collapsed caves containing items tentatively identified as pottery jars with scrolls, an urn, animal ashes, metals, and gemstones—a veritable unclaimed treasure trove.[15] Archaeologist Dr. Gordon Franz declared that excavation of this ledge was unnecessary to determine the nature of these anomalies, because a small camera inserted through a drill hole would obtain suitable results.[16] Nevertheless, exploratory trenches were dug on the site to examine these anomalies in 1993. The work was soon stopped by Yitzhak Magen on technicalities. Shortly afterward the Israeli Antiquities Authority, under

Amir Drori, launched "Operation Scroll," a massive artifact retrieval project initiated in light of the expected return of the area to Palestinian rule. Collett's plateau was one of the first to be examined by this project (as was Jones's site), and Drori placed the base of operations near Collett's dig at Qumran.

In January of 1994, after the project had completed its excavations on the plateau, I visited the site with Dr. Collett to assess the results. The excavators had dug up several of the anomalous areas and revealed the predicted storage bins lined with river rocks and plastered with lime (*see photo section*). These had been located using Collett's geophysical survey map. As far as is known, these bins were empty, although one of those present during the excavation reported that a silver bowl had been unearthed on the plateau near these pits. (This information was not reported in any published account of the operation.) Antiquities Authority dug up only a few of the anomalies, and according to Collett, not the ones containing possible Temple treasure because they did not have access to his more detailed map. In the summer of 1994, Dr. James Strange, whose excavations at Sepphoris in the region of Galilee are well known and who has added his professional sponsorship to Collett's dig, will begin new excavation at the site.[17] In addition, infrared scans of the site by helicopter also are planned to help pinpoint the exact location of any artifacts buried on the plateau. Perhaps the future will soon reveal exciting developments that will advance the possibility of uncovering lost Temple treasure.

The Search in Jerusalem

Just as the only legitimate place for the restoration of the Temple is Jerusalem, so do many people contend that the only possible hiding place for the lost Ark is within the boundaries of its own home town. As we have seen, such a location has the support of both Scripture and tradition. Several sites have been proposed for the Ark in Jerusalem, but most of them are quite speculative and have been included here for the sake of completeness. One location, Mount Calvary, has received much attention in America and therefore merits a thorough critique.

The Search in the Hinnom Valley

In conversations with Dr. David Allen Lewis, an author who has made more than 50 trips to the Middle East, I learned of an incredible theory that the Ark may be within a fully constructed Temple buried in the Hinnom Valley at a site visible from the Abu Tor observation point. The theory comes from several sources familiar to Dr. Lewis, as well as from Dr. Yehuda Oppenheim, whose recent work has been with the Ezekiel Tablets housed at the Yad Ben-Zvi Institute in the Rehavia section of West Jerusalem. These tablets consist of the book of Ezekiel on 64 marble and four basalt tablets. The Hebrew writing is of square (Aramaic) character and is in form of raised relief (that is, the letters rise above the writing surface). Based on Dr. Oppenheim's investigation of these curious tablets—unofficially rumored to be of Babylonian origin although officially designated as medieval—there is supposedly a coded message in the Hebrew text indicating the location of Ezekiel's Temple. According to the message, this location in the Hinnom Valley south of the Temple Mount had an entrance on the northwestern slope of the Mount of Olives guarded by two red-painted lions and inscriptions on the walls in the form of a wheel-within-a-wheel (cf. Ezekiel 1:10, 16).

According to Dr. Lewis, a group that believed this story bored a hole at the proper location in the valley, discovered a tunnel, entered it, and found precisely these items. They told Dr. Lewis that the shaft they discovered was filled with reconstituted rock and that they could go no further, but they believe there is an underground building located beyond this point.[18]

I decided to investigate this intriguing story myself, and along with an archaeologist went to explore the area. We walked through the Hinnom Valley from the village of Abu Tor to the Silwan village. Most of this area is a garbage dump and the topographical features did not easily lend themselves to such an undertaking. We discovered no evidence of any structures that might confirm this story, so for now it must be relegated to the realm of rumor.

The Search on the Mount of Olives

Zvi Hoffman, an archaeologist and former deputy minister of the Israeli Ministry of Religious Affairs, has suggested that the Ark might be hidden in a cave on the Mount of Olives directly across from the Temple Mount. His theory is based on a statement in 2 Maccabees that tells of Jeremiah taking the Ark from the Temple Mount. The account in Maccabees says the Ark was taken to "the mountain where Moses climbed up and saw the heritage of God" (usually interpreted as Mount Nebo). But Hoffman conjectured that because Jeremiah was seen going over the Mount of Olives—the last visible area from upon the Temple area—and then seen returning from the Mount of Olives empty-handed, the Ark was buried somewhere on this mountain. Hoffman also suggested that because 2 Maccabees contains historical embellishments, the Mount Nebo location was only a guess as to where the prophet had gone.

There is evidence that the Ark was brought to the Mount of Olives during ceremonial pilgrimages in the later monarchial period because the Shekinah had come from this site to fill the First Temple (*see* Ezekiel 11:23) and because traditionally God was worshiped there. In addition, the offering of the red heifer took place on the eastern slope of this mountain, directly across from the Temple Mount's Sushan Gate. Furthermore, some Christians consider the Mount of Olives to be the place of Jesus' crucifixion, and consequently find the prospect of the Ark hidden in the same spot an intriguing symbolism.

There are many caves on the Mount of Olives that date from the First Temple era, and the mountain on both sides of the Kidron Valley has been covered with Jewish and Christian (and later Muslim) tombs and crypts. Owing to Jewish laws of purity, however, it seems unlikely that Israel's holiest object would be buried in the midst of a cemetery. The lack of any clear tradition advocating this location further decreases the theory's plausibility.

The "Discovery" at Mount Calvary

American Ron Wyatt, in his self-published book *Discovered—Noah's Ark*, claims that on January 6, 1982, at 2:00 P.M. he discovered the Ark of the Covenant under the escarpment of Mount Calvary, which he believes to be what is known as "Jeremiah's Grotto." He states:

> I broke into a chamber beneath the Calvary escarpment, north of the city wall of Jerusalem. In that chamber is the Ark of the Covenant, the Table of Showbread—that I didn't see—they were covered with animal skins, with boards, and then stone.[19]

This most novel of sites has been proposed as the hiding place because Wyatt believes it fits the concept of Jesus as the High Priest offering the final blood atonement. To accomplish this, Wyatt figured, would require the Ark. So Wyatt speculated that when Jesus was crucified on the top of this hill, His blood must have run through a socket hole in which the cross was set, dripped down through a crack in the mountain (caused by the earthquake recorded in Matthew 27:51), and finally landed on the mercy seat of the Ark, which was positioned in a subterranean chamber some 60 feet beneath the mountain.

Wyatt sells a videotape of his various adventures. One segment shows him standing within a cavern inside Gordon's

Calvary at a box-shaped rock within which he claims he discovered the Ark! On this video, narrated by Wyatt's wife, Mary, the claim is made:

> In January of 1982, after steadily digging in a cave system since 1979, he busted through the rock into a chamber which contained a gold table and several other artifacts which Ron believed to be from the First Temple. Then, further back, he saw the top of a stone case which appeared to be the correct size to contain the Ark of the Covenant. Overwhelmed with emotion and double pneumonia, Ron passed out in that chamber for 45 minutes. He knew what was in that case, but now what? He attempted to photograph it with a Polaroid camera, a 35mm camera, and video. In every case, the photos were a white-out. He returned home to recover and work until he could afford to return. In May, he borrowed a colonoscope and went back. Drilling a small hole through the case, he was able to see enough to positively identify the contents of the stone case—it was the Ark![20]

In his July 1993 newsletter, Wyatt published drawings of an unconventional-looking Ark, based on his supposed personal examination of the Ark using a colonoscope.[21]

Because Wyatt has gone public with his "discovery" in churches and seminars throughout the United States and abroad, his claim must be subjected to scrutiny.

Evaluating the Claim

I wrote to Wyatt with the hope of obtaining a statement that I could include in this report of his work, but Wyatt never answered my letter. As a result, my evaluation of his claim does not have the benefit of interaction and discussion. His claim alone, however, provides much to doubt.

My main objection is this: Why would such a holy object as the Ark be purposely put under such a place of defilement as an execution site? It might be argued that this location was not an execution site at the end of the monarchial period when the Ark was hidden. But ultimately we are forced to admit that God would allow such an act of desecration since He, in His omniscience, knew that it would become such a place. Theology aside, we have to remember that the Garden Tomb (which is a part of Mount Calvary) dates to the First Temple era, so the site itself was already a burial grounds before the Ark would have been put into hiding. Because the Ark was hidden specifically to *preserve* it from defilement, the Garden Tomb would have been disqualified as a potential hiding place.

Credibility Problems

Bill Crouse, founder of Christian Information Ministries International, has carefully researched Wyatt's credentials and claims. Perhaps his evaluation best summarizes the controversy surrounding Wyatt:

> Evidence generally stands or falls on its own merits. Rarely is there a need to delve into the nature and character of the one making a claim. A careful evaluation of the facts is usually sufficient. Unless, of course, the one making the claim calls attention to himself in such a way that makes us openly skeptical. Would you . . . not question someone who not only claims to have found Noah's Ark, but also every archaeological site of interest to Christians?[22]

Some of the sites Wyatt claims to have discovered are the true Mount Sinai, the spot where the ground swallowed up Korah and his followers, the exact location where the Israelites crossed the Red Sea, the site of the crucifixion, and the tomb of

Christ. His claims to archaeological discoveries include Noah's Ark, the chariots of Pharaoh under the Red Sea, the 12 altars built by Moses, and Abraham's family tomb in Hebron (*not* under the 2,000-year-old shrine!). In addition, he claims to have solved the mystery behind the construction of the Egyptian pyramids, cracked the code of the Copper Scroll, and discovered how the Shroud of Turin was forged. In light of these fantastic assertions, Crouse concludes, "Is Ron Wyatt the greatest archaeologist who ever lived? Or is there another explanation?"[23]

Part of the answer may be found in Wyatt's dubious credentials. His professional training is as a nurse anesthetist, not as an archaeologist. While this does not disqualify him from finding an archaeological site or artifact, it does raise questions as to how he could have solved historical and scientific problems and made discoveries that have baffled the greatest professional archaeologists of all time!

But there is another more disconcerting report that casts suspicion on Wyatt's credibility. Wyatt hired Jeff Roberts and Associates, a public relations firm in Hendersonville, Tennessee, to arrange his speaking engagements. This firm produced for Wyatt a packet of materials that stated he was a Korean War veteran, that he had graduated from the University of Michigan with honors in pre-med, and that he had completed all the requirements for both M.A. and Ph.D. degrees in antiquities. When others investigated these credentials, they found none of these statements to be accurate. There is no record that Wyatt served in Korea and no evidence that he worked toward any degree at the time these materials were printed, although he did attend *Western* Michigan University for several years.

A Damaging Report

Further doubt as to Wyatt's credibility was supplied by Dr. Jim Fleming, founder and former director of the Jerusalem

Center for Biblical Studies (located at Tantur) and an editorial advisor to *Biblical Archaeology Review*. He told me in the summer of 1993 that he had originally been asked by Wyatt to be his archaeological advisor during his excavations at Mount Calvary. Because Dr. Dan Bahat, a Jerusalem archaeologist and lecturer at Hebrew University, had agreed to sponsor the dig, Fleming tentatively agreed. After spending time with Wyatt at the site, however, Fleming became alarmed at both his claims and techniques. In one instance, Fleming saw Wyatt drop a hammer down into a large crack in the mountain. Later, Wyatt offered as proof that he had discovered the Ark a metal-detector reading that indicated a metal object within the rock. Fleming says he left after this incident. Others have given similar disturbing reports concerning Wyatt's conduct at the site. One such observer, the Reverend John Woods, noted, "I saw him explaining to a group that a piece of metal embedded in the face of the Garden Tomb was part of the seal Pilate had placed upon the tomb. In fact it was a piece of shrapnel from the war [in 1967]."[24]

Wyatt does tell amazing stories and apparently receives generous support from uninformed churches where he speaks. What he and other explorers like him have *not* done is discover the Ark!

10

The Secret Beneath the Stone

All the foundations of the Holy Temple have gone into secret hiding places, none have been lost, not even one. And when the Holy One Blessed be He returns, and restores Jerusalem to her original place, those original stone foundations will return to their places. [1]

—Pe'kuday

Could it be that the quest to find the lost Ark is really nothing more than a romantic treasure-hunter's dream? I admit I felt this way until about five years ago, when I began to investigate a story that had reached me through many reliable sources. The more I learned about this story, the more I was convinced that this was surely the greatest—and in my opinion, the most promising—of all the searches for the Ark! In order to set the proper stage for this story of the secret beneath the stone, let us first consider the city of two tales.

A City of Two Tales

Charles Dickens's classic *A Tale of Two Cities* turned upon the tragedy of a great exchange. For both of his main characters, the exchange brought release from bondage and the beginning of a new life.

During the past quarter century another classic has been in the works that we might call "A City of Two Tales." But in this story, the tragedy of exchange is reversed from that in Dickens's fiction. The city in this story is Jerusalem, and the tragedy is a twofold tale of conflict between religious expectation and political expediency.

For religious Jews concerned with the national and spiritual redemption of Israel, these two tragedies are enshrined in infamy. The first was the loss of control of the Temple Mount in July of 1967, and the second was the loss of access to the underground Temple Mount Gate in July of 1981. Both incidents involved the same sacred area, with the same holy hope, and to some extent the same contenders.

The Tragedy of the Temple Mount

In 1967, the feeling of tragedy was mixed with betrayal as Defense Minister Moshe Dayan removed control of Judaism's most holy site from Rabbi Shlomo Goren and returned it to the Wakf (the Islamic authority). The Temple Mount had been captured from Jordanian forces only a month earlier during the final days of the Six-Day War. A jubilant Israeli army occupied the site and hoisted the flag of the State of Israel to the top of the Dome of the Rock. The Arab world, as well as the world at large, expected to see the soon erection of the long-awaited Jewish Temple. Rabbi Shlomo Goren was placed in charge of the Temple Mount and he immediately assigned a corps of engineers a two-week task of measuring and mapping the area. He also opened a synagogue on the Mount and brought Torah scrolls, prayer books, and other items of worship in expectation of a revival of Jewish presence at the site. But after only one month, Dayan ordered Goren to close down the synagogue and to evacuate the site. He announced that it had been given back to the Muslims as a gesture of peace. Rabbi Goren explains the exceptional nature of this act and of his feelings on that day:

> I had a fight with Dayan for us to remain on the Temple Mount. But Dayan was pro-Arabic, and religion was meaningless to him and the Temple Mount was unimportant to him. I said to him, "Who gave you permission to hand over the Temple Mount—the Holy of the Holies of Israel—to them [the Arabs]?" He said, "This is the decision of the government!" It was not true. He acted [on his own authority] and [Prime Minister] Begin accepted whatever he did.[2]

It is thought that Dayan believed many religious Jews intended to destroy the Islamic structures on the Mount and prepare for the rebuilding of the Third Temple. For his part, Rabbi Goren insisted he would not have touched these buildings; he had confined his synagogue to the area permitted in Jewish law at the corner of the Mount. Nevertheless, Dayan considered that a Jewish occupation of the Temple Mount would only lead to a greater threat of war with the Arab League, and so took the initiative that has only postponed the inevitable contest for the site between Arab and Jew.

The Tragedy of the Temple Gate

In 1981, Rabbi Goren again felt betrayed by an Israeli government official. This time it was Joseph Berg, who allowed Muslim Arabs to force a conflict within Goren's secretly excavated tunnels beneath the Temple Mount. The ensuing melee resulted in the permanent closure of the dig, an excavation that Goren had proclaimed would lead to the greatest discovery of all time, the Ark of the Covenant.

If it had been feared in 1967 that Israel's access to the Temple Mount might result in a rebuilding of the Temple and the provocation of Islamic *Jihad* (holy war), you can imagine the reactions that would result if news got out that the Ark of the Covenant had been found under the Temple Mount. Could this be the event that would finally incite the postponed war?

The Israeli reaction to the first tragedy of the Temple Mount was the revival of an Israeli-based worldwide movement to rebuild the Temple. These efforts were further intensified in response to the beginning of the Palestinian *Intafada* in 1987, whose goal includes the return of all Jerusalem. I described this movement in 1992 in my first book, *Ready to Rebuild: The Imminent Plan to Rebuild the Last Days Temple.* Since the publication of that book and others like it, the Christian public has been made more aware of the strategic significance of the Temple Mount to the present Middle East conflict and especially of its central role in the Bible's predictions concerning the final chapter of human history.

This brings us to the second tragedy that took place at the Temple Mount. This story has been carefully guarded for the past 13 years and the full tale has never been told. Yet it is the most recent and best documented of all the modern searches for the Ark. Here, revealed for the first time, is the story of the secret beneath the stone.

The Stone and Its Secrets

We learned earlier that some rabbis believe that when King Solomon built the Temple, he foresaw its eventual destruction and constructed a secret chamber deep within the Temple Mount to serve as a security vault in such times of danger. Jewish tradition maintains that the Ark has been housed in this secret chamber underneath the Temple Mount ever since King Josiah instructed the Levites to place it there some 36 years before the destruction of the First Temple (2 Chronicles 35:3). If the rock within the present Muslim Dome of the Rock is the ancient *'Even Shetiyah* ("Foundation Stone") that was within

Artist's conception of the Ark within the secret chamber, based on the
testimony of Rabbi Mati Dan Hacohen in 1982.

Re-creation of the Ark's transport to the battlefield by Kohathite Levitical priests. Courtesy of Desperado-Secrets Films, Inc.

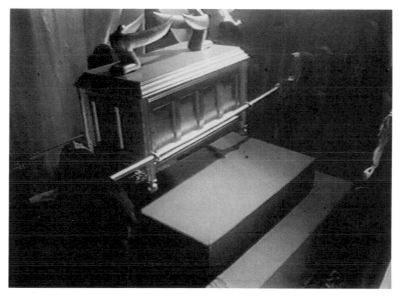

Re-creation of the Levite priests hiding the Ark in the subterranean chamber beneath the Holy of Holies prior to the Babylonian invasion. Courtesy of Desperado-Secrets Films, Inc.

The author points to the non-Jewish base on the menorah in a copy of
the relief on the Arch of Titus in Rome. The original Mosaic menorah
had a three-legged base, and this difference may indicate that the
treasures taken by the Romans in A.D. 70 were not the actual Temple
treasures.

Some people believe that the Temple treasures captured by the Romans in A.D. 70 were stored in vaults beneath the ancient Nea Church in Jerusalem's Jewish Quarter. Courtesy of The History of Jerusalem Museum.

The *'Even Shetiyyah* ("Foundation Stone") within the Muslim Dome of the Rock. Some people believe this is where the Ark once rested within the Holy of Holies in the First Temple.

The author with a modern Torah-ark in the synagogue of Rabbi Getz, which is located above Warren's Gate (now sealed over). During the construction of this synagogue the gate and tunnels beyond it were discovered.

Rabbi Meir Yehuda Getz, Chief Rabbi of the Western Wall and Holy Places in Israel, standing in front of the now-sealed Warren's Gate. Rabbi Getz conducted an underground excavation here, digging through a tunnel in the direction of the Holy of Holies in search of the Ark.

Gershon Salomon, founder and director of the Temple Mount and Land of Israel Faithful, in his office (adorned by a banner depicting the Ark). Involved in the secret excavation beneath the Temple Mount, he believes the Ark will be brought out in the near future.

The author inside the Dome of the Rock, standing by the entrance to the cave known as the "Well of the Souls." Tradition says that a passageway beneath this cave leads to the subterranean chamber which houses the Temple treasures. It was in this cave that the Parker expedition attempted to find the Ark in 1911.

The author and Rabbi Shlomo Goren, former Chief Rabbi of Israel, who governed the Temple Mount in 1967. Rabbi Goren, along with Rabbi Getz, directed the secret excavation beneath the Temple Mount in 1981.

One of the storage bins revealed by the excavations at Dr. Gary Collett's site during Operation Scroll in December 1993. A silver bowl was discovered nearby and may indicate the presence of additional ancient treasures.

Inset. Using ground-penetrating radar to locate buried objects under the Qumran plateau in 1991.

The author in Cave III at the spot where the Copper Scroll (*inset*) was discovered in 1953. It lists 64 separate hiding places for Temple treasure. The site is high in the cliffs above the Wadi Jafet Zaben north of the Dead Sea.

The author and Dr. Gary Collett inside Qumran Cave IVb, where many of the Dead Sea Scrolls were discovered in 1948. Dr. Collett believes the Ark was temporarily stored here by Jeremiah before the Babylonian destruction.

Inset. The Wadi Qumran, identified by Dr. Collett and Aubrey Richardson as the Wadi Ha-Kippah of the Copper Scroll. Note the dome-shaped mountain in the background, the *kippah* (dome), and Caves IVa and IVb (foreground), which, according to Collett, represent the First and Second Temples and served as markers to the enlightened that the Temple treasure was buried on the opposite plateau.

Poster in the Jewish Quarter of Jerusalem announcing the expected arrival of the Messiah, whom the Lubavitchers believe is Menachem Mendel Schneerson. He is their present spiritual leader and currently resides in New York. The Hebrew text reads, "[Long] live our master, our teacher, and our rebbe King Messiah forever and ever!"

Hebrew graffiti on the Golden Gate at the east of the Temple Mount, which reads as a prayer: "Come Messiah!" Jewish tradition says that in the end times Elijah and the Messiah will lead the Jews triumphantly into the Temple through the eastern Temple gateway. Muslims have built a cemetery along the eastern wall to prevent Elijah (who is a priest) and the Messiah from entering, because going through a burial ground would defile them.

the Holy of Holies, then immediately beneath this stone should lie the secret chamber containing the holy Ark.

Rabbi Mayer Yehuda Getz, official rabbi of the jurisdiction of the Temple Mount, believes that the Dome of the Rock is the site of the Great Altar and that the Holy of Holies was located 210 feet forward from the rock. He argues that "when the altar was built, they built a gigantic wall around the Moriah mountain. They dug tunnels from the sides of the mountain to the wall around it. One of these tunnels was made to store the Ark of the Covenant in times of trouble or distress."[3]

In support of Rabbi Getz is the fact that both the Temple Scroll and Ezekiel's Temple locate the altar in the center of the Temple Mount. However, the Mishnah tractate *Middot's* description of the Second Temple does not agree with this location. Rabbi Goren is of a similar opinion, based on his 1967 survey of the surface area of the Mount.[4] Nevertheless, Dan Bahat insists that the rock under the Dome is the only possible place for the Holy of Holies:

> There is no doubt that the Dome of the Rock is part of the Temple itself, and in my opinion, the Holy of Holies. Some others believe that this was the place of the altar of sacrifice, but I think that this is impossible; it won't fit with the natural features of the mountain. It is an axiom that the rock which can be seen in the middle of the Dome of the Rock is nothing but the rock of the Holy of Holies, the top of Mount Moriah, the place where Abraham . . . attempted to sacrifice Isaac.[5]

Regardless of which theory is correct, the rabbis have based their estimates on the assumption that Warren's Gate stood west of the Temple and opened almost directly in front of the Holy of Holies. With this in mind, let us consider Warren's Gate itself.

A Description of Warren's Gate

Warren's Gate was discovered by accident more than a century ago by Charles Warren during the first probes ever attempted underground at the Temple Mount. However, its exact location was not clearly specified in Warren's excavation reports and maps. Warren never revealed how he had found it or how he knew it to be one of the four ancient entrance gates to the Temple. It was later rediscovered and identified by the British explorer and excavator Charles Wilson (who named it Warren's Gate). It was located beneath the obscure Gate Bab-el-Mat'hara, which had been used as an Arab latrine until 1967. The vaulted passageway within was partially used as a water reservoir or cistern until recent times. Historical sources tell us that this gate led directly onto the Temple courts and was used for bringing in wood, sacrifices, and other materials needed for the Temple rites. Dr. Dan Bahat notes the historical significance of this site:

> This [gate] is a threshold to the Temple Mount and . . . one of the gates to the Temple.[6] This gate is the most important of all the gates because it is the nearest gate to the Holy of Holies. The eastern extremity of this passage is even nearer to the Holy of Holies, and this is why it was preferable for Jews to pray inside this vault. For over 450 years it was the holiest place where people came to pray, or in other words, from the Arab conquest of A.D. 638 till the Crusader conquest of A.D. 1099, it was the central synagogue of Israel's Jewry. It was called "the Cave" because it has the form of a cave, a kind of an underground vault penetrating into the Temple Mount, and thus it played a very important role in Jewish life in Jerusalem in the early Arab period simply because of its proximity to the Holy of Holies. When the Jews returned to Jerusalem after

> the Crusader rule, the Jews wanted to come back
> into [Warren's Gate], but the whole area was filled
> in with Islamic buildings, so they chose the second
> best site, the Western Wall further down [from the
> site of the Temple].[7]

This account by Bahat confirms the sanctity accorded to this
area in previous centuries—a sanctity that may well have been
enhanced because of the site's proximity to the hiding place of
the Ark. Bahat acknowledged this when he noted the attention
the early British explorers gave to this site in connection with
the Temple treasures when they searched for the Ark. These
early hunters had based their excavations on the ancient Jewish
accounts that mentioned the hiding place of the Ark. It was
these same sources that directed Rabbi Shlomo Goren to
excavate in this place and no other. He confirmed to me that his
initial leads came in part from the information given in 2
Chronicles 35:3, Jeremiah 3:16, and the Talmudic references to
the hiding of the Ark:

> Jeremiah's statement gives us a hint of what
> really happened to the Ark in the days of Josiah ben
> Amon. He became afraid that the Babylonians
> would take the Ark into captivity, so 36 years before
> the destruction of the First Temple, he dug very
> deep beneath the Holy of Holies—on the same line
> with the Holy of Holies—and hid it together with
> the tablets [of the Law], the pot of manna, and the
> stick of Aaron. I believe that it is still there, but we
> have to dig hundreds of meters down in the cham-
> bers that exist beneath the Temple Mount.[8]

Warren's Gate, which Josephus tells us provided the most
direct access to the Temple from the west, may have connected
with other subterranean passageways used by officiating priests
in the Temple to reach *miqvahs* (ritual purification pools)

located both north and south of the Temple complex. If so, it is conjectured that Warren's Gate might also have connected with a tunnel that entered the hidden passageway that led from under the "wood store" to the chamber of the Ark. While no official archaeological exploration has been done of this area, a clandestine search of the tunnel behind this gate was made during the early excavations at the site. Those who entered the site at that time testify that this conjecture is indeed correct.

The Excavations Behind Warren's Gate

In July of 1981, Rabbi Meir Yehuda Getz, chief rabbi of the Western Wall and all holy places in Israel, was in the process of constructing a new synagogue behind the Western Wall that would face the Temple Mount. As his workers were knocking out a place in the stone to affix a Torah cabinet, they accidentally rediscovered Warren's Gate and the open area behind it. Rabbi Getz details this discovery and explains why he is convinced that this entrance leads toward the Ark:

> After we traced the leaking water to its source, we discovered this large opening [Warren's Gate] 25 meters long, 30 meters high, and 8 meters wide. [I believed] it was from the First Temple. When we found this entrance [gate], I ordered the wall to be opened and we discovered a giant hall shaped like the Wilson Arch, but with exit tunnels running in different directions. The length [of this hall] was about 75 feet. There were some stairs that we descended for about 30 feet, however, at the bottom everything was full of water and mud. When we pumped this away I found an insect. This insect verified that this place was the place opposite the Holy of Holies [because] it is recorded in [the Mishnah] tractate *Yoma* that if the priest was found unclean, and therefore unable to get out of the Holy

of Holies, [he] should release an insect that would go under the veil. I have discovered this insect![9]

Rabbi Getz guessed that the large vaulted room was from the First Temple period. Rabbi Goren, however, put the discovery in its proper historical context:

> When King Solomon built the Temple, he built the Western Wall as a frame. . . . Between this frame and the actual wall of the Temple there was a [stone] filling to fill the gap in between. We discovered that underneath this frame all the stones are connected with the frame of the Temple. When our workers first entered [the gate] they thought that these kinds of rooms might have been built by the Turks for just collecting water, [but then] they saw an arch . . . and a beautiful hall[way]. This big vault that we saw was one of the main entrances to the Temple, probably the Second Temple.[10]

Once the rabbis realized the opportunity of actually entering the secret priestly passageways hidden for 2,500 years, they assembled a select team of ten men to further the excavations. This group, which included students of the Ateret Cohanim Yeshiva, began clearing the great hall that once had served as a cistern to the Mount. They expended a great deal of time and energy in clearing and cleaning this area. Ze'ev Bar-Tov, now treasurer of the Temple Mount Faithful organization, later observed this vaulted area and testified, "It looked just like a big cleaned apartment—not like most digs; it was very clean!" Behind this room the team began work on one of the passageways that led to the northeast. Rabbi Getz explains the location of this passage:

> From [the place where the insect was discovered] we saw several openings. One entrance was toward

the gate. It was closed, but we opened it. From there we saw a wall that was later built and was about 9 to 12 feet away from the warning wall of the Western Wall, which itself was only 15 feet from the Holy of Holies.[11]

The excavators proceeded onward in the direction of the Holy of Holies, underneath which they believed lay the chamber of the Ark. Describing this arduous operation, Rabbi Goren gives here for the first time the most complete account of those dramatic moments:

> We decided together with Rabbi Getz to start digging beneath the Temple Mount in the direction which, according to my measurements [taken in 1967 after the Six-Day War], we had to go in order to reach the Holy of Holies. It took us a long time— a year and a half—and it was very hard work. We found chambers half-filled with water and there were swamps and such which we had to drain. I had hoped that if we had enough time—another year and a half—we would have been able to reach the surface of the Holy of Holies beneath the Temple Mount.[12]

In an earlier interview, Rabbi Goren explained his thoughts at this point in the excavation:

> We were very close to the place on the Temple Mount where the Holy of Holies was located. We were very close, beneath the Holy of Holies. We believe that the holy Ark made by Moses, and the table from the Temple, and the candelabra made by Moses, along with other very important items, are hidden very deep underneath the Holy of Holies. We started digging and we came close to the place; we were not more than 30 or 40 yards away.[13]

Rabbi Goren has since revised his initial statement to express greater reserve as to the extent of his actual proximity to the expected Ark chamber:

> I imagined that [I was there] when I had dug in about 50 yards in a straight line from the place where the chamber of the Ark was. But it was still very deep—maybe 100 meters. If [Charles] Warren dug over 100 meters and he didn't get to the end [bedrock], what can one say about the Temple, its foundation, and the chambers beneath it! I believe that the Ark is somewhere beneath the Temple and the problem [now] is one of digging down a hundred meters.[14]

The Secret Shattered

The excavation of the tunnel had been a carefully guarded secret. Before the details were released to the public, Rabbi Getz said in 1991: "[It has now been] ten years since its discovery, and it is [still] a secret." Rabbi Goren also stressed this point with me. He insisted:

> [This work] was very secret. Nobody on the outside knew what we were doing inside. No news of our dig had been revealed to any journalist; we did not reveal the story to anyone. We had a budget and only a few people—about ten—were engaged in the work, but they took a vow not to tell anything about their work.[15]

Despite the cloak of secrecy that Rabbis Goren and Getz had maintained over their clandestine excavation, news eventually leaked to the media and public exposure forced a quick end to the work. Reports published at the time say that when word came to the Muslim Wakf that the Jews were about to uncover the Ark, the Wakf stopped the excavations by sending a Muslim mob to attack the excavators. Chaim Richman of the Temple Institute suggests that the Wakf had definite motives for the attack:

> They were afraid that if the Jews found these objects it would be the surest sign of all of a Jewish presence on the Temple Mount—that it wasn't some sort of mystical tradition. They were afraid that if these things were uncovered that we would rebuild the Temple. [It is part of] an orchestrated effort to destroy and eradicate any semblance of Jewish presence around the Temple Mount.[16]

The border police and the army say they had to intervene to keep Getz, Goren, and their men from being killed. Even after the riot had been stopped by the arrests of the students from the Yeshiva, another Arab riot occurred later at the site. That, in turn, was followed by a general strike called by the Muslim Council to protest the search for the Ark.

Rabbi Goren claims that the entire riot scenario was part of a political conspiracy to close his diggings in deference to Arab sensitivities following the Camp David peace accord between Israel and Egypt. Detailing the events of that time, the rabbi added, "This is the original story that no one else knows, not even Rabbi Getz." Here, then, for the first time is Rabbi Goren's full account of what transpired and of his strong feelings about it:

> One day a journalist who was a good friend of mine came up to me and told me that he knew what we were doing beneath the Temple Mount. I asked him to promise not to reveal it to the media and he promised me that he wouldn't, provided no other journalist found out. However, several months later he told me that a television journalist had learned of

our secret and that he was going to broadcast it on television. Because [my friend] wanted to be the first [to announce it], he said that his promise was no longer valid. I begged him not to do it, saying that he would destroy the entire work. He [went ahead and] announced on the radio that we were digging beneath the Temple Mount to get the direction of the Holy of Holies in order to find the holy Ark.[17]

What happened next must be told from two different vantage points—namely, from inside and outside the tunnel. Gershon Salomon, who took part in the excavation, recounts what happened inside the tunnel at the time of the attack:

We had just discovered another wall which blocked our continuance [into the tunnel]. I remember that the workers, along with Rabbi Getz, started to break down this wall, since beyond this point [Rabbi Getz conjectured] it continued to the place under the floors where the Ark of the Covenant, the Menorah, and the other vessels were. We were so very, very close! [But] at this moment the Arabs started to demonstrate against our activities. . . .[18]

Meanwhile, on the outside, Rabbi Goren continues the story by telling of his encounter with government officials who sought to close the project:

After he [the newsman] announced it, the Arabs got together on the Temple Mount and prepared to open the entrances [on the Temple Mount] to go down [inside the tunnels] and prevent our work. But while they [the Arabs] were still talking about it, Joseph Berg, the Minister of the Interior and of the police, suddenly came to me at my office and said that he would like to prevent the Arabs from going down to stop our work. He promised to put police at every entrance on the Temple Mount and to put an iron chain on the opening of these entrances so that no one could go down. But I didn't trust him. I knew that Berg would, if he could, hand over the Temple Mount to the Arabs—to the Wakf. So I asked him to sign an agreement, which he did, but before he had even left the building on the elevator I got a call from the [Western] Wall, saying, "Did you know that there is a fight at the Wall with your people where they are digging? There are hundreds of Arabs that have gone down into the chambers and there could be bloodshed!" I knew then that Berg had concocted the story [his offer of help] to camouflage his real intention of opening the entrances to the Arabs and telling them to go down to get us.

When I arrived at the Wall there were hundreds of police—even the chief of police [was there]—and I was happy that they were there because [I thought] they [the Arabs] would not be able to do anything. I asked them to come with me to see what was going on inside the dig. Some of the top officers followed me, [but] when I reached the place there were hundreds of Arabs inside—coming in from both sides and crying and shouting. . . . I went to get the police to arrest the Arabs and take them out, but when I turned all of the officers had disappeared. When I came outside [of the tunnel] to the Wall there were no police to be found. There are always police at the Wall to protect the people—to be on the safe side. But this time there were none! I became afraid because we were alone, so I called Berg at his office and told him that he had betrayed me! I asked him to send the police to protect us because otherwise we would be killed. When the police [still] could not be found, I called him again and told him he would be [held] responsible and that I was going to mobilize the boys of the Yeshiva Ha-Kotel and my Yeshiva [Ha-Idrah] and they were going down with pistols—with weapons—and there will be bloodshed! So I called to General Ariel Sharon, the defense minister, and told him the story and said if you do not send soldiers to evacuate the Arabs from the chambers, there will be bloodshed. But he said that he had foreign guests and could not do anything.

Finally, I called to the boys from the Yeshivot and a few hundred came with weapons. Meanwhile a cry came from Rabbi Getz's wife: "They are killing my husband!" At that moment the police appeared from where they were [apparently] hidden on the Temple Mount. The radio had reported that three Arabs had been killed and many wounded [in the riot], but it was a lie! It was simply an excuse for the police to exercise authority over us and to close down our dig. The police arrested the boys from our Yeshiva and put them in prison. They did nothing to the Arabs. Then they gave orders to immediately erect a new wall [over the entrance to the tunnel] and to close the chambers to prevent any [Jewish] access. [As a result] we lost all connection with the chamber which we were digging [that led to the Ark].[19]

A Site Sealed and Sequestered

Rabbi Goren added that on the following day, a Friday morning, he was invited to the airport for an official send-off for then Prime Minister Menachem Begin, who was going to

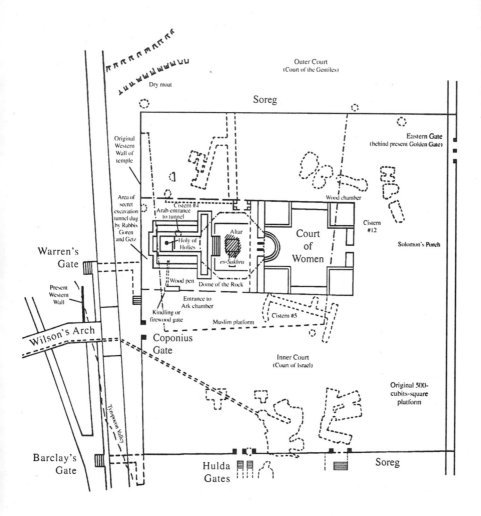

Map of the ancient Temple and surrounding courtyards superimposed upon the modern-day Temple Mount. This diagram shows where Rabbis Goren and Getz conducted their secret excavation and the proposed location of the Ark chamber (beneath the Holy of Holies).

Credits:

1) Placement of Temple and courtyards (with the Dome of the Rock at site of the altar)—Rabbis Goren and Getz
2) Temple Mount topography—B. Mazar and L. Ritmeyer

the United States to meet with President Reagan. At the airport Goren once again confronted Berg (in Begin's presence) about what he believed was an organized effort to close down his politically sensitive excavations. Goren says that he finally gave both officials an ultimatum that his Yeshiva boys be released from prison within the hour—and they complied! However, not only was access to the site not restored, but the original seal placed over the massive Warren Gate entrance was further reinforced with steel and a plaster wall by the government's Ministry of Religious Affairs. The surface of this wall was reworked in 1992 to give the appearance of rough natural rock because the contrast of smooth plaster drew too many questions from tourists.

This action may have resulted in part from the new focus the site received as a result of my story about the excavations for Sun International Pictures, which aired nationally in a segment about the Ark on the first CBS television special "Ancient Secrets of the Bible."[20] Supported by filmed interviews with Rabbis Goren and Getz, this televised account of the excavation won a 13-percent share of the audience on the night it aired and pushed CBS ahead to win the annual ratings "sweeps week."[21] The producers told me that based on audience response, the Ark segment was by far the most controversial and the most appealing part of the program.

Why Suppress This Story?

The rabbis still say that they know exactly where the Ark is located. They had not made such a full disclosure prior to this book, and even now have not revealed the Ark's precise location for fear that others might steal or destroy the Ark and other Temple treasures.

Yet this story has been suppressed for over a decade for other reasons as well. Rabbi Getz admits that the Ark's hiding place is known to the Israeli government, but that it has decided the matter is too politically volatile to go public. The announcement would likely cause worldwide media attention to be focused on the already sensitive Temple Mount area and provoke "premature" action by fringe groups wanting to build the Temple. In view of the prospect of a negotiable peace in the Middle East, the present actions of the government are decidedly against any disclosure of what it knows.

This may be precisely the reason the rabbis have chosen to break their long silence and tell the world of their discovery. Rabbi Goren is especially frustrated with what he sees as a secular government working against the will of God. Perhaps by exposing the secret beneath the stone he will be able to force the government to acknowledge the sanctity of the site and not relinquish it further to the Arabs.

Absolute confirmation of the rabbis' story is currently impossible because the Wakf and the Israeli government have sealed up the entrance to Warren's Gate. However, keep in mind that these men are leading political and religious figures in Israel and have nothing to gain by spreading a false rumor of this magnitude. Neither can we doubt that as trained rabbis they understand the details of what they have discovered. (In testimony to the sanctity of the site, Rabbi Getz still maintains his synagogue built directly on the wall above the sealed entrance.)

There are rabbis in Israel, most notably Rabbi Nahman Kahane of the Institute for Talmudic Commentaries, who have told me they doubt that Goren and Getz know the true location of the Ark. Yet there are others, such as Rabbis Yisrael Ariel and Chaim Richman of the Temple Institute, who are convinced the story is true.

I believe that Rabbi Goren and Rabbi Getz, who have honorable and impeccable credentials as scholars and rabbis, are telling the truth about their excavation. However, I suspect that they have told only as much as they want known about the now-14-year-old incident. Allow me to list some of the reasons for that possibility.

The Problem with the Media

One reason for believing that the rabbis might withhold some details is the natural reluctance interviewees have about how their words will be used. For instance, the Israeli media has developed a bad reputation with those who desire to re-build the Temple because it has taken serious interviews and placed them within a context that mocks the idea. Unfortunately, some Christian media have likewise acted without proper respect and sensitivity to those who have granted them interviews. Rabbi Chaim Richman of the Temple Institute has complained of seeing a Christian publication that featured a photo of his institute's founder, the acknowledged Torah scholar Rabbi Yisrael Ariel, with the caption, "Getting Ready for Jesus!" To orthodox rabbis who not only reject the messiahship of Jesus but also remember a long heritage of Christian anti-Semitism, such acts give them good cause to be cautious.

Second, the rabbis believe that holy matters like the Ark do not belong in a common discussion with secularists and Gentiles. In addition, both Rabbi Goren and Rabbi Getz believe that the secret of the Ark belongs to the future time of redemption and the Messiah's appearance. They may fear that a premature disclosure of the facts could possibly delay these events. There may be some evidence of this thinking reflected in Rabbi Goren's comment to writer Louis Rapoport made only one year after the closing of the gate: "The secret will be revealed just prior to building the Third Temple."[22]

On the other hand, it's possible that Rabbi Goren may have come public with these new details because he feels the time is right. If there are further secrets, it is doubtful that either he or Rabbi Getz would discuss them—even with other orthodox rabbis. No doubt they would act as they did during the dig, discussing details with only a trusted few.

The Problem with the Opposition

A third reason for suspecting that the rabbis are moderating what they know is the tremendous opposition to their project from both the religious sector and the Israeli government. Concerning the matter of religious approval, Rabbi Getz admitted to me, "What I did was not approved by many others." He then acknowledged that great rabbis of the past and present (including Goren's *rebbe*, Rabbi Kook) have rejected, on religious grounds, any search for the Ark. As an example, Getz told me of one encounter he had with Lubavitcher rabbis. They said to him, "What will you do with it if you find it? Will you bring tourists to look at it? You had better leave it closed until its time will come!"

Dan Bahat claimed this traditional attitude on the part of the orthodox Jews as the reason for the government's closing of Warren's Gate:

> Why don't we penetrate [the sealed gate] and go in? It is not merely a problem of politics or because behind this wall exists a modern Muslim cistern. This is not the problem. The problem here is that many of the people who are so ardent in keeping the purity of the Temple Mount are afraid that if they trespass the [religious boundary] line . . . they may come to places which they are not supposed to [enter]. [This is] because these places are too holy, and since we are [ceremonially] impure, it is impossible for them to go inside. This is the reason why observant Jews do not go up to the Temple [Mount]. Unfortunately the Muslims [mis]understood this [as saying] that we don't have any interest in the Temple Mount.[23]

Rabbi Goren strongly disagrees that this prohibition of religious Jews had anything to do with the closing of the gate: "It was Berg; it was his plan; he sent down the Arabs and gave the orders to close down our digging."[24] According to Rabbi Getz, the shutdown was entirely the decision of the Israeli government because of its desire to maintain good relations with the Arabs: "[Egyptian] President [Anwar] Sadat had been in Israel [after the Camp David peace accord] and we were in a peace process. The government did not want to disturb it [the peace with the Arabs] and therefore ordered the diggings stopped."[25]

Gershon Salomon gave a combination of these views when I asked for his opinion on the matter. He stated:

> Joseph Berg gave the order by decision of the government of Israel to close the gate to not incite the Arabs and to stop their demonstrations. It was not because of the orthodox Jews; they were not involved; and none of them could say [that is, none had the clout] to the government to stop it. When the government of Israel wanted to do something she did it, and so to say today that this [the closing of the gate] is because of the orthodox Jews is to rewrite history.[26]

The concern over government intervention in issues of religious importance is a crucial matter for the rabbis. They have already lost access to the Temple Mount above and below ground because of such government control. It may be that the rabbis are keeping quiet about the real extent of their dig in order to retain the possibility of future excavations and avoid conflicts before the opportune time. I was especially impressed with a statement Rabbi Getz made at Warren's Gate when we were filming the video companion to this book. He said, "Since the government said that we are not to go in [to the gate], we are not going in, because we do not go against the government."[27]

The Problem with the Muslim Wakf

The greatest opposition to Goren and Getz's dig came directly from the Muslim Wakf, who ordered the digging to stop, orchestrated the riot to stop the excavators, and sealed off the entrance from their side. I suspect that if the rabbis are withholding any information, this may be the key reason. Rabbi Getz observed that this was the underlying motive for keeping the dig a secret from the beginning: "The Muslims were against the idea that we would do any kind of digging in general. They said that it [the Temple Mount] is theirs."[28] This was again confirmed by Gershon Salomon, who presented to Israel's Supreme Court an appeal to keep the gate open. The court's decision to permanently close the excavation was explained by Salomon in succinct terms: "It was closed because of the Arab demonstrations and because of the fear from the Arab reaction."[29]

It was for these reasons that the government sealed off the excavation entrance from the Israeli side. Soon afterward, the Ministry of Religious Affairs removed a dedication plaque at the Western Wall Tunnel entrance because it connected the site with aspirations for rebuilding the Third Temple. The ministry later replaced the plaque with a less inflammatory one. According to Dan Bahat, "This [Warren's Gate in the Western Wall] is the outer limits of our [Israel's] possession. The [boundary of the] Temple Mount was decided by the early government following the Six-Day War in 1967 and is held by the Muslim authorities to this very day."[30]

But if the Muslim Wakf is aware of the Jewish attempt to find the Ark, what keeps them from reaching the site first and taking it for themselves?

Why Don't the Muslims Get the Ark?

The Wakf authorities have access to the secret tunnel through the cistern entrances located on the Temple Mount. Today, 25 of the original 36 cisterns mentioned in the Mishnah are still in use. One of them (cistern #4, which is entered from the western side of the Haram close to the Dome of the

Prophet) was used by the Arabs who attacked Rabbi Getz and his workers inside the tunnel in 1981. The Wakf officially states that the excavations under the Temple Mount have discovered only Islamic or pre-Islamic remains and that it is concerned about the possibility of damage to the foundations of buildings in the Muslim Quarter above. Their sealing of the entrance from the Jewish side of the tunnel may, of course, simply be a demonstration of their authority over the site both above and below ground. Since the Wakf claims that Jews did not previously occupy the Haram in 4,000 years of history, they cannot be expected to look for an Ark buried beneath the site of a Temple that they say never existed!

On the other hand, if Rabbi Goren's estimation of the chamber's location is correct, the Wakf would have to undertake a long and difficult excavation just to reach the Ark. The Wakf is not known for having an interest in conducting such archaeological work. Furthermore, if it did perform such an excavation and it became known, the orthodox Jews would start an even greater riot than did the Arabs!

Gershon Salomon, an Oriental specialist, has yet another suggestion to explain the Wakf's reluctance:

> This secret place underneath the floors of the Temple itself has been closed for over 2,000 years. Occupiers of Jerusalem like the Romans, Byzantines, Mamelukes, Arabs, and Muslims were afraid to touch them. We know that some occupiers and Gentiles have tried in the last 2,000 years to reach these underground chambers, but [tradition says] they immediately died strange and mysterious deaths. Others who tried to build something there [that is, over the site of the Holy of Holies] experienced an earthquake or fire and died together with their buildings. The Turks which used part of this tunnel [behind Warren's Gate] as a cistern did not dare to continue through the tunnel to the area

beneath the Temple, but used only the first part close to the gate.[31]

Salomon believes that due to the legends associated with the underground tunnels, as well as recorded problems of the past, Muslims are afraid to attempt to reach the Ark. Indeed, the early British excavators reported certain difficulties arising from the superstitious beliefs of the resident Turkish authorities. The cave beneath the rock *es-Sakhra* is called *Bir el-Arwah* ("the Well of Souls"), and it is believed that the prayers of the dead can be heard in the netherworld located directly below. While the Muslims know the legend that the vaults beneath the Temple complex (and especially below the es-Sakhra cave) contain treasures, they also believe that the vaults are guarded by fearsome demons.[32]

In addition, if the rabbis are afraid to come into contact with the Ark because of their own ritual impurity, how much more might this be expected of Gentiles who know that their very presence would be a desecration of sacred space? On the night that the entrance was sealed, Rabbi Goren told Rabbi Hacohen that he was not concerned about their inability to retrieve the Ark because "the Moslems revere the Ark as much as we do and they would be afraid to touch it."[33] Even so, Rabbi Goren confided to me, "Frankly, I do not want the Arabs to know the exact location [of the Ark]. They may dig and destroy evidences."[34]

Therefore, the rabbis are careful about what they say not out of concern for Muslim religious sensitivities nor fear of Muslim threats, but rather because they want to prevent any Muslim desecration of this holy place. Their concern is not unrealistic; it is based on the official finding of the Israeli Supreme Court. On September 13, 1993—the same day that Prime Minister Yitzhak Rabin and Yasser Arafat, chairman of the Palestine Liberation Organization (PLO), signed the Declaration of Principles on the White House lawn—the court issued a 99-page decision concerning the intentional destruction of ancient evidences of Jewish occupation on the Temple Mount. Ruling on a petition filed by the Temple Mount and Land of Israel Faithful in 1990, it concluded that—

> The Arabs did in fact destroy important holy remains and built new structures on the Temple Mount [and that] the authorities [the government police and Antiquities Authority] closed their eyes to those illegalities of the Wakf and did not enforce the law.[35]

It is quite probable, then, that these rabbis want to preserve their secrets intact and not provoke the Wakf by showing interest in the site until favorable circumstances permit their reentry into the excavation area.

Has Anyone Seen the Ark?

I personally have heard of two stories connected with individuals in the excavation who claimed there were eyewitness sightings of the Ark. The first such story was told by Rabbi Matiyahu (Mati) Dan Hacohen, founder of the Ateret Cohanim Yeshiva, shortly after the excavations were closed. This account was given to Dr. David Lewis, noted author and founder of Christians United for Israel. He recorded Rabbi Hacohen's statement and reported it as follows:

> Hacohen told of how they were excavating along the lower level of the Western Wall of the Temple mountain. At one point during the night, they came to a doorway in the Western Wall. Passing through this doorway, the crew entered a fairly long tunnel. At the end of the tunnel, Rabbi Hacohen said, "I saw the golden ark that once stood in the Holy Place of the Temple of the Almighty." It was covered with old, dried animal skins of some kind. However, one

gold, gleaming end of the ark was visible. He could
see the loops or rounds of gold through which the
poles of acacia wood could be thrust so that the ark
could be properly carried by four dedicated Levites.
Hacohen and his friends rushed out to the home of
Chief Rabbi Shlomo Goren. They awakened the
rabbi and excitedly told him that they had discovered the holy ark of the covenant! Goren said, "We
are ready for this event. We have already prepared
the poles of acacia wood and have Levites who can
be standing by in the morning to carry out the ark in
triumph."[36]

I asked Rabbi Goren about the factual nature of this account,
since it was supposedly reported to him. His response was
nothing short of emphatic:

They are all liars! They are just telling you stories! How can anyone say they saw the Ark? The
Ark is hundreds of meters down. . . . If [anyone]
would see the Ark he wouldn't remain alive even for
one minute![37]

Today, Rabbi Hacohen also denies that he ever told such a
story and says his statements were misunderstood. Hacohen's
present position (as well as that of his Yeshiva Ateret Cohanim,
is that the Temple Mount is off limits to prayers, according to
rabbinic injunction. If he held this same conviction in 1981
when the alleged sighting took place, it seems unlikely that he
would have entered the holiest of all holy places and gazed
upon the holiest of all objects.

The second story is told of Rabbi Getz. While my initial
exposure to this story was from Jimmy DeYoung, who had
interviewed Rabbi Getz for his video *Ready to Rebuild*, it was
also substantiated by another rabbi who knows Getz, but the
details of this account are rather sparse. Supposedly, Rabbi

Getz said that when the chamber leading to the Ark was discovered, he was afraid to go in and look upon the Ark. So he used a mirror to look around a corner of the tunnel, and beheld the reflected image of the Ark.

I also heard a rather mystical allegation that during the excavation, Rabbi Getz had heard the sound of a bellows or breathing, which Jewish legend associates with the presence of the Shekinah. This sound was said to have indicated to Rabbi Getz that the excavation team was close to the Ark, which was still attended by the divine immanence.

I went with my rabbi friend, who had also heard these stories, to ask Rabbi Getz for clarification. When I repeated what we had heard, he was surprised that such comments were circulating. Wanting to set the record straight, he said:

> No . . . no . . . that is not what I said. These are all
> stories. . . . I am not responsible for someone else's
> remarks. It is important to know the truth, since
> millions of Christians and people who love Israel
> read such material.[38]

My own evaluation of these accounts is mixed. Some of the details do not coincide with the biblical and rabbinic descriptions of the Ark or with the reports given by the excavators who participated in the dig. Let us briefly weigh some of the allegations against the evidence.

First, the poles for transporting the Ark, according to divine command, were *never* to be removed from the Ark (Exodus 25:15). The Gemara (*Yoma* 72b) states that the poles could be shifted, but they could not be completely removed. Some rabbinic commentators have said the poles *couldn't* be removed because they were wedged into the rings that held the poles—wedged in such a way to keep the Ark from slipping backwards or forwards. Of course, it is possible that an exception was made when the Ark was put into hiding; or, perhaps after 3,000 years in a dank environment, even acacia wood, normally not subject to decay, might have rotted away. Also, the Ark was said to have always been covered with a blue-dyed cloth and badger skins, not animal skins. Again, however, it is possible that the blue cloth had been lost or had rotted away, leaving only the dried badger skins. So the two accounts about the Ark's sighting might be plausible, yet another significant problem remains.

Both stories claim that the excavators reached the site of the Ark itself. According to Rabbi Getz's calculations, however, the excavation party reached within some 96 feet of the Holy of Holies. And Rabbi Goren contends that the chamber which houses the Ark is located deeper still beneath the Holy of Holies. He believes they would have to dig not a few meters, but hundreds of meters to reach it. He estimated that it would have taken the group another year and a half to reach the chamber in which the Ark is believed to be hidden.

Again I pressed Rabbi Getz as to whether he had actually been in the room where the Ark was stored. His reply was consistent with Goren's statement:

> We know where it is, but we did not discover it. According to the [rabbinic] writings it is called the *Gear He'Etzem* ("Chalk of the Bone") and is located deep within the ground. I wanted to go through the tunnels [and reach this area], since I knew the direction—I might be off only 15 to 18 feet—but it is impossible [to reach] because it is deep under the water [which flooded the tunnels].[39]

If we take Rabbis Getz and Goren, who *directed* the excavation, at their word, then there is no way they could have possibly come close to the Ark, much less seen it. Furthermore, there is the question of whether or not they *would* have looked at it. Some Christians suppose that the Shekinah is no longer present with the Ark, so it's a harmless relic. After all,

Bezalel (and Oholiab?) had touched the Ark while constructing it. Yet the rabbis believe the Shekinah never left Jerusalem. Also, the Mishnah tractate Shekalim records the instant death of a priest who sought to reveal the location of the Ark. Thus, Rabbi Goren categorically denies that Rabbis Hacohen or Getz or anyone else could ever have seen the Ark.

Perhaps the closest we will come to the actual thoughts of these rabbis is the honest statement reflected in Gershon Salomon's answer to the question of whether anyone had seen the Ark:

> I did not hear anyone say that they found it. What I heard is what Rabbi Getz said very clearly in those days: "We are at an important point in history. After 2,500 years we are marching to the place of the Ark of the Covenant, and we must do it quickly!" He was wonderful, and he was determined to do it![40]

For the time being, the Ark may remain locked in secret behind an entrance sealed with three meters of concrete and steel. Rabbis Getz and Goren agree that the matter cannot be resolved by human agency and are willing to wait for the Messiah to reveal it. But *if* the possibility later comes to further these excavations and retrieve the Ark, we can be certain that these rabbis—or their students—will seize the day. Indeed, it became clear that Rabbi Goren's resolve matches that of Rabbi Getz when he declared, "I will give everything in my life to get to the Ark, to get to the tablets [inside the Ark]."[41]

There may yet be secrets beneath the stone, and in a day not far away we may be privileged to learn the greater story. As conditions on earth, and especially in Jerusalem, allow renewed excavations, perhaps soon these men will finally bring to light the long-lost Ark!

PART THREE

*Closing in
on the
Future*

11

The Ark and
the Temple

The Ark of the Covenant cannot be put in a museum, nor in a synagogue, but in only one place, the Temple. We know that the generation of the destruction of the First Temple hid the Ark of the Covenant for the time of the Third Temple, the last and eternal Temple.[1]

—Gershon Salomon, leader,
the Temple Mount Faithful

There is no other reason for the existence of the Temple but the Ark. While this may appear to be an oversimplification, it is scriptural. In 1 Chronicles 28:2, King David declares to all the assembly of Israel his purpose for the Temple: "I had intended to build a permanent home for the ark of the covenant of the LORD and for the footstool of our God. So I had made preparations to build it." David's primary concern with the Temple was the same as that of Moses with the Tabernacle: to house the Ark. Moses had the Ark made to fulfill God's design to dwell among His people (Exodus 25:8). That this was God's intent is seen in that He gives instructions for constructing the Ark prior to any word about building the Tabernacle itself (Exodus 25:10-22).

This is also seen by the parallels between Moses' and David's actions. Just as Moses had made preparations for the Ark through the people's offerings (Exodus 25:2-7) and the construction of the Tabernacle by craftsmen (Exodus 31:1-11), so also did David's preparations for the Ark include an offering for construction materials (1 Chronicles 29:2-9) and the provision of skilled workers (1 Chronicles 28:21) for the Temple. And just as Moses had received the plans for the Tabernacle directly from God (Exodus 25:8-9), so also did David receive such blueprints and pass them on to Solomon (1 Chronicles 28:11-19).

Indeed, the linkage we have observed between the Ark and the Temple is an intrinsic and essential one.

Ark and Temple as One Concept

When we consider the form and function of the Ark with that of the Tabernacle and Temple, we find the latter are a projection of the former. One would expect this correlation, since in function all of these served alike as a place where God's presence was manifested, sacrifice was offered, and divine guidance was received. In form, some have seen a correlation between the Ark as a portable "house" for God and the Tabernacle and Temple by extension as "the house of God." One way this correlation seems to be confirmed is in the archaeological discovery of ancient, miniature pottery temples. These shrines seem to represent portable temples in which the resident god could be transported from place to place.

One such miniature shrine was found at Megiddo and dates from the time of Solomon, who built up the defensive fortifications of that city (1 Kings 9:15). Because this pottery temple is decorated with cherubim in relief, it is thought to be analogous to the description of Solomon's Temple in 1 Kings 6, which mentions decorations featuring cherubim (verse 29, 32). On the basis of such artifacts, higher-critical scholars like Herbert May once concluded that "the ark was the temple in which the deity sat or dwelt."[2] However, rather than the Ark being a miniature temple, the Temple appears to be an extended Ark.

We can observe in Scripture some connections between the Ark and the Temple. For example, God's glory or divine presence inhabited both (compare 1 Samuel 4:22 with 1 Kings 8:11). Likewise, the Ark and the Temple both were "called by the name" of God, an expression used to signify dedication (*see* 2 Samuel 6:2; 12:28; 1 Kings 8:43; 1 Chronicles 13:6; 2 Chronicles 6:33; cf. Isaiah 4:1; Jeremiah 7:10-14). While these passages show a relationship between the Ark and Temple, it is not because the Ark is to be identified as a temple but rather because the Temple is associated with the Ark. Remember that after the Ark disappeared from the Second Temple, the glory of God was also said to have disappeared from the Temple. The association of the Ark and Temple as one concept may be further seen in the placement of the Tabernacle (the earlier association) within the Temple (the later association).

The Tabernacle in the Temple

Like the Ark, the Tabernacle was said to have been brought into the First Temple (1 Kings 8:4; 2 Chronicles 5:5), and like the Ark, its final outcome is never recorded in Scripture. However, just as the Temple was vitally connected with the Ark, so also was the Tabernacle. Thus we should expect that this sacred structure, popularly and royally venerated until the Temple, would not disappear without some notice. Some scholars have sought to find the Tabernacle in the Temple in the sense that the Tabernacle represented the Temple on a reduced scale. However, this thinking is based on the higher-critical hypothesis that the Tabernacle was an artificial projection of authors writing after the fall of the Jerusalem Temple.[3] By any calculation, the Tabernacle's dimensions are so different from those of either the First or Second Temple that any idea of imitation must be rejected. What the biblical text *does* imply is that the Tabernacle was in the Temple.

A careful comparison of the measurements of the Tabernacle with the dimensions inside the Holy of Holies in the Temple does reveal a near-exact correspondence. Interestingly, this space in the Holy of Holies is located beneath the wings of the large olive wood cherubim that guarded the Ark in the First Temple. Richard Friedman, a scholar who has studied this relationship, observes:

> According to the description of the Temple construction (1 Kings 6; 2 Chronicles 3) the Holy of Holies (or *debir*) is 20 cubits in length and 20 cubits in width (1 Kings 6:20; 2 Chronicles 3:8). Within are the two cherubim, each 10 cubits high. Their wings are spread . . . and the wingspread of each is 10 cubits, so that the tips of the wings of each touch the walls of the room on each side and touch each other in the center of the room (1 Kings 6:23-27; 2 Chronicles 3:10-13). Thus the space between the cherubim is 10 cubits in height, 20 cubits in length, and less than 10 cubits in width (as the bodies of the cherubim take up a portion of the center space). The measurements of the Tabernacle, as pictured in Exodus 26 and 36, are just this: 10 cubits in height, 20 cubits in length, and 8 cubits in width.[4]

This arrangement, however, may only represent the Tabernacle by a *symbolic* spatial correspondence at the Ark. This may be because the Tabernacle, or Tent of Meeting, was considered to be the ordained place of sacrifice (*see* 2 Chronicles 1:3-4), and therefore it had to be included within the Temple's construction, even if only symbolically. Yet it has been argued by some—based on the scriptural texts as well as extrabiblical literature—that the actual Tabernacle was placed within the Temple.[5]

The Tabernacle Beneath the Temple

In order for us to understand these descriptions of the Tabernacle's presence in the Temple, it is important to know that the Tabernacle and the Tent of Meeting were in fact one single structure composed of two separate parts. According to Numbers 3:25 the inner fabric of this structure was called the *mishkan* ("Tabernacle"), and the outer fabric was referred to as the *'ohel* ("tent"). The relationship between these two parts was conveyed in the biblical text through a literary device known as *hendiadys*, a pairing of terms to express one unified thought.[6] That's why 2 Samuel 7:6 can note that God always went about "in a tent, even in a tabernacle."

When we examine the book of 2 Chronicles, we find that the Temple is referred to as the house of the tent (2 Chronicles 24:6) or even as the Tabernacle of the Lord (2 Chronicles 29:6-7). In the Psalms, the Tabernacle is likewise pictured within the Temple precincts.[7] For instance, Psalm 74:7, a verse lamenting the destruction of the Temple in 586 B.C., literally reads: "They cast your Temple into the fire; they profaned Your name's Tabernacle." In Psalm 61:4 there may be an allusion to the Tabernacle's spatial relationship to the Ark when the verse notes: "Let me dwell in Thy tent forever; let me take refuge in the shelter of Thy wings [that is, of the cherubim]."

The reason for this mention of the Tabernacle within the Temple is made for us by the extrabiblical writers. Josephus states that the Tabernacle was brought into the First Temple (*Antiquities* 8. 101, 106), and that the effect of the spread-winged cherubim was to make it appear as a tent (8. 103). Rabbinic tradition further asserts that the Tent of Meeting was stored away in the subterranean vault beneath the Holy of

Holies (*see* Babylonian Talmud, *Sota* 9a; *Yoma* 21b; Rashi on Gen. 9:27). Friedman again interprets this for us:

> It is possible that the Tabernacle was in fact stored in the manner which the Talmud describes, while the appropriately measured space beneath the wings of the cherubim meanwhile corresponded to it above.[8]

What this means is that the outer Tent of Meeting was deposited in the chamber Solomon constructed to house the Temple treasures, while directly above it in the Holy of Holies the Tabernacle was represented at the Ark. Some have even argued that the inner tent of the Tabernacle was physically present with the Ark, appearing in the form of the dividing or covering curtain known as the *paroket*. The purpose of this arrangement may have been to testify to the immanence (Ark/Tabernacle) and transcendence (Tent) of God. What it reveals is that the prior sanctity of a structure can continue to sanctify whatever contains it—in this case, the Temple. Therefore, just as the Tabernacle was present beneath the First Temple yet continued to provide a sanctity to the Holy of Holies above it, so also in the Second Temple, when the Ark joined the Tent of Meeting in the secret chamber, it too could provide this function for the empty Holy of Holies. This, then, provides further evidence that the Temple treasures may have been hidden and that one day the Ark may be recovered.

What the Future Holds

If the Temple is to be literally rebuilt in the future, then the close connection between the Temple and the Ark suggests that the Ark will also be present with this future Temple. Let us first review one New Testament reference to this future rebuilt Temple, a reference in which the Ark also appears:

> There was given me a measuring rod like a staff; and someone said, "Rise and measure the temple of God, and the altar, and those who worship in it. And leave out the court which is outside the temple, and do not measure it, for it has been given to the nations; and they will tread under foot the holy city [Jerusalem] for forty-two months [three and a half years]" (Revelation 11:1-2).

This text's historical description of a Temple that exists at the beginning of the first three-and-a-half-year period, then is desecrated at the start of the second three-and-a-half-year period, and finally gets trampled for the remainder of that period can only place this building in the context of Daniel 9:27. Based on Jesus' use of this passage in the Olivet Discourse—Matthew 24:15 and Mark 13:14—it must have a future end-time reference.[9] This identification is also confirmed by the mention that the sacrificial system (indicated by "the altar" and "worship" in Revelation 11:1) will be interrupted (verse 2), just as in the Daniel text. There is simply no way to fit these time distinctions into the historical account of the Temple's destruction in A.D. 70.[10]

Literal Temple or Symbolic?

Some people have questioned whether Revelation 11:1-2 talks about a literal, earthly Temple because they assume that the use of symbolism throughout the book of Revelation requires that a symbolic meaning be attached to terms such as "temple."[11] Because these people are arguing from a nonfuturist perspective, they cannot conceive of John writing about the literal Jerusalem or Temple because both had already been in ruins for over 20 years when Revelation was written. They say that when John measured the Temple, he did so in an allegorical sense intended to point to the church.[12] They also insist that the Temple in Revelation 11 is the church because they believe the literal Temple was abandoned by Christ, the Spirit was transferred to the church, and in previous chapters of Revelation the church had been symbolized by the 12 tribes, the seven golden lampstands, and the priests.[13] But such reasoning is based on theological analogy rather than a careful analysis of the biblical text.

Let's look at some of the reasons the futurist view makes more sense than the symbolic view:

1. While some New Testament passages use the Temple as a metaphor for the spiritual composition of the church and the spiritual nature of the Christian, all other references to the Temple in the New Testament, taken in their normal sense, refer to the literal, earthly Temple in Jerusalem (or the heavenly Temple).[14]

2. The noun describing the Temple is definite: "*the* Temple of God" is used only with reference to the Jerusalem Temple and *never* to symbolize Christians or the church.[15]

3. The Temple in Revelation 11:1-2 is clearly described as the Jewish Temple in Jerusalem (note the use of "holy city" and "nations . . . will trample under foot"). Such a description would not be a suitable symbol for the church, which is predominantly Gentile.[16]

4. The "altar" has no corollary to the church nor to the church age, and therefore would make no sense as a symbol of anything Christian. On the other hand, it is a literal part of the Temple complex.[17]

5. John speaks of the outer precinct being trampled by the Gentiles, which would better suit an earthly Temple than a symbolic or heavenly one.[18]

6. John's references to an altar, the outer court, Gentiles, and the holy city all indicate that the setting is Jewish, not Christian.[19] Note also that the outer court and the entire city are trampled by the Gentiles. This indicates that the Temple and the city must be something *other* than Gentile (that is, something Jewish).[20] Thus Revelation 11:1-2 talks about a period of Jewish history and does not relate to the church.

7. John's viewpoint in this book is prophetic, and because predictions that the Temple would be restored were expected, he is showing how these expectations of the end times are to be fulfilled.[21]

8. As stated earlier, the "forty-two months" is clearly a reference to Daniel's seventieth week (Daniel 9:27; 12:11), which is divided into two sections of forty-two months (three and a half years) each. In addition, the context here is the end of the sixth trumpet judgment, which would corroborate this being the middle of the seventieth week.[22]

9. If the Temple here represents the church, then who is represented by the worshipers in the Temple (Revelation 11:1)? It would be inconsistent to make the Temple the church and then identify the church as these worshipers.[23] Because the worshipers are measured in *addition* to the Temple, they must be seen as distinct from it, or else John has been told to measure a group of people whose being is only a part of themselves.[24] The distinction between the Temple and its worshipers is best explained as between the Jewish people as a whole and a remnant who are true to God.[25]

10. The measurement of the Temple in Revelation 11 is like that in Ezekiel 42:2. Because Ezekiel measured a literal earthly Temple, the Temple in Revelation should also be understood in this manner.[26]

The Fate of the Future Temple

According to the literal understanding of the earthly Temple in Revelation 11:1-2, the Temple's court and the city of Jerusalem will be given over by divine command to the Gentiles for the last half of the seventieth week. This period coincides with the period of the Great Tribulation, which is characterized by Gentile domination and an escalating persecution of the Jewish remnant. Apparently these verses describe the pivotal period in the middle of the seventieth week in which the Temple is initially desecrated by the Gentiles, leading up to the trampling of Jerusalem. By supplying details from other prophetic texts, we can plot the fate of the Temple as described in Revelation 11.

First, according to Daniel 9:27 and 12:11 the cessation of the daily sacrifices pollutes the altar.[27] Second Thessalonians 2:4 reveals that the Antichrist and his image will then enter the Holy of Holies, resulting in the abomination of desolation. Following this, Revelation 13:4, 8 predicts the whole world will be forced to worship the Antichrist.

This series of events may indicate why John was told not to measure the Gentile court. The first half of the seventieth week sees Jerusalem at peace, with Jewish worshipers in the Temple and the sacrificial system in place. But the second half sees the trampling of Jerusalem. This corresponds with the treatment given to the two witnesses (11:7-10), who have direct relation to the Temple and represent the Jewish remnant. Their deaths may provide the opportunity for the Temple's desecration (11:8-10), which leads to the judgment of the nations (11:13, 18)—a judgment continuing through the campaigns of Armageddon and concluding with the advent of Messiah and the battle for Jerusalem. Because the Gentile nations are to be judged at a later time, there would be no reason to include them in the preliminary spiritual evaluation reserved for Israel in Revelation 11:1.

An Ark in the Future Temple?

In Revelation 11:19, following a reference to the planned destruction of the nations (verse 18) and before a section dealing with war on earth (12:1-6, 13-17), we find mention of the Ark: "The temple of God which is in heaven was opened; and the ark of His covenant appeared in His temple, and there were flashes of lightning and sounds and peals of thunder and an earthquake and a great hailstorm."

It has been argued by some people that the words "in heaven" are an editorial insertion and not original to John's text. They insist that "it is the earthly (not the heavenly) Temple that is referred to, and the meaning of the statement is that the Ark which was hidden (so tradition variously said) by Jeremiah or Josiah, shall suddenly reappear in the sanctuary in the latter days."[28]

While we may agree with the *conclusion* of this interpretation, there is *no support* for viewing this Temple and Ark as anything but the heavenly originals of the earthly counterparts. That the phrase "in heaven" belongs here is affirmed by Revelation 11:15, which introduces the setting as "in heaven." The revelation of the Temple and the Ark serves as an assurance that the messianic kingdom will come, as promised, to reward the faithful saints on earth (verse 18). It also serves as an announcement of God's coming judgment upon the earth (11:18; 12:13-17). It seems that the heavenly Temple appears here, as elsewhere, as a sign of God's sovereign reign with respect to Israel; and the heavenly Ark, which appears only here (but is implied in Revelation 15:5-8), indicates God's presence coming to earth in judgment (as with the earthly Ark in battle).

Furthermore, the accounts about heaven and earth in Revelation reveal a cause and effect action—heaven responds to earth. If this is so, then perhaps the appearance of the heavenly Temple and Ark corresponds to the earthly Temple and Ark in some way. Perhaps the earthly Ark will be brought out as a precursor to the messianic era, which the Jews say will begin with the signing of the covenant that permits the building of the Temple. With the Ark installed in the Temple, Israel will attempt to restore the ceremonial system. But the restoration will be cut short when the Antichrist desecrates the Temple and the Ark. For this reason, heaven reveals its undefiled Temple and Ark and a revelation ensuring the destruction of those who have desecrated the sacred, earthly counterparts.

This pattern of desecration and restoration is evident throughout the Old and New Testaments in passages that deal with the Temple, national Israel, and the program of the Messiah (*see accompanying chart*). Therefore, it is possible on the basis of Revelation 11:1-2, 19 that the future earthly Temple will temporarily house the recovered earthly Ark.

Objections to the Ark in the Temple

Some people use Revelation 11:19 to try to prove that no earthly Ark exists. They claim that the Ark's appearance in heaven indicates that its purpose has been eclipsed by the ministry of Christ, yet in chapter 7 we saw why that is not necessarily so. What is interesting is that some of those who say no earthly Ark exists still believe that a literal Temple will be rebuilt in Jerusalem. Such reasoning seems inconsistent. On the one hand, they argue that the Ark must have been destroyed by the Babylonians because it only symbolized the presence of God, which Christ fulfilled at the incarnation (*see* John 1:14). On the other hand, they argue that a Third Temple must be built because Daniel 9:27 predicted the cessation of sacrifice at the midpoint of the seventieth week, and this action requires that a Temple and a sacrificial system be in place.

However, if the Ark was no longer needed because its symbolic function had been fulfilled, then why would a Temple with sacrifices be needed, since its role would also have been fulfilled? After all, the original purpose for erecting the Temple was to house the Ark. This implies that that which is housed is *greater* than that which houses it (cf. Hebrews 3:3). If so, then the return of the Ark should be at least as necessary as the rebuilding of the Temple.

It might also be argued that since the presence of God had departed from the Ark (Ezekiel 9:3), the Ark no longer retained its original sanctity and therefore would not be necessary. But the same argument must be applied to the Temple

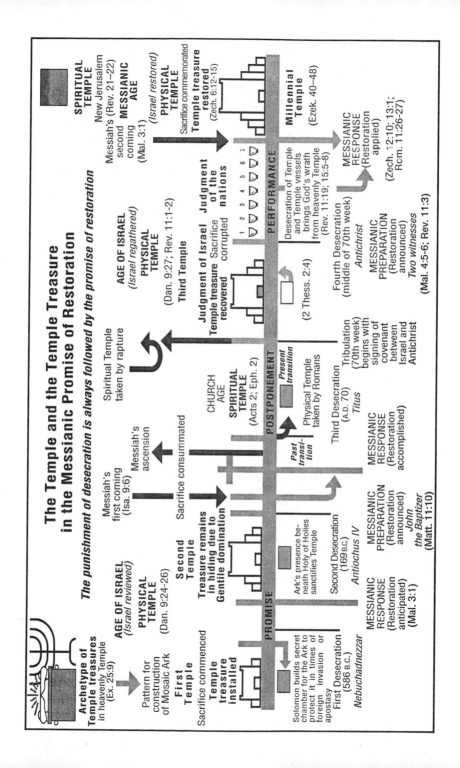

The Temple and the Temple Treasure
in the Messianic Promise of Restoration

The punishment of desecration is always followed by the promise of restoration

(Ezekiel 10:4, 18-19; 11:23), which *continued* to bear its spiritual significance long after this event. Along this line it might also be argued that the consummating nature of Christ's atonement for sin ended the need for the Ark's mercy seat (*see* Hebrews 9:3-26) and consequently ended its sanctity for Christians. Yet it is apparent that the Temple had sanctity for Jesus during His life (*see* Luke 2:49; John 2:16) and continued to do so for the early church and Paul after the resurrection of Jesus (cf. Acts 2:46–3:1; 21:26; 22:3, 17; 25:8). If the presence of the Ark gave sanctity to the Temple, then would not it have been as highly regarded and significant as the Temple itself?

A Dual Hope

If the Ark of the Covenant is truly beneath the Temple Mount awaiting the proper time for rediscovery, then that day of discovery will also see the rebuilding of the Third Temple. Perhaps the Ark will first be discovered and become the catalyst that begins the rebuilding of the Temple. Or perhaps the rebuilding of the Temple will occur first and generate a search for the lost Ark in order to return it to its historic place within the Holy of Holies. Whichever scenario comes about, I believe that both the Ark and the Temple will see that day together. This is the dual hope of many in Israel today who expect the fulfillment of these events within their lifetime and can confidently boast:

> The Ark of the Covenant is under our control. We have it! And in the day when the Third Temple will be rebuilt, all of us will have the wonderful privilege to be close to this holy Ark.[29]

12

The Messiah Connection

It was a common belief among the rabbis of old that the Ark would be found at the coming of the Messiah. [1]

—*Catholic Encyclopedia*

If I would have found the Ark of the Covenant, it would have been a sign that the Messiah was on my side. [2]

—Rabbi Meyer Yehuda Getz, chief rabbi of the Western Wall

To speak of any sacred or prophetic article or act without thinking of its messianic connection is impossible. Not only is the Messiah a Savior in the spiritual sense, but for Israel He is also a Restorer of the national order. This order includes the spiritual as well as the political and requires that the Messiah restore the lost Temple treasures. Almost every person who has searched for the Ark has understood this connection and hoped in some small measure that his actions might contribute to the day of Messiah's coming. Temple movements in Israel, while remaking sacred items for future Temple worship, have no concern for rebuilding the Ark because they believe it will be brought out from the Temple Mount by the Messiah Himself.

Today, for the first time in modern history, one segment of Judaism has revived the expectation of the Messiah and is seeking to motivate all of world Jewry to help make the advent of Messiah possible. One of the proofs connected with this expected appearance is the belief that the Temple treasures, and especially the Ark, will be discovered by the one who will be identified as Messiah. Gershon Salomon, leader of the Temple Mount and Land of Israel Faithful, believes that the Messiah's coming might have been planned to occur within our present generation but was postponed because of the unwillingness of the Israeli government to follow God's will. He explains:

> God is waiting for us to do things in order to give us the Messiah. When our government gave back the Temple Mount to our enemies, we delayed the coming of the Messiah. We could [almost] hear his steps on the Moriah Mount, but we lost the opportunity. [This opportunity was renewed] the moment when we discovered the gate to the place of the Ark of the Covenant, but we lost it again.[3]

The Revival of Messianic Expectation

Not since the seventeenth-century debacle surrounding the messianic claimant Shabbetai Zvi has a revival of Jewish messianic expectation appeared on the scale of that recently displayed in the United States, England, Europe, and Israel. *Time* and *Newsweek* have both reported on the Lubavitchers' widespread publicity campaign to prepare for the coming of the Messiah.[4] (The Lubavitchers are a Hasidic Jewish group.) Books on the Jewish doctrine of the Messiah,[5] "prophetic" newsletters,[6] international newspaper advertisements,[7] banners, posters, electric signs atop cars, and national messianic information hotlines[8] are among the many visible signs of this astounding movement.

The basis for this new messianism is in part drawn from Maimonides' Code of the Jewish Law called the "Principles of Faith." Number 12 of these 13 fundamental principles reads, "I believe with complete faith in the coming of Messiah. Though he tarry, nonetheless I await him every day, that he will come." Such belief has been bolstered by the conviction that ours is the first age that has been identified for the fulfillment of the messianic prophecies. Recent events are believed to have demonstrated that the time of the messianic redemption is at hand. A central feature of this modern messianic hope is the rebuilding of the Third Temple; it is believed that through this climactic event the identity of the long-awaited Messiah will finally be revealed.

This Jewish messianic awakening with its concomitant awareness that these are the final hours of Gentile domination ("the times of the Gentiles," Luke 21:24; cf. Romans 11:25) before the Messiah arrives is a significant sign that we are living in the last days. This was a sign that Jesus Himself predicted for the era beginning the fulfillment of Daniel's seventieth week: "Many will come in My name, saying, 'I am the [Messiah],' and will mislead many. . . . And many false prophets will arise, and will mislead many" (Matthew 24:5, 11). Jesus also predicted that after the Antichrist has revealed himself, these false messiahs will be accompanied by convincing proofs: "If anyone says to you, 'Behold, here is the [Messiah],' or 'There He is,' do not believe him. For false [messiahs] and false prophets will arise and will show great signs and wonders, so as to mislead, if possible, even the elect" (Matthew 24:23-24).

Planting the Seeds

The current messianic movement first began in Israel as a response to the almost disastrous Yom Kippur War in 1973. In this war Israel was surprised by an Egyptian attack and would have seen the Soviet Union join with its Arab allies had the United States not intervened in favor of the Israelis. In the aftermath of this conflict an orthodox Jew within the settlement group called *Gush Emunim* ("Bloc of the Faithful") said:

> We [Jewish messianists[9]] were born out of the Yom Kippur War. . . . Our Bibles told us that before Messiah comes, Israel will experience great distress. So while other Jews were depressed over the outcome of the war, we were encouraged. We believed this was the beginning of the redemption of Israel. Our belief is quite simple, really; when we possess all of the land historically held by the Jewish people, the Messiah will come.[10]

One sign of the prophetic fervor that surrounded the Yom Kippur aftermath was the popularity of a bumper sticker that began appearing on the streets of Jerusalem: "We Want Moshiach [Messiah] Now!" These were the product of the ultraorthodox Hasidic organization Habad,[11] whose 250,000 followers worldwide have swelled the messianic revival to international proportions.

The Revival Goes International

If the Yom Kippur War sparked the revival, all that was needed to set it on fire was another melee of prophetic proportions in the Middle East. The Persian Gulf War was heralded as just such an event by those in the messianic movement; it was the catalyst that moved the revival to international status. The religious authority who inspired this recognition was the

Lubavitcher Rebbe, Rabbi Menachem Mendel Schneerson, a Russian-born Jew whose accomplishments in Hasidic philosophy moved him into the Lubavitcher line of ascendancy. The Talmud discusses the signs that will mark the time of Messiah's return and the Day of Redemption (Sanhedrin 97-98),[12] and Schneerson declared that the present world conditions fit this description precisely. When the Gulf War hostilities were threatening Israel, Schneerson predicted that "Israel would be the safest place in the world." Although 74 Israelis died as a result of the Scud missile attacks, all but six died from heart problems, and it did indeed appear that Israel had been spared by God as Schneerson predicted.

International recognition of Schneerson's predictions was achieved through an aggressive campaign that placed full-page ads in major newspapers and newsmagazines (as well as campus newspapers at universities where Habad student organizations existed). One such ad in the *Jerusalem Post* pictured the word *Moshiach* ("Messiah" in Ashkenazi-accented Hebrew) as a connect-the-dot pattern, with each dot being a recent current event. The caption asked the reader to "draw your own conclusion." In the text of the ad was this message:

> Yes, we are living in the most extraordinary times—as our world evolves toward a state of peace, and mankind thrives toward a state of perfection. The times are changing—not just for the better, but truly for the best. A cornerstone of Jewish faith is the belief that, ultimately, good and peace must triumph. This is the essence of "Moshiach," who will usher in the final redemption ordained in the Torah. The Lubavitcher Rebbe, Rabbi Menachem Mendel Schneerson, emphasizes that these remarkable events are merely the prelude to the final Redemption, culminating in unity among people, domestic harmony, and cessation of

hostilities between races, neighbors and nations.
... The era of Moshiach is upon us.[13]

A Highly Visible Campaign

Lubavitcher leaders in Israel announced that with the end of
the Gulf War the Messiah would soon appear.[14] Throughout
the war, banners on highways in Tel-Aviv had read "Trust in
HaShem" ("the Lord," literally, "the Name"), but these were
soon replaced with new banners: "Prepare for the Coming of
Moshiach" emblazoned in black letters on 100-foot-long yellow signs which depicted a red sun rising from the horizon.

Menachem Brod, who oversees public relations and publications for the Habad Youth Organization in Israel, said the
purpose of these massive billboards was "to put Messiah into
the national consciousness." With thousands of Israeli mo-
torists passing these signs daily, the indoctrination is well
underway. Brod, who is serious about the outcome of this
"messianic campaign," stresses that getting people excited
about the coming of Messiah and spurring them to action will
help hasten the arrival of the long-awaited era. In a *Jerusalem
Post* interview, he announced to readers, "Dear Jews, Moshiach is about to arrive! The dream of millions of Jews for
centuries is upon us, and we all need to be ready for it!"[15]

In a paper entitled "Waiting in the Wings," which was
distributed all over Israel, the appeal was made to give Messiah
the signal to come. The article, in part, read:

> We must show him we want him with all our
> heart. He is ready. He is just waiting for the signal
> from us. Moshiach is waiting in the wings. He is
> ready. When he comes the curtain will rise on the
> most magnificent stage set we could imagine—
> world peace and disarmament, glory and honor for
> the Jews, the end of strife and jealousy. We must
> show him through our good deeds, through our

tangible anticipation, through our longing for him, that we are ready.[16]

In 1993 the massive yellow banners were supplemented with signs bearing pictures of Schneerson and the caption, "Welcome King Messiah." To prepare for "Messiah Schneerson's" coming to Israel, a unique (for Israel) administration building has been constructed in Kfar Habad, near the Ben Gurion airport on the Jerusalem/Tel-Aviv highway. This building is an exact duplicate, inside and out, of the international headquarters building at 770 Eastern Parkway in Crown Heights, Brooklyn (New York), where Rabbi Schneerson currently resides. When I toured this building at Kfar Habad in January of 1994, I found it contained numerous offices—one reserved for Schneerson—a library, several study centers, and a bookstore.

While Schneerson has never been to Israel, he gave permission for his followers to build him a house in Kfar Habad. When he comes, his arrival will be heralded as the advent of the Messiah and the moment of redemption for Israel. Moshe Kruger, who participated in the groundbreaking for the house, declared that this was a sign that the time is near: "The Messiah will come any day!"[17]

Today, Schneerson's campaign has moved to the background and the signs of messianic greeting have all but disappeared from the street corners in Jerusalem. But it is clear that this activity marks a new chapter in Jewish history—a chapter in which a Jewish group has sought to identify the Messiah and provoke the anticipation of their fellow Jews and Israelis about his coming.

Identifying the Messiah

The Lubavitcher promotion of a coming messiah who will be a strictly human, nonmiracle-working Jewish leader has opened the field for many such messianic candidates. The Lubavitchers are preparing the Jewish world to accept as messiah whoever is instrumental in bringing about the erection of the Third Temple. Israeli Lubavitcher campaign leader Menachem Brod defines this messiah as "a great leader of the Jewish people; he will be such a great charismatic leader that the whole world will unite behind him."[18] However, Brod believes he will not be identified as messiah immediately: "The people may only realize that he has come after the fact—after we see his actions."[19] What actions are expected to be performed in confirmation of messiahship? Rabbi Manis Friedman, interviewed by University of Maryland professor Susan Handelman in the Hasidic journal *Wellsprings*,[20] reveals the Lubavitch opinion:

> If he goes on to build the Temple and gather all Jews back to Israel, then we will know for sure that he is the Moshiach. Moshiach comes through his accomplishments and not through his pedigree. Maimonides says that once he builds the Temple and gathers the Jews back to Israel, then we will know for sure that he is the Moshiach. He doesn't have to say anything. He will accept the role, but we will give it to him. He won't take it to himself. And his coming, the moment of his coming, in the literal sense, would mean the moment when the whole world recognizes him as Moshiach . . . that both Jew and non-Jew recognize that he is responsible for all the wonderful improvements in the world: an end to war, an end to hunger, an end to suffering, a change in attitude.[21]

This new Jewish concept of the messiah, then, is that of a mortal man and a leader with sufficient charisma to capture and command the admiration of the world—if not its devotion. He will be recognized not by his lineage (as the biblical

Messiah—a descendant of the Davidic dynasty), but by his acts of global significance. The arrival of this messiah will supposedly take place during a time of military threat to the Jewish people. Hasidic writer Naftali Loewenthal has observed that war has always been an expected precursor to the advent of the Messiah. She writes:

> Throughout history Jewish leaders have seen international events and especially wars as expressing Messianic portents. The Book of Daniel prophesies wars as preceding the Messiah. The Midrash states, "If you see nations battling together, you can expect the feet of the Messiah" (Gen. *Rab.* 42:7). ...many Jews in our time saw the Second World War as the war of the "birthpangs of the Messiah." Recently the Gulf War excited similar speculation...."[22]

Beware the Counterfeit

While some aspects of the Hasidic messiah have a biblical basis, the expectation of a human leader who will arrive in a time of war, resolve the conflict, deliver Israel, and then rebuild the Temple also fits the Old and New Testament descriptions of the coming false messiah. Many have sought to identify this counterfeit messiah with *the* Antichrist, since the Antichrist will probably be responsible for constructing the Third Temple through his covenant with Israel (Daniel 9:27), and this role is predicted of the Messiah (Zechariah 6:12). However, while this false messiah will undoubtedly be an antichrist (1 John 2:18, 22; 4:3), he will not necessarily be *the* Antichrist. That's because the long-awaited Messiah is expected to be Jewish, and the Antichrist appears to be Gentile. While Jews in the past have on occasion accepted a Gentile as messiah (for example, Napoleon Bonaparte), ever since the

State of Israel was formed it became a mandate among Hasidic Jews that the true Messiah would make his appearance as a Jew (generally as a rabbi) in Israel.

The best candidate for false messiah would be the Jewish lieutenant of the Antichrist, "the false prophet" (*see* Revelation 13:11-18). This false prophet is called a "beast," as is the Antichrist (Revelation 13:1, 11). He exercises a counterfeit divine authority and power for the purpose of eliciting faith in the Antichrist, who will apparently claim the status of deity (Revelation 13:12-13). While he is said to deceive the earth-dwellers or Gentiles (Revelation 13:12), he is also shown to perform "signs" which are peculiar to Israel (Revelation 13:12-15). Because these "signs" include the ability to restore life (verse 12), to call fire down from heaven (verse 13), and to create (verses 14-15), his actions recall those of the prophetic messianic forerunner Elijah (*see* 1 Kings 17:14-16, 21-23; 18:36-38). Perhaps this implies that the false prophet will act only as a messianic forerunner like Elijah (*see* Malachi 3:1-2; 4:5) and proclaim the Antichrist as Messiah. However, because the Antichrist receives worship (Revelation 13:4, 8), it seems his status is elevated even above that of Messiah.

Whoever it is that fills this counterfeit role in the future, it is possible that the activities of the Hasidic Jews are now unwittingly preparing the Jewish people to accept both the Antichrist as a coming world ruler and the false prophet as a miracle-working messiah.

Embracing New Age Concepts

In their messages exhorting people to prepare for the coming Messiah, the present Lubavitcher leadership are embracing New Age concepts of reality. Rabbi Schneerson, in a message based on Isaiah 11:9 ("The earth will be full of the knowledge of the LORD as the waters cover the sea"), said:

The prophet tells us that the redemption will herald a new reality for humankind. A reality in which the Divine intention underlying all of creation, and the Divine purpose inherent in everything, will become revealed to the world, enlightening all humankind.[23]

What do terms such as "a new reality," "inherent in everything," and "enlightening all humankind" have to do with Isaiah's portrayal of a millennial age where harmony is restored to the created order and the Gentile nations submit to Messiah (Isaiah 11:6-10)? Rabbi Friedman explains this New Age style of interpretation when he says:

> The coming of Moshiach can't be one of these glassy-eyed, overwhelming experiences like the Exodus from Egypt or the giving of the Torah at Sinai, because those things just don't last. Because again, it's G-d doing it, not us . . . it's just another good event in our long history of miracles and revelations. In order for Moshiach to come without disrupting us, without blowing us away, we have to have some awareness or some readiness, or some ability to handle the idea that the world is becoming good, that evil and suffering are going to end. Like the bumper sticker that says, "Visualize world peace." If you can't make it happen, visualize it; at least be able to conceive of it. So if we get more and more people thinking, "Yes, it is time for the world to become good," maybe we could actually realize that which everyone has always insisted and believed: that the world will someday be good.[24]

Friedman also believes that the present world order is progressing toward this potential state of utopia:

In *Yemos ha-Moshiach* ("the Days of Moshiach") nature does not change. You don't have any resurrection of the dead, and you don't have any disruption of nature. All you have is total universal goodness and morality. And that would mean that nation does not oppress nation, and that there is no suppression of religion, and so on. And we're beginning to see that today.[25]

Rabbi Schneerson has urged a similar course of action: "Now he says the world is much closer to being ready for Moshiach, but he says it depends on us. If we expect more, if we ask the Holy One to make it happen, it will."[26] What Friedman appears to be saying is that the messianic advent is always possible but will not be realized until it has been adequately prepared for by men. Supposedly the Messiah will come in response to a world that has attained a new level of spiritual reality—through visualizing a world of goodness—and that is working to bring about a peaceful order politically and religiously.

The Biblical View

The millennial kingdom envisioned by the biblical prophets is indeed to be a world of righteousness (Habakkuk 2:14; Zechariah 14:9), but it will come by divine spiritual power, not human work (Zechariah 4:6; 13:1-4; 14:3, 9). The only "millennium" that will come by human means will be the pseudo-peace brought by the Antichrist during the first half of the Tribulation period.

Rabbi Friedman has stated that the core message of Moshiach is *teshuva* ("repentance"): "As Rav in Talmud (*Sanhedrin* 97) stated all that Jews need is to do *teshuva* and Moshiach comes, for all the predestined dates for the redemption have already passed."[27] But what is the nature of this "repentance"? Friedman has in mind a return of worldwide Jewry—or at least a majority of the Jewish people—to biblical and Mishnaic legalism. This ritualistic "repentance" is a far cry from the biblical call to turn from sin and to the messianic Savior (Zechariah 12:10-14). Yet this "repentance" for a new world order (which will include the resumption of ritualistic worship without regeneration) will be made possible by the Antichrist's covenant with Israel.

An Imminent Sign?

Rabbi Schneerson, at age 92, does not fit the expected image of a messianic deliverer. In 1992 he suffered a stroke that left him partially paralyzed and unable to speak. In 1994 he suffered another stroke that placed him in critical condition. Rather than view these tragedies as disqualifying the rabbi from a messianic role, Lubavitchers have proclaimed this suffering a sure sign. The fact that his two strokes fell on the same day, the twenty-seventh of the Jewish month of Adar, was interpreted as a providential act that had support from the Torah. Schneerson's followers explain that it was on this day that King Jehoiachin was released from Babylonian captivity (2 Kings 25:27). The word translated "release" is literally "raised up the head" (*nasa'* . . . *'et rosh*). This same phrase was used when the second set of tablets was given to Moses. Between the first set of tablets and the second was the incident of the golden calf. Schneerson himself was said to have commented on this text shortly before his first stroke, noting that this negative experience led to a positive result.

In a letter dated March 13, 1994, advocates of Schneerson's messiahship (in Habad) stated that their Hasidic founder, Rabbi Zalman, had predicted a time of discord and divisions between Torah scholars, just before the coming of Messiah—and that this would affect the body of Israel much like a stroke.

Zalman, however, found encouragement in this, observing that it is darkest just before the dawn. He believes this experience of suffering will prepare Israel for a greater revelation thereafter.

Schneerson's followers had made a similar connection between suffering and messiahship after the rebbe's first stroke. They referred to the messianic text of Isaiah 53:7: "He was oppressed and He was afflicted, yet He did not open His mouth." They applied these words to Schneerson's paralysis, believing he would recover miraculously as the passage predicts: "[I] will prolong His days, and the good pleasure of the LORD will prosper in His hand" (verse 10).

As Passover arrived in April of 1994, Lubavitcher followers of the rebbe were hopeful for his full recovery and announcement as the Moshiach. That's because the Baal Shem Tov (Rabbi Yisrael ben Eliezer), the seventeenth-century founder of Hasidism, had a vision in which he was told the Messiah would appear on the last day of Passover. Ever since, Hasidic Jews have celebrated this day with a *S'udat Ha-Mashiah* ("Messianic Meal") in anticipation of its fulfillment.

Stepping Up the Effort

Rabbi Nahman Kahane, the brother of the late Kach party leader Meir Kahane and head of the Young Israel Synagogue (the synagogue closest to the Temple Mount) and the Institute for Talmudic Commentaries, has long been at the forefront of religious efforts to see the Temple rebuilt. For years his activities were scholarly in nature and he publicly distanced himself from activist organizations, choosing rather to quietly compile a computerized list of all qualified *cohanim* ("priests") in Israel. Recently, however, he has shifted to a semiactivist stance and reported the formation of a Jewish fundamentalist organization in response to similar groups existing in Christian and Islamic circles.[28] He has stated seven goals for this organization:

1. The return of the Israeli nation to a monarchy.
2. The return of the Israeli people to a classic Jewish (biblical) lifestyle.
3. The restoration of the Sanhedrin to elect a high priest.
4. The formation of a government with a reigning prophet.
5. The liberation of all the land promised to Israel.
6. The making of G-d the center of the universe.
7. The rebuilding of the Third Temple.

Like Rabbi Joel Lerner of the Sanhedrin Institute and Rabbi Shlomo Goren, who has constructed a fully furnished meeting place for the restored Sanhedrin adjacent to the Temple Mount, Rabbi Kahane advocates returning to the rule of sages with a Torah-based government, which must—in order to perform properly—exist in relation to a functioning Temple. This messianic or theocratic government cannot be properly effected until the Messiah appears. Rabbi Kahane may also believe that this appearance will be attended by a messianic recovery of the Ark.

Reviving an Ancient Ceremony

Reuven Prager, the founder of *Beged Ivri* ("Hebrew Clothing"), believes that it is his destiny to assist in returning Israelis and all Jews to a biblical lifestyle in preparation for the advent of the Third Temple era. Indeed, a sign with that very announcement greets visitors to Prager's shop in the ultraorthodox Jewish section of Jerusalem. A Temple Mount activist in his own right, Prager has worked for years toward the revival of an ancient Jewish marriage ceremony which takes place on the Temple Mount. Prager explains the reason for this revival:

> Between the First and Second Temple period, there existed an ancient marriage ceremony which was performed primarily in Jerusalem. This beautiful and colorful event fell into disuse after the destruction of the Second Temple and the loss of the Land. With the return of the Jewish people to the Land of Israel, preparations are paving the way for the establishment of the Third Temple and with them, the revival of Temple consciousness—hence the . . . proposal for the reinstitution of the ancient Jewish marriage ceremony.[29]

To realize this goal, Prager established a nonprofit organization registered with the Ministry of the Interior, constructed an ancient bridal crown made of pure gold, and raised funds to build the *Apiron* or Royal Wedding Litter, originally described in the Song of Solomon. With the completion of the *Apiron* last year, Prager has successfully entertained numerous Jewish families outside of Israel with the prospect of conducting their weddings in Jerusalem on the Temple Mount. His belief, like all in the Temple movement, is that increased religious devotion (the fulfillment of *mitzvot*, "commandments") toward the Temple will hasten the day of its rebuilding. Like the Ark, which was transported with poles, the *Apiron* is carried by Levites in a sacred procession (*see photo section*).

It is the acts of people like Prager who, as part of a religious revival, may help move the collective consciousness of Israel toward the Third Temple era, and with it, a national call for the Ark.

There has never before existed such an extensive movement to prepare the Jewish people for the end-time leader who, in reality, will counterfeit the messianic office. Already this movement has contributed toward the Jewish recognition of the Messiah as a human political and religious figure whose calling card will be the rebuilding of the Temple. Indeed, in its own way, this revival may be hastening the day when that signal event will be realized: the day that the true Messiah returns and the Ark of the Covenant is set in the millennial Temple.

13

The Last Days' Ark

At the end-time the Ark, with the stone tablets,
will resurrect first: it will come out of the rock and be
placed on Sinai. There the saints will assemble to
receive the Lord. [1]

—*The Lives of the Prophets* 2:15

As a young boy I grew up in the southern part of Texas. One day my father gave me an old, odd-looking bill and said, "Son, save your Confederate dollars—the South shall rise again!" Although I now know he was simply having fun with me, at the time I took his advice seriously. As the years went by I kept that Confederate bill in my secret treasure chest against the day when it would again be legal tender. In time, however, I came to realize that all rebel hopes were vanquished, that old Dixie would never wave again, and that the South would never rise.

Just like my Confederate dollar—now merely a collector's curiosity—some people have regarded the Ark as a long-lost relic doomed to the dust of decay. As we have seen in previous chapters, however, there has been a revival of interest in the Ark and it may yet rise again to resume a pivotal place in history. Like the nation of Israel, itself once thought to be a fossil civilization but now the center of international concern, the Ark may be destined to appear in the last days as the rediscovered treasure of prophetic prediction.

The Ark as a Sign of the End Times

In the opening chapter concerning the Temple treasures, I emphasized a prophecy made during Israel's first exile (Jeremiah 27:22): the Temple vessels would be taken to Babylon and remain there until God restored His people to their land. In that passage a pattern was revealed for the way God would relate to Israel concerning its Temple and worship: with desecration would come destruction, but with repentance would come restoration. This text, and the majority of restoration passages in the prophets, indivisibly bind the Jewish people with their ordained form of Temple worship.

In Jeremiah, God is said to have protected the Temple vessels in Babylon (*see* Daniel 5:2-6) just as He did His own people (*see* Esther 9:1-19). In this same light, in the *Paralipomena of Jeremiah*, God did not allow the Temple to be destroyed until the vessels had been safely removed (1:4-8; 4:1-2). When the people were in exile, so were the vessels. And as the people returned, so did the vessels.

Today as the Jewish people end their long exile and return to Israel from every nation on earth, should we not expect to see a restoration of the Temple, its vessels, and most of all the Ark? The current fascination over the lost Ark may in fact serve as a signpost along the prophetic path to indicate the nearness of the predicted Jewish age and Daniel's seventieth week (Daniel 9:24, 27). Does the Bible give us any clues that the Ark may one day resurface to play a role in end-time events?

Will the Ark Be in
the Millennial Temple?

Daniel and Jesus both prophesied that during the Tribulation period the "abomination of desolation" would be erected

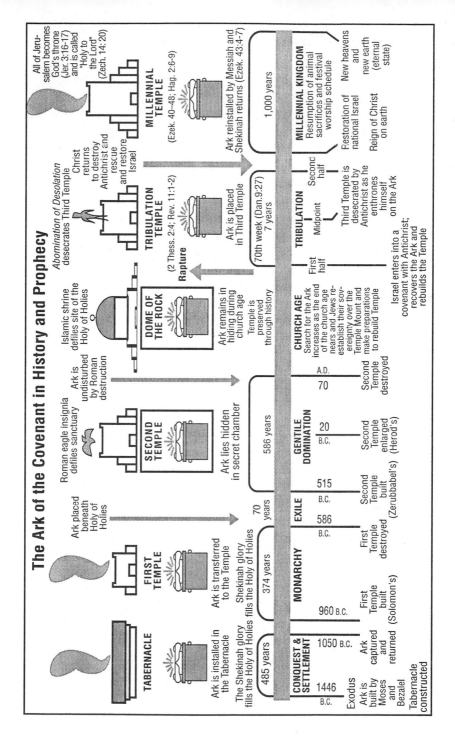

The Ark of the Covenant in History and Prophecy

in the Holy Place of the rebuilt Third Temple, thereby defiling the Temple (Daniel 9:27; Matthew 24:15; Mark 13:14). Paul, commenting on Daniel's text, explained in 2 Thessalonians 2:4 that the Antichrist will seat himself in the Holy Place, usurping the place of God. Historically, the divine presence in the Holy Place was above the Ark, since the Ark represented the footstool of God. It is possible that in order to manifest himself as deity the Antichrist will require the presence of the Ark in the rebuilt Temple (more details on this are given in chapter 13).

Although Ezekiel's prophecy of the millennial Temple does not *explicitly* refer to the Ark, I believe there are some *implicit* references to the Ark's presence. Before we look at those references, let's consider a general deduction drawn from the prophetic relationship of Ezekiel's Temple to that of the Second Temple.

The Greater Glory of the Millennial Temple

The millennial Temple was prophesied to replace the Second Temple as a place of legitimate Israelite worship. In Haggai 2:9 we read that "the latter glory of this house will be greater than the former." While this statement might appear to compare the First and Second Temples, a careful look at the description of the "latter house" reveals that it *cannot* be the Second Temple. First, Haggai 2:5 tells us this "latter house" Temple has the divine presence (or "Spirit") that is visibly present, just as it was during the exodus (*see* Exodus 19:4; 29:45-46). Second, Haggai 2:6-7 place this Temple in an era that follows a time of divine judgment—a time in which earthly and heavenly disturbances have forced the Gentile nations to bring their wealth to the Temple (*see* Zechariah 14:14).[2] And third, in Haggai 2:9 we're told this Temple is a Temple wherein God will provide universal peace (*see* Isaiah 2:2-4).

Many Christians want to spiritualize Haggai 2:5-9 and apply it to Jesus' first coming and the peace He established "through the blood of His cross" (Colossians 1:20). Jesus, as the Prince of Peace, did teach in the Temple and give personal peace to those who heard and believed. As Messiah, He also made it possible for men to have peace with God through His work on the cross near the Temple site. But, He clearly taught that the Temple would be destroyed because the Jewish nation had not recognized Him as the Messiah. He did not promise a divine peace in Jerusalem. Rather, He predicted that for Jews, as well as for Christians, the time to come would be one of trouble (Matthew 24:21; Mark 13:8; John 16:33) and wars (Matthew 10:34; 22:36). In contrast, the millennial Temple era is clearly a time during which troubles are forgotten (Isaiah 65:16), instruments of war are turned into instruments of productivity, and all nations are at peace (Isaiah 2:4).

The Failure of the Second Temple

In relation to the historical fulfillment of Haggai's prophecies (and all other biblical prophecies) concerning Israel's national restoration, the Second Temple must be considered a failure. If we attempt to make the Second Temple fulfill these extensive restoration prophecies, then either we must abandon any sense of literal interpretation (which the details of the text cannot bear), or admit that the Word of God itself has failed (which orthodox theology cannot bear!). Consequently, Jewish interpreters have explained that the Second Temple was not built according to Ezekiel's plan because they realized that *it was not yet the time* to build this Temple (*see Tosefta Yom Tov*). Rashi, one of the greatest medieval Jewish commentators, explains how they knew the time was not right at the first return from exile:

> The return to Israel in the days of Ezra could have been like the first time the Jewish people entered Israel in the days of Joshua. . . . However, sin prevented this, for their repentance was imperfect.

> Since they were not worthy, they did not have per-
> mission to build the Temple which was designated
> as the Temple for the eternal redemption, for when
> it will be built according to this design, the [divine]
> glory will rest upon it forever.[3]

Historically, only a small remnant of 50,000 Judeans (mixed
also with remnants of Israelites) returned in 538 B.C. to rebuild
the Temple. However, the work was delayed for 15 years because of foreign opposition. Even after that, Ezra and Nehemiah had to confront the sins of the people, which included
spiritual apathy, unlawful marriages, violations of the Sabbath, and extortion. Also, we must not forget that at that time
the Jewish nation was not independent (as it had been during
the First Temple era), but was subject to the Persians. This
subjugation continued throughout the entire time of the Second Temple under the Seleucids, Ptolemies, and finally the
Romans, until these last rulers destroyed the Temple in A.D. 70.
In view of these historical realities, there is no way that the
"glory" (as described by Haggai) of the Second Temple could
be considered "greater" than that of the First Temple.

According to *Tosefta Yom Tov* (paragraph 60), the reason
the future Temple will have a greater glory than the Second
Temple is because the Second Temple lacked five things that
had been in the First Temple (one of these being the Ark).
These five elements evidently will be reinstated in the Third
Temple.

The Glory Returns . . . to the Ark?

Ezekiel does clearly state that the divine presence will
return to the new Temple. In fact, this return, described in
Ezekiel 43:1-12, is the climax of the book and therefore the
most important feature in Ezekiel's prophecy. When God's
glory initially entered the First Temple, it came to a rest at the
Ark, dwelling between the cherubim. It seems reasonable to

expect that this will also happen in Ezekiel's Temple, since it is considered a restoration of the First Temple. If that were not so, we should expect the text to point out this departure from the historical pattern. Yet as we examine Ezekiel's record of this prophetic return, we see that every element of the earlier account is duplicated (compare Ezekiel 43:5, 7 with 1 Kings 8:10-12; 2 Chronicles 7:2). Ezekiel also said that the glory will come to the Temple by way of the eastern gate. Remember, God's glory departed from the First Temple by this same gate. Since the latter is the reversal of the former, and the Ark was lost after the First Temple, we should expect to see the Ark restored and made part of a future Temple wherein God's glory dwells (*see* 1 Kings 8:6-12).

Some people have expressed concern over Ezekiel's failure to make a direct reference to the Ark. They assume that such an important object would have been mentioned. But the seeming failure to include an object does not mean that it is excluded. There are other lost items Ezekiel does not mention, such as the Menorah or the Golden Altar of Incense. However, they are thought to be in the millennial Temple because other vessels, such as the Table of Showbread (Ezekiel 41:22), are described. Ezekiel only states what he needs to specify, and apparently it wasn't essential to mention the Ark. For instance, Ezekiel says cherubim decorate the walls of the Holy Place (the partition before the Holy of Holies; Ezekiel 41:18-20). If there are yet to be depictions of cherubim leading into the Holy of Holies, why should not the two cherubim of the Ark also be in the Holy of Holies? I believe Ezekiel's lesser inclusions (cherubim on the walls) point to the greater inclusion (the Ark).

The Ark and the Millennial Feasts

Ezekiel also says that in the millennial Temple, *all* the appointed Jewish feasts will be observed (Ezekiel 44:24). In at least one of these feasts—the Day of Atonement—the Ark served a central and indispensable function. While the Day of

Atonement and the Feast of Weeks are not mentioned by name, neither are many of the other distinctive feasts. However, their omission does not mean that they will not be observed. Ezekiel does not mention the Feast of Booths, but Zechariah does (Zechariah 14:16). On the other hand, Ezekiel does mention that regular atonement would be made for the house of Israel (Ezekiel 45:15-17), even though he does not state when these offerings would be made (such as on the Day of Atonement). Apparently those who were familiar with these details felt that specific details would not be necessary. If a person is inclined to reject the Day of Atonement on the premise that Jesus fulfilled this feast, then why would Ezekiel include the Passover (Ezekiel 45:21)? This service will be performed by Zadokite Levitical priests (Ezekiel 44:15; cf. Revelation 7:7), who last officiated in the First Temple when the Ark was present.

Although no high priest is mentioned by Ezekiel, this might be assumed. I find some difficulty in relegating this Temple task to Jesus, since His High Priesthood was of a special order, the order of Melchizedek (Hebrews 5:10). Even though this was "in the days of His flesh" (Hebrews 5:7), God stated that this office was "forever" (Hebrews 5:6). It's possible that Christ may accept the Aaronic office since His glorification (*see* Hebrews 5:5); however, we have no evidence that He will do so. At any rate, whoever will serve as high priest will probably continue officiating at the Ark. We must remember that this is an earthly Temple for earthly people, and therefore sin must still be atoned for in order for men to have communion within a ritually holy community. In addition, because God's glory has returned, it will be necessary to protect the holiness of God as in the former days of the theocracy—that is, by the sacrificial system (*see* Exodus 40; Leviticus 1:1–10:20; 23:26-32).

The reinstitution of the sacrificial system should not be a matter of concern for Christians.[4] Many people have taught that a return to the sacrificial system would be a return to the

Old Covenant and a rejection of Christ as the supreme and final sacrifice for sin (Hebrews 9:23; 10:14, 18; 13:10-13). Yet we must remember that sacrifices were instituted before any covenant was made, any Law was given, or any Jewish nation existed (*see* Genesis 4:3-4; 8:20; Job 1:5; 42:8). The purpose of even the Mosaic sacrifices, especially those offered before the Ark on the Day of Atonement, was not to save anyone but to set apart, in a ritually purified manner, the covenant community (Israel). The ultimate goal of such a system was to enable Israel to function as a holy nation and a royal priesthood. This ministry for the nation will be fulfilled in the millennium, just as the prophets predicted (*see* Isaiah 61:6). In token of the fulfillment of this promise to that remnant of Israel who will believe on Jesus as their Messiah in the Tribulation and enjoy this service under the New Covenant in the millennium, believers in Jesus at the present time, especially Gentiles, function in this capacity (*see* 1 Peter 2:7-10; Titus 2:11-14; Hebrews 9:14) to provoke Israel to jealousy (Deuteronomy 32:21; cf. Romans 9:3-5, 24-26; 10:19; 11:5, 11-14). However, once Israel is saved and returned to service, the sacrificial system will permit them to properly worship Christ in His theocratic position on earth.

In summary, then, nothing in Ezekiel's description of the millennial kingdom appears to deviate radically from the theocratic instructions previously given, including the place of the Ark.

The Tribulation in the Old Testament

For our Jewish readers there is perhaps no more confusing and disagreeable concept than the future seven-year period Christians refer to as "the Tribulation." Rabbis have told me, "One Holocaust in the past was enough; why do you want to punish us with an even greater one in the future?" But as we'll see in a moment, warnings about the Tribulation date back to

Moses. And because the next events on the prophetic calendar may very well usher in the Tribulation, it is imperative that we clarify what will happen so that those who are willing can make an escape before this dreadful day arrives.

The concept of the Tribulation is largely drawn from the Jewish scriptures themselves, where it is referred to by terms such as the "tribulation" (Deuteronomy 4:30 KJV), "the day of the LORD" (Isaiah 2:12-22; 13:6-16; Joel 1:15-20; Zephaniah 1:14-18), "the time of Jacob's trouble" (Jeremiah 30:7 KJV), the seventieth week of Daniel (Daniel 9:27), "the day of [Israel's] calamity [or, disaster]" (Deuteronomy 32:35; Obadiah 12-14), "a time of trouble" (Daniel 12:1 KJV), and "a day of wrath" (Zephaniah 1:15). It is these Old Testament terms which are generally used in the New Testament (*see* Matthew 24:21, 29; 1 Thessalonians 5:2, 9; Revelation 11:18; 15:1; 16:1). In addition, not only is the concept of the Tribulation originally Jewish, it also continued to be developed by Jewish thinkers from the prophetic period through the Middle Ages.

During the Second Temple era some groups of religious Jews clearly held to the teaching that the Tribulation texts spoke of an end-times Jewish punishment. Jewish apocryphal and apocalyptic writings of this period also spoke frequently about this terrible day at the conclusion of the age. One of the primary themes in the Dead Sea Scrolls is the Tribulation. In the Dead Sea document known as *The War Scroll* a battle between "the sons of darkness" and "the sons of light" is described: Satan, Belial, and the evil angels will come against Israel, and God and the Messiah will defeat these oppressors of righteousness and restore Israel to its promised glory. One of the terms employed for this period is "the birth pangs of the Messiah" (Hebrew, *chevlo shel Mashiach*) because Israel in her suffering is thought to be like a mother in labor, whose delivery will bring forth the Messiah. This period is well explained by the standard Jewish reference work, the *Encyclopedia Judaica*:

In general, the intertestamental literature depicts the period preceding the coming of the Messiah as one of terrible distress: plagues and famine, floods and earthquakes, wars and revolutions, accompanied by such cosmic disturbances as the darkening of the sun and the moon and the falling of the stars from the sky. In part, these ideas were derived from contemporary events, such as the dispersion and persecutions suffered by the people of Israel, and in part from descriptions of the Day of the Lord found in the writings of the earlier prophets. The purpose of these terrifying pictures was to encourage the faithful in Israel to bear their afflictions patiently as God's will for them, for only when the cup of evil was filled to the brim would the Messiah come to bring salvation.[5]

The Purpose of the Tribulation

As terrible as this day will be, the Tribulation is designed within the plan of God to fulfill a glorious purpose. This purpose encompasses both Jew and Gentile, but is centered on bringing Israel into the promised age of messianic blessing. In order to accomplish this, the Tribulation will produce three changes desperately needed in the present-day order of the world.

First, it will bring about a messianic revival among Jewish people scattered throughout the world. During the first half of the Tribulation, 12,000 believing Jews from each of the 12 tribes (144,000 in all) will attempt to reach their fellow Jews and the Gentiles with the gospel of the coming messianic kingdom (Revelation 7:1-4; cf. Matthew 24:14).

There is a modern-day complaint among orthodox Jews that the majority of Jews in Israel as well as in the Diaspora are totally unconcerned with the Torah and therefore do not consciously seek to hasten the messianic era. "To this day," writes

Rabbi Walter Wurzburger, "orthodoxy has never been able to resolve the dilemma that a considerable section of Jewry today no longer obey the *halakhah* [religious law]." Problems with assimilation, intermarriage, and spiritual defection to the New Age movement and other cults have seriously threatened the prospect of a universal Jewish return to Israel as required by the prophets before the Messiah and the promised blessings can arrive.

What is needed is a heaven-sent repentance (Hebrew, *tsuvah*), evidenced by a return to the God of Abraham, Isaac, and Jacob and a new heart to live as God's chosen people. While today there exists no successful mechanism to bring this kind of universal Jewish repentance, during the Tribulation the Jewish remnant throughout the world will experience a massive spiritual revival that will lead to national restoration. Just as out of the horrors of the Holocaust God brought refuge for the Jewish people with the establishment of the State of Israel, so even in the midst of the Tribulation God will establish the Jewish people and afterward their messianic kingdom.

Second, the Tribulation will provoke the Jewish nation to pray for their Messiah, resulting in a national regeneration (Isaiah 59:20-21; Jeremiah 31:31-34; Ezekiel 20:34-38; 36:25-27; 37:1-14; Daniel 12:5-7; Zechariah 12:10–13:1). This restoration will result in a massive return of Jews to Israel (Ezekiel 36:24; 37:21; Zechariah 8:7-8) to enjoy the blessings of the kingdom after Messiah's advent.

Third, the Tribulation will purge the earth of wicked people and end the period of Gentile domination in order to establish the Jewish messianic kingdom in righteousness (Isaiah 11:9; 13:9-10; 24:19-20; Ezekiel 37:23; Zechariah 13:2; 14:9). This violent eradication of the world's unbelieving population will result from the divine judgments unleashed throughout the Tribulation (Revelation 6–18), climaxing with the battle of Armageddon under King Messiah (Revelation 19).

Having seen the biblical events which characterize the Tribulation, let's look to the Middle East and Europe to see the now-transpiring political and religious events that may usher in this predicted period.

Tension on Every Side

Currently the government of Israel is led by the left-wing (liberal) Labor party. It has taken greater and faster steps to negotiate with Israel's enemies than all previous governments combined. Its policies of trading land for peace and for pacifying Arab religious and political demands—even at the expense of a united Jerusalem and the loss of the Temple Mount—have brought violent protests from every quarter of the Israeli population.

Assuming the present Labor government survives further no-confidence votes, it will be faced with one of two equally difficult situations. If it is successful in maintaining its self-rule compromise agreement (signed in Cairo on May 4, 1994) with the Palestine Liberation Organization (and later with Syria), and compels the settlers to leave the Gaza Strip, West Bank, and Golan Heights, it will face the likelihood of a civil war for Judea and Samaria. If the party is unsuccessful in maintaining its negotiations and the peace process fails, it will be forced to engage in another war with its Arab neighbors—a conflict on a scale far greater than any it has yet seen.

After the self-rule pact was signed, Syrians and radical Palestinian groups said, "This is a false peace and it adds new justification for an all-out war against Israel."[6] This attitude has led Middle East analysts to view the situation as only trading land for time, making for a pessimistic prognosis for peace:

> Let us also be under no illusion as to what has happened, or what will happen hereafter. The Palestinian Arabs as a whole have not changed their minds one iota about what they regard as a great

historic wrong, nor have they abandoned their hope of rectifying it.[7]

Benjamin Netanyahu, a front-line leader of the Likud party, has stated that the agreement with the PLO has turned back the calendar to 1947. At that time a temporary "peace" resulted from the United Nation's partition of Palestine into a Jewish and Arab state. This peace was short-lived, for when the independent state of Israel was established on May 14, 1948, the Arab world went to war against the Jews.

The resultant Israeli victory left a displaced Arab population which had fled Israel's borders under Arab command. Later they were allowed to return to the areas formerly known as Palestine, and many took up residence in the West Bank territories (which at that time belonged to Jordan), while others became citizens of Israel and lived within Israel proper. These Arabs were designated as "Palestinians" (just as Jews were also once designated) although today their ranks have been joined by a great number of militant Arabs living outside the borders of Israel. These "Palestinians" claim allegiance with the original Arab League charter dedicated to the removal of all Jews from the land.

So while the world hopes for peace in the Middle East, seasoned analysts are forecasting just the opposite. One writer, comparing the similar context of history, put it this way: "Weakening Israel territorially or spiritually . . . will soon force it to face the choice Chamberlain faced when appeasement failed and Hitler invaded Poland: fight a desperate war or perish."[8]

One of the most disturbing events taking place as political leaders implement the supposed peace plan in the Middle East is the continual buildup of weaponry throughout the Arab League. Russia is one of the largest suppliers of submarines and other armaments to Iran; China has supplied reactors and nuclear technology to Iran and Algeria; and France has sold massive numbers of tanks to the United Arab Emirates. As a result of allied assistance during the Persian Gulf War, the United States and Great Britain have granted the use of many jet fighters and bombers to Saudi Arabia.[9] It is also well known that Iraq, Iran, Libya, Pakistan, Syria, and Algeria have all sought to produce or have produced nuclear and chemical/biological weapons.[10] Reports that Egyptians have located uranium sites concealed by Israelis in the Sinai have also caused recent concern.[11] One must wonder why there is a proliferation of arms pouring into these Arab countries if peace is truly a prospect.

The Return of Russia

In Ezekiel 38–39 we read of an end-time battle of Gog and Magog. Gog is a military leader that arises from "the northern region" (from Israel's vantage point) of Magog (ancient Scythia). Today this area comprises the former Soviet republics of Kazakhstan, Kirghiza, Uzbekistan, Turkmenistan, and Tajikistan. According to Ezekiel, other nations which will ally themselves with Magog to invade Israel are Rosh (Russia), Meshech and Tubal (territories in Turkey), Gomer (Germany), Togarmah (Turkey), Persia (Iran), Cush/Ethiopia (Sudan), Put (Libya), and Egypt (*see* Daniel 11:40-42). While there is a difference of opinion among prophecy scholars as to the precise timing of this war, most now place it sometime before or during the Tribulation period (cf. Ezekiel 38:8, 16; 39:9).[12]

Many orthodox Jews today also believe that this as-yet-unfulfilled conflict looms large on Israel's horizon. I have in my library a book (in Hebrew) of some 125 pages published in Tel-Aviv in 1973 entitled *The War of Russia and Israel: Gog and Magog.* In this book the Israeli author holds that this climactic conflict is imminent and that the events of the Yom Kippur War set the process in motion. He teaches that a coming invasion of

Israel will result in God's intervention and the final redemption of Israel. Can it be only coincidental that the balance of power in this part of the world has for decades depended on Russia and the Arab countries?

Since the dissolution of the Soviet Union, six of the former southern republics have become independent Islamic nations: Azerbaijan, Kazakhstan, Uzbekistan, Kirghizia, Turkmenistan, and Tajikistan. All of these new nations are included in Ezekiel's prediction, have a militant Islamic movement, and are virulently anti-Jewish. All also have economic hardships which have forced alliances with other Islamic nations; and at least some have nuclear weapons at their disposal.

In mother Russia there is also a growing anti-Semitism among nationalists. This has been exemplified by ultranationalist leader Vladimir Zhirinovsky, who has gained popular support. While the White House seeks to downplay the viability of his political career, former KGB counterintelligence chief General Oleg Kalugin has said, "Both you Americans and we Russians had better prepare ourselves to deal with Zhirinovsky as president of Russia."[13] Zhirinovsky has called for a restoration of Greater Russia's primacy and has even threatened to use atomic weapons to achieve his ends. In this light he has written a book entitled *The Final March to the South,* which proclaims it is Russia's destiny to capture the lands to the south, including Israel. However, his interests are not in the destruction of Israel but its control. As Richard Judy writes:

> Zhirinovsky sees the world as one of great powers destined to exercise hegemony over specific spheres of influence. . . . Russia's sphere of influence includes . . . the remainder of the Middle East not already included in Russia proper, plus East Africa and its horn. . . . Iraq, also a friend of Russia, will exercise suzerainty over the Arabian peninsula

> (except for Israel, which quixotically will be permitted to exist)....Under Russian hegemony, the Muslims would be pacified and those threats [Islamic fundamentalism] eliminated....Russia would also guarantee (or co-guarantee) the security of the State of Israel.[14]

Zhirinovsky's outline of world power is remarkably close to the prophetic sketch of the end-time, one-world government divided into ten regions of power presided over by a supreme leader who arises from their ranks (see Daniel 7:24; Revelation 17:12-13). Russian control of Arab countries will perhaps give it the power to negotiate with Israel, although the conjecture here is that Russia will invade Israel and control it by guaranteeing its security (by a covenant of peace?). This seems to fit Ezekiel 38:8 and Daniel 11:41, which both picture a nondestructive invasion of Israel from the north.

It appears that the groundwork for this plan has even now been laid through political and economic circumstances in Russia. Since Russia cannot produce a sufficient industry to survive economically, its only course has been to align itself with third-world countries. An axis has been formed between Iran, Syria, Sudan, and Ethiopia to overthrow the United States and its allies. Russia has already forged alliances with some of these countries and others: Iran, Syria, Pakistan, Libya, and Turkey. In addition, the Central Asian republics of Kazakhstan, Turkmenistan, Tadzhikistan, Uzbekistan, and Krygzstan have signed a military-assistance pact with the Russian federation. These countries are all Islamic and have been confirmed to possess nuclear weapons. Perhaps Zhirinovsky, or another like him, will move to act on this vision; if so, the war prophesied by Ezekiel may be close at hand.

Arabs and the New World Order

At the same time, the Palestinians and the Arab League are

hastening to position themselves as part of the expanding new world order that has emerged with the unification of Germany, the collapse of the iron curtain, and the rise of the European Economic Community. Essential to this network is a peaceful coexistence that fosters the principle of unity. Yasser Arafat, the leader of the new Palestinian state, has made acceptance by this community one of his top priorities; it is his primary motivation for making "peace" with Israel. He says, "For many years I have been asking the Israelis to start making peace. . . . There is a new world order. We want to be part of this new order, as Palestinians, and as an Arab nation."[15]

For this reason Arafat demanded that an international force be stationed in the Palestinian territories to police the Israeli settlements nearby. His action drew the Palestinian state into the protective custody of the international community, while at the same time set Israel apart from it. The Arabs perceived this demand as an important guarantee for their security because they had interpreted the establishment of diplomatic relations between Israel and the Vatican as a move against Muslim solidarity.[16]

The Future Scenario

When the Russian-Arab alliance moves against Israel, the European community will be compelled to intervene. When the battle turns to favor Israel, the Europeans will join with the Israelis and their leader will perhaps claim credit for what is, in fact, divine intervention.

It is incredible enough to believe that Israel's nearly five million inhabitants will hold their own against 22 Arab nations of more than 200 million, but the added numbers of Russia and her satellite republics will convince the world that Israel's survival is nothing short of a miracle. For a time, this anti-Semitism, even now spreading through Europe, will give way to an acknowledgment of this phenomenon. But once Israel asserts her independence from the rule of Antichrist, anti-Semitism will explode on a worldwide scale and Israel will truly be "hated by all nations" (Matthew 24:9).

Because the Russian-Arab conflict will leave Israel on top in the Middle East, the European leader (the Antichrist) will move to make a covenant with the Jews (Daniel 9:27). For the first time in modern history there will be no Muslim opposition to Israel's sovereignty over Jerusalem. It is possible that orthodox Jews will take over the government because secular Jews will recognize that Israel's success was a result of divine intervention. These new spiritual-political leaders will announce that Israel's victory marks the start of the messianic era. The Third Temple will then be erected and the sacrificial system reinstituted (Daniel 9:27; Revelation 11:1-2). And in the new Holy of Holies will most likely be placed the ancient Ark, which will serve as proof that the age of restoration has begun.

During the first half of the Tribulation period, while God's wrath is displayed elsewhere on earth (Revelation 6:1-2), Israel will enjoy a pseudomessianic era. Yet this time of calm in the Middle East, which may be the political maneuver that propels the Antichrist into world ascendancy, is described by the Bible as a false peace (Jeremiah 6:14; 8:11). In 1 Thessalonians 5:3 we read, "When they shall say, Peace and safety; then sudden destruction cometh upon them, as travail upon a woman with child; and they shall not escape" (KJV). It may be that during this time the false prophet (Revelation 13:11-18) will appear and eventually be accepted by many Jews as the Messiah (Matthew 24:24). The false peace will evidently end with the desecration of the Temple by the Antichrist and the worldwide persecution of Jews at the midpoint of the Tribulation.

How Will It Happen?

The current mix in the Middle East makes it hard to see how the scenario described in Scripture will happen. Nevertheless,

I believe there is good reason to think that the events concerning Israel during the Tribulation will be spearheaded by a dedicated minority of religious Jews. They will unknowingly enter into the contract with the one who will later be revealed as the Antichrist in order to build the Third Temple.

Even now we can see how the minority movements in Israel (messianic and Temple movements) influence world events. The 1990 Temple Mount incident with the Temple Mount Faithful (which drew a response from Saddam Hussein) and Baruch Goldstein's 1994 mosque shooting have revealed that it does not require a majority to make a big difference in the Middle East. One writer has said this concerning the disproportionate influence of minority organizations in Israel: "Although small in absolute numbers, the power of these splinter groups to derail international initiatives and to reignite conflict on the West Bank is magnified by uninhibited ideological fanaticism."[17]

It is significant that many of these groups have had a part in or have knowledge of the Israeli search for the Ark. Should they, despite the present restrictions on their movements, be able to renew the quest, perhaps their efforts will result in an even greater conflict over the Ark. After the battle of Gog and Magog (Ezekiel 38:1–39:20) and before the erection of the millennial Temple (Ezekiel 40:1–48:35), Ezekiel mentions the national restoration of Israel at the end of the Tribulation (Ezekiel 39:21-29). God declares that during this time He will "set [His] glory among the nations" (verse 21) and restore Israel's blessings in connection with His holy presence (verse 25). The result will be that Israel will thereafter live securely (verse 26). This description seems to recall the functions of the Ark: the "glory" attended the Ark (1 Samuel 4:21) and brought blessing to Israel (2 Samuel 6:11-12), which in turn secured the land for Israel (Numbers 10:33-36). If such language is intended to include the Ark, then this may be further evidence that the Ark will indeed be present in the last days.

While the old South will certainly never rise again, the ancient Ark, as a part of Israel's destiny, may soon rise to take its role in the last days. Let's move now into these last days and look at those scriptures which may reveal the drama about to be enacted between the Antichrist and the Ark.

14

The Ark and the Antichrist

---

*Let no one in any way deceive you, for it [the
second coming of Christ] will not come unless the
apostasy comes first, and the man of lawlessness is
revealed, the son of destruction, who opposes and
exalts himself above every so-called god or object of
worship, so that he takes his seat in the temple of
God, displaying himself as being God.*

—2 Thessalonians 2:3-4

When God chose Israel, His enemy chose them as well.
The future will see a time of Jewish persecution
and religious deception. The figure who instigates this tribulation is the Antichrist, joined by his false prophet, who will
eventually dominate Jerusalem and desecrate the newly built
Temple. In this chapter we will study the Antichrist in detail
and his relationship to the Temple, which may one day house
the restored Ark of the Covenant. We will also look in Scripture for any indication that the future may see a link between
the Antichrist and the Ark.

Because Hollywood and Christian fiction have often dis-
torted the biblical picture of the Antichrist, let us first consider
this image of evil incarnate in its scriptural context.

A Portrait of the Antichrist

The conflict of the ages is between Christ and Satan, and therefore we find throughout the biblical record a satanic corruption and counterfeit of the divine plan—particularly in relation to Israel and their Messiah. Just as the Bible gives a progressive revelation of the messianic program, so there is also an unfolding of the antimessianic program. The apostle John stated the long-held belief that "Antichrist . . . is coming" (1 John 4:3). Jewish readers often react negatively to the Christian idea of the Antichrist because they associate it with anti-Jewish thinking. Without a doubt some misguided people have used the epithet "antichrist" to speak of the Jews, yet in the New Testament the term was applied to Gentiles.[1]

Properly understood, *antichrist* means "antimessiah," since the word *Christ* (Greek, *Christos*) is the translation of the Hebrew word *Messiah* (*Mashiach*). Therefore, the Antichrist should properly be understood as a Gentile adversary of the Jewish Messiah and not be dismissed as an invention of anti-Semitic thinking.

In fact, the figure of the Antichrist is implied in the Old Testament and appears under various names in the Jewish apocryphal and pseudepigraphal writings that date from before the birth of Christ. This last-days opponent of the Jewish people and the Messiah is especially prominent in some of the apocalyptic texts of the Dead Sea Scrolls. Michael Stone, a leading Israeli expert on this literature, has observed that "the background to this figure lies in Jewish eschatology."[2] The same conclusion was drawn by Hebrew University professor David Flusser. As an expert on the origins of Christianity, he categorically states, "The idea of Antichrist is strictly Jewish and pre-Christian."[3]

In later Jewish commentaries, the legendary name given to the antimessiah is Armilus. A brief summary of his characteristics, as given in such works as *Sefer Zerubbavel* and those by Saadiah Gaon, reveals close similarities between the Jewish and Christian concepts of the Antichrist:

> This Armilus will deceive the whole world into believing he is God and will reign over the whole world. He will come with ten kings and together they will fight over Jerusalem. . . . Armilus will banish Israel "to the wilderness" and it will be a time of unprecedented distress for Israel; there will be increasing famine, and the Gentiles will expel the Jews from their lands, and they will hide in caves and towers. . . . God will war against the host of Armilus. . . . and there will be a great deliverance for Israel and the kingdom of Heaven will spread over all the earth.[4]

Other references further describe Armilus as arising from the Roman empire, having miraculous powers, and being born to a stone statue of a virgin (which is why he is called "the son of a stone"). It is also interesting that he makes this statue "the chief of all idolatry" with the result that "all the Gentiles will bow down to her, burn incense and pour out libations to her." This parallels the Antichrist's "abomination of desolation," which is worshiped by the nations (Daniel 9:27; 11:31; 12:11; Revelation 13:14-15).

We should not be surprised that the New Testament places the Antichrist in the context of the Jewish nation and the Temple. Indeed, the satanic strategy has been to desecrate and destroy every holy thing that would enable the Jewish nation—as God's representatives—to fulfill their ordained role as a light to the Gentile nations of the world (Isaiah 43:10; 45:4-6). Since the Ark of the Covenant was the most holy object given to reveal God's presence with Israel, it is reasonable to expect that it might be targeted by Satan and his Antichrist in their campaign against the end-time Jewish remnant who have revived Temple worship. Before we move to consider specific biblical texts which suggest this notion, let us further survey the biblical teaching concerning the Antichrist.

The Appearing of the Antichrist

The Antichrist will appear at the beginning of the Tribulation, which will be marked by the signing of a seven-year covenant between himself and the nation of Israel. This covenant is described in Daniel 9:27: "He will make a firm covenant with the many." The original Hebrew text may refer to either the initial "making of a covenant" or the "confirming" (literally, "strengthening") of a preexistent one. It may be that because God had promised to establish a "covenant of peace" with Israel in the end times (Ezekiel 37:26), the Antichrist will move to do the same.

This event cannot take place until *after* the church is raptured and at least three other historical conditions are met: Israel must be established as a nation, the Antichrist must rise to power, and Israel must have a need for such a covenant. Today it is possible that the latter three of these conditions have been met. Israel has been a nation since May 14, 1948. Since that time it has been in a state of war with most of its neighboring Arab states since that time, conditions for a covenant have particularly existed since 1987 when the Palestinian Intafada escalated the move toward a final war over the possession of historic borders.

On September 13, 1993 the Intafada was suspended with the signing of a declaration of principles between Israel and the PLO. This agreement offered a peaceful resolution by establishing an autonomous Palestinian state in Gaza and Jericho. Perhaps the covenant of Daniel 9:27 will be a similar peace covenant except on a broader scale. Certainly the present Middle East conflict requires such. However, the issue in Daniel is the status of Jerusalem and the rebuilding of the Temple, which tells us that the covenant may help to resolve these historic problems. To be sure, any covenant that favors Israel and allows for the rebuilding of the Temple will have international ramifications, such as implied in Daniel (cf. Zechariah 12:2-3).

On May 19, 1993, a document called "The Jerusalem Covenant" was signed by Israeli officials and Jewish leaders worldwide. It is a reaffirmation of the historic unity of Jerusalem and a declaration of the prophetic blessings accompanying the rebuilding of the Temple on the Temple Mount. Some have considered this covenant (a copy of which is enshrined in a special exhibition at the Western Wall Tunnel) the very document the Antichrist will one day ratify with Israel. Of this we cannot be certain, but it may be a treaty like this one which guarantees Israel's sovereignty over Jerusalem and the Temple Mount.

The Antichrist may well be in the world today and in a place of power, but he will be prevented from exercising dominance until the rapture of the church. Although present conditions permit a treaty like the one Daniel describes, it cannot yet be enacted. For this reason, many prophetic observers believe that the rapture—which can occur at any moment—may be close at hand.

Antichrist in the Old Testament

As we survey the Old Testament, we can see Satan preparing for the advent of the Antichrist during the Tribulation through a series of "antichrists" who appear as opponents of the Jewish people and as desecraters of the holy Temple that housed the Ark. While the term "Antichrist" is not used until the New Testament, the apostle John's reference to present-day antichrists and the coming end-time Antichrist (1 John 2:18) encourages an examination of the Old Testament for imagery that encompasses both figures.

In the Old Testament the imagery of a human being (usually a monarch or military commander) set in direct opposition to

God often takes on superhuman proportions by virtue of the divine/human contest. In this way he serves as a prefigurement or type of the end-time Antichrist. Prominent examples of such antichrists are the unnamed pharaoh who oppressed the Israelites in Egypt (Exodus 1:11, 22; 5:2) and the Babylonian king Nebuchadnezzar, who destroyed the Temple in Jerusalem (2 Kings 24:13-14). Other suggested types may include the serpent in Eden (Genesis 3), Nimrod (Genesis 10:8; 11:1-9), Amalek (Exodus 17:8-16; Deuteronomy 25:19; 1 Samuel 15:2-3), Balaam (Numbers 22–24), and Sennacherib (2 Kings 18:13–19:37).

Later figures develop the typological connection with the Temple specifically. The book of Daniel appears to predict the historical desecration of the Temple by the Syrian king Antiochus IV Epiphanes (Daniel 8:11-14; 11:31) and perhaps the Roman general Titus (Daniel 9:26). Daniel's description of Antiochus (Daniel 8:9-25; 11:21-35) and especially of his abominable desolation of the Holy Place (Daniel 8:11-14; 11:31) casts the mold for the New Testament's portrayal of the future Antichrist (Daniel 11:36-45; cf. 2 Thessalonians 2:3; Revelation 13:1-10; 17:11-17) and the abomination of desolation (Daniel 9:27; 12:11; cf. Matthew 24:15; Mark 13:14; 2 Thessalonians 2:4). By comparing the more obvious types (the antichrists) with the antitype (the Antichrist), we can observe a progressive development of opposition to God centering on the desecration of the Temple.

In the accompanying chart, the development toward the antitype (Antichrist) reveals that the movement of the type's (antichrist's) actions is toward Temple desecration. Notice that the development begins with *both* opposition to the divine program and the oppression of God's people. Pharaoh sets the basic plot that will be progressively enlarged by a desecration against the Temple. Nebuchadnezzar cast the third element; his desecration was that of removing the Temple from Israel and the Israelites *from* the Land. This act was more

Typological Development of the Antichrist Imagery

TYPOLOGICAL FIGURE	TYPOLOGICAL ACTIVITY
PHARAOH	OPPOSED TO GOD (EXODUS 5:2) OPPRESSED PEOPLE (EXODUS 1:11, 22)
NEBUCHADNEZZAR	OPPOSED GOD (HABAKKUK 1:6—11) OPPRESSED PEOPLE (2 KINGS 24:14) **DESECRATED TEMPLE (2 KINGS 24:13)**
ANTIOCHUS IV	OPPOSED GOD (DANIEL 11:36) OPPRESSED PEOPLE (DANIEL 11:41) DESECRATED TEMPLE (DANIEL 11:31) **ABOMINATION OF DESOLATION (DANIEL 11:31)**
TITUS	OPPOSED GOD (DANIEL 9:26a) OPPRESSED PEOPLE (DANIEL 9:26c; LUKE 21:23) DESECRATED TEMPLE (DANIEL 9:26b; LUKE 21:24) **ABOMINATION OF DESOLATION (HADRIAN)**
ANTITYPE	ANTITYPICAL ACTIVITY
ANTICHRIST	OPPOSES GOD (REVELATION 13:6) OPPRESSES PEOPLE (DANIEL 9:27; REVELATION 13:7) DESECRATES TEMPLE (2 THESSALONIANS 2:4) **ABOMINATION OF DESOLATION (DANIEL 9:27;** **MATTHEW 24:15; MARK 13:14; REVELATION 13:14-15)**

severe than Pharaoh's persecution of Israel *in his land*. But it was not as severe as what Antiochus did—persecute Israel and desecrate her Temple *within her own Land*. That's because the Babylonian exile offered the opportunity of return to Israel, but the Antiochean persecution offered only a succession of further persecution without escape.

The Abomination of Desolation

The next element in the typological/apocalyptic scheme is Antiochus' setting up of the abomination of desolation. His invasion made it possible for Rome to acquire Israel when it conquered the Greeks, thus rendering the Roman empire "the people of the prince who is to come" (Daniel 9:26). When Titus as a successor-oppressor to Antiochus destroyed the Temple in A.D. 70 he did not implement this fourth element, but left it to his typological successor, "the . . . prince who is to come" (the Antichrist). It was this ultimate act of desecration that was predicted by Jesus in His Olivet Discourse, Paul in his Thessalonian correspondence, and John in his Apocalypse.

What is important for us to note is that the activity of the Antichrist centers on desecrating the holiness of the Temple, and in the past, *the holiness of the Temple depended on the presence of the Ark*. While this logic merely implies the possibility of the Ark in the Third Temple, we will now consider biblical evidence that more clearly suggests the Ark's presence during the Antichrist's act of desecration.

Its Connection to the Ark

The primary passages that suggest the Ark's presence during the Tribulation are those dealing with the abomination of desolation. This term, used by Jesus in His Olivet Discourse, was first used in the book of Daniel (9:27; 11:31; 12:11). Yet Daniel was not the first to introduce this concept. The two words that make up Daniel's expression "abomination of desolation" are derived from Jeremiah and Ezekiel's discourses about the desecration of the Temple (Jeremiah 7; Ezekiel 5:11; 6–8). Daniel reveals that he studied the book of Jeremiah while in Babylon (Daniel 9:2), and since Ezekiel was a fellow exile, he also was familiar with his message. Daniel may have used this expression to summarize the entire Old Testament prophetic truth touching any future events earmarked by this phrase. That may explain why Jesus could simply use the phrase "abomination of desolation" to describe the signal event that would serve to warn the Jewish citizens of Jerusalem of the coming final judgments.

Jesus' message was a continuation of what the biblical prophets proclaimed. His frequent citations from Jeremiah and Zechariah make it certain that He and His disciples saw their generation and Jerusalem's future in light of these prophecies. Jesus' cleansing of the Temple harks back to Jeremiah's famous Temple sermon. The Olivet Discourse contains striking resemblances to the prophetic judgment passages of Ezekiel and Zechariah. Thus we see a pattern of dependence upon prophetic texts that were themselves dependent upon one another. In this manner, the Old Testament's teaching on the Antichrist was transmitted through the ages and finally crystalized in the term "abomination of desolation."

Its Meaning

The Hebrew term *shiqqutz*, translated as "abomination," refers to objects used in the Jewish Temple service which have become contaminated and thus are unclean (*see* Zechariah 9:7). Specifically this has in view the abominable or repulsive nature of idols and idolatrous practices (cf. Jeremiah 7:30-32). The character of this abomination is described by the word "desolation." In the Hebrew text of Daniel 9:27 this word appears as the *Pol'el* participle *meshomem*, which has a range of meanings: "devastate, desolate, desert, horrify, appall"—

usually as the result of divine judgment.[5] The verbal construction implies that someone has actively caused this condition. Thus, this work of desecration is a willful act that deliberately renders the Temple unfit for the worship and service of God.

The Hebrew grammatical form of the phrase "abomination of desolation" in Daniel 9:27 is actually a linguistic impossibility (a plural noun with a singular participle). If this were an early error in copying the original manuscript, why didn't the ancient citations of this verse (in 1 Maccabees and the New Testament) attempt to correct this form in light of the other correct forms in Daniel? The reason may be that the authors and copyists saw this unique construction as an intentional device to alert the reader to a hidden message that pictured the action of the Antichrist.[6] This hidden message takes the form of a play on words, a method often used by the biblical prophets to dramatize a particularly wicked or idolatrous act.[7] In Daniel 9:27, the plural form *shiqqutzim* ("abomination") could be a substitute for the word *elohim* ("God"), which is plural in form, but treated as singular.[8]

Some Bible scholars have seen even more in this wordplay. They suggest that the phrase was meant as a deliberate substitute for the title of the chief pagan god, whose name would translate as "lord of heaven."[9] The intended message would then be that the Antichrist, who pretends to be God, is in fact only an abomination. This may be why Matthew 24:15 adds the words "let the reader understand" after Jesus cites Daniel 9:27. Only those who understand this meaning in Daniel's words while beholding the actions of the Antichrist in the future Temple will be able to avoid the deception of his counterfeit miracles. They will realize that the Antichrist's deeds are not a display of the attributes of deity, but rather an idolatrous abomination against God—one that is repulsive, horrifying, and destructive (*see* Matthew 24:23-26). This would explain Jesus' admonition to these informed people to immediately flee the city (Matthew 24:16). Since their insight into the true identity of the Antichrist will prevent them from joining the world in his worship, they are certain to face a fatal persecution if they remained (Revelation 13:8, 15).

Daniel and the Antichrist

Higher-critical scholars claim that the book of Daniel was written long after Daniel's lifetime (about 605-536 B.C.). They date the book of Daniel to the Maccabean period (165-63 B.C.) and say that Daniel's figure of the Antichrist must have been fulfilled by the Syrian king Antiochus IV Epiphanes. In this way they discount any future figure of the Antichrist, limiting Daniel's statements to past fulfillment. But it is Babylon, not Syria, which occupies center stage in Daniel, making Daniel's concept of the Antichrist correspond more readily with King Nebuchadnezzar of Babylon. For example, the idea of Babylon as an anti-God world system is epitomized by Nebuchadnezzar's self-deification (Daniel 2–3) and godless arrogance (Daniel 4). He made a great statue of gold, a 90-foot image, and commanded that all under his rule worship at its feet (Daniel 3:1-12). Then in the book of Revelation, where Daniel's idea of Antichrist is carried forward to the future, Babylon appears as the oppressive end-time center of abomination (Revelation 17–18).

Another problem with restricting Daniel's prediction to Antiochus IV Epiphanes is that this figure did not completely fulfill the details of the Antichrist type as presented in the seventy-weeks prophecy (for example, ratifying the covenant, destroying the Temple). We also know that Antichrist's destruction will come at the hands of the Messiah (Daniel 9:27; Revelation 19:19-20). For these reasons, the figure of the Antichrist remains to be fulfilled in a future opponent of God.

We are now prepared to return to Paul's statement in 2 Thessalonians 2:4, where the Antichrist seats himself in the Temple "displaying himself as being God." I believe this verse implies that the Antichrist will enter the Holy of Holies in the rebuilt Temple and seat himself in position to the recovered Ark. Let us carefully examine Paul's statement to see what connection it might have with Daniel's prophecy of the rebuilt Temple and the abomination of desolation. A further look at Daniel 9:27 will show that the phrase "on the wing of abominations" may refer to the cherubim on the Ark and serve as the background to Paul's concept of the Antichrist's enthronement.

Paul and the Antichrist

Second Thessalonians chapter 2 has been called "the tale of the two comings" because it contains both the coming of Christ and the Antichrist.[10] The event Paul describes here as preceding "the day of the Lord" (verse 2) is called "the apostasy" (verse 3), a time of moral defection and spiritual declension on a universal scale. The coming of Christ *to* this earth cannot occur until after the coming of the Antichrist *on* the earth.

In Jewish apocalyptic literature, a final rebellion by the wicked against the righteous in Israel is predicted to occur at the last day (*see* Jubilees 23:14-23; 4 Ezra 4:26-42; 6:18-28).[11] A close parallel to Paul's passage in 2 Thessalonians 2:3-9 is Psalms of Solomon 17:13, 23-27, which describes "the son of David" delivering Israel by destroying "the lawless one" with "the word of his mouth," purging Jerusalem and restoring the Promised Land to the Jews.

In these accounts, the forces of the wicked are led by "Belial" in an end-time conflict with the forces of righteousness led by the Messiah.[12] In a similar fashion, Jesus in the Olivet Discourse predicted an apostasy during which many would defect from the true faith and betray one another to deceiving false prophets (Matthew 24:10-11; Mark 13:21-22).[13] Only after the coming of the Messiah will this apostasy end (Matthew 24:30-31; Mark 13:26-27; Luke 21:27-28).

It is important to note that the Antichrist assumes the place of God in his blasphemous act of self-deification. This is seen in the words Paul uses to describe his nature and character. In 2 Thessalonians 2:3 the Antichrist is called "the man of lawlessness" and "the son of destruction." The word "lawlessness" apparently describes his opposition to the divine order (verse 4), while the word "destruction" refers to his destiny— perdition. Because verse 3 states that this one is "revealed" (the Greek word *apocalypsis*), it is thought that his "revelation" (or "coming") is a counterfeit to that of Christ's (verse 9). In this way the Antichrist appears as a rival to Christ, even though he may not assume the messianic role himself. Rather, as one commentator has said, "Obviously the man of lawlessness . . . is a quasi-divine figure, a kind of evil 'divine man', some intermediate figure between God and humanity."[14] This role, I believe, will be accorded to the false prophet because the contemporary Jewish concept of the Messiah does not permit any sense of divinity, and this is the ultimate claim of the Antichrist.

The character of the Antichrist is further defined as he "who opposes" (verse 4). The Greek word here is the same one used in the Septuagint in 1 Kings 11:25 to translate the Hebrew word *satan* ("adversary"). This points to Antichrist's link with Satan, which affirms Paul's statement that the Antichrist's coming is "in accord with the activity of Satan" (2 Thessalonians 2:9). Since Satan's adversary is God and his original goal was to become like God (*see* Isaiah 14:14; Ezekiel 28:17), the Antichrist attempts to fulfill this by usurping God's place as the focus of worship (Revelation 13:4-8). The Antichrist does this because he is energized by Satan. Revelation 13:2 says the Antichrist will receive "his power and his throne and great authority" from the great red dragon (a symbol of Satan—Revelation 12:9).

Antichrist's claim to deity will convince the world to follow him because, as 2 Thessalonians 2:9 states, he will back his words "with all power and signs and false wonders." (It may be that people will attribute this demonstration of power, signs, and wonders to the Antichrist, even though these "miracles" are actually performed by the false prophet—*see* Revelation 13:13-15.) Ultimately, the Antichrist's goal is to present himself as God in order to complete the satanic strategy of receiving worship in the place of God.

Antichrist's Abominable Act

The Antichrist's abominable deed in 2 Thessalonians 2:4 is clearly an act of self-deification. Paul shows this by his use of the middle voice with its reflexive nuance: "exalts himself." The sphere of Antichrist's self-elevation is "above every so-called god or object of worship," meaning that he elevates himself above all other claimants and that his "sanctity" exceeds even the holy Temple vessels themselves. And because he wants to elevate himself above the true God, the God of Israel, he will manifest himself in the rebuilt Jewish Temple.

We can know with certainty that Paul is talking about the Temple as a physical structure in Jerusalem and the Antichrist's act as a literal deed. This is evident from Paul's use of the definite article, "the Temple,"[15] and his use of the verb "to sit down," which suggests a definite locality.[16] This literal interpretation was accepted by most all of the early church fathers. For example, Irenaeus (about A.D. 185) wrote:

> When this Antichrist shall have devastated all things in this world, he will reign for three years and six months, and sit in the temple at Jerusalem; and then the Lord will come from heaven in the clouds, in the glory of the Father, sending this man and those who follow him into the lake of fire; but bringing in for the righteous the times of the kingdom.

By contrast, the symbolic or "spiritual" interpretation of the Temple as the church does not fully appear until the third century A.D. with Origen, who was influenced by the allegorical interpretations of the Hellenistic idealist school of Philo. Perhaps another reason for the Antichrist's abominable act in the Temple is to announce himself as a fulfillment of prophecy.[17] According to Malachi 3:1, the Jews expect the Messiah to enter the Temple and perform a sign when He appears. Rabbis have interpreted this to mean that Messiah would physically walk into the Temple to judge those who desecrated the worship service and to purify the Temple workers and their offerings (Malachi 3:3).

Jesus acted according to this messianic expectation in John 2:13-21 when He walked into the Temple precincts (the Women's Court) and overturned the tables of the money changers. The crowd, who had made the messianic connection with Malachi 3:1, asked Him, "What sign do you show us?" Jesus answered with the sign of resurrection. I believe this resurrection can be understood in relation to the nation of Israel (Ezekiel 37:1-14), the resurrection at the last day (Daniel 12:2), and Jesus' own resurrection because it is by His resurrection that He will raise all others and be their Judge (John 5:27-29).

Since Satan has an understanding of this truth, he might seek to counterfeit it through the Antichrist. Perhaps the Antichrist's "resuscitation" (Revelation 13:3, 12-14) will attempt to duplicate Christ's resurrection, and the Antichrist's murder of all who defy him (Revelation 13:8-10) will be an attempt to counterfeit "divine" judgment.

An Old Testament Precedent

The Antichrist's act in the Temple also reveals Paul's dependence upon Daniel 9:27, with allusions to Daniel 11:31-36 and 12:11.[18] It is important to note that Paul (like Jesus) assumed that his readers were familiar with the terms he used and the concepts they represented. Paul does state that he taught them previously about this prophecy (2 Thessalonians 2:5), and that the teaching itself was usually derived from the Old Testament, unless otherwise stated (*see* Romans 16:25-26; Ephesians 3:3-5). A first-century audience could not have understood Paul's predictions except by reference to Daniel's prophecy.

Jesus' direct use of the phrase "abomination of desolation" from Daniel 9:27 sets the precedent in the New Testament for references to the desecration of the Temple. It is clear in Matthew and Mark that an idolatrous object is set up or a defiling activity takes place within the Temple: "standing in the holy place" (Matthew 24:15); "standing where it should not be" (Mark 13:14).[19] That Paul is also drawing from Daniel's "abomination of desolation" can be seen from his use of the Greek term "lawlessness" (2 Thessalonians 2:3), which is parallel to the Septuagint's use of Daniel's term for "abomination." It would appear, then, that Paul's phrase "man of lawlessness" is analogous to Daniel's "abomination of desolation."[20]

The second term in Daniel's phrase, "desolation," is used in the Septuagint primarily to depict the condition of Israel and its land as a result of desecration and exile (*see* Leviticus 26:34-35; 2 Chronicles 30:7; 36:21; Psalm 73:19; Jeremiah 4:7). This may imply that the Antichrist will attempt to reverse the demonstration of divine blessing (evident with the 144,000 and the two witnesses—Revelation 7:1-8; 14:1-5; 11:3-12) by returning the whole nation to an exilic or scattered state. This is indeed portrayed by the worldwide Jewish persecution that follows the Antichrist's act of desolation (Revelation 12:13-17) and further explains Jesus' warning for the Jews to flee from Jerusalem after the abomination of desolation takes place (Matthew 24:16-22; Mark 13:14-18).

Now that we see how Paul's teaching in 2 Thessalonians 2:3-4 draws from what the Old Testament tells us about the

Temple and the Antichrist, we are ready to see how the Ark might be included in this drama of desecration.

Detailing the Desecration

In the Temple

In 2 Thessalonians 2:4, the Greek word Paul uses for the Temple is used almost exclusively to refer to a particular part of the Temple: the Holy of Holies. The Temple was the place where divine authority was authenticated; this was so because the presence of God was resident between the cherubim on the Ark. In order for the Antichrist to duplicate this act of divine authentication and usurp the place of God, he would have to enter the Holy of Holies (unscathed) and display his own presence between the wings of the cherubim on the Ark. If this counterfeit extends to every detail of the Old Testament reality, he may actually enthrone himself above the cherubim in such a manner that the Ark itself serves as a footstool. Perhaps only such an act as this could serve as a sufficiently convincing display of deity with the potential to deceive "even the elect" (Matthew 24:24).

If the Antichrist is the antitype of the Temple desecrater, then by this act he would climax all the typical figures throughout biblical history who entered and violated the Temple through physical contact. Notice that when he does this, he will blaspheme God and His heavenly Tabernacle that are represented there (Revelation 13:6).[21] Consequently, this violation of the earthly Ark could parallel a satanic attempt to attack the heavenly Ark in the heavenly Temple (Revelation 11:19; cf. Isaiah 14:13-14). This would then correspond with the point in the Tribulation where the war on earth is seen as a counterpart of the war in heaven (Revelation 12:7-12; 13:7-10).

Perhaps one reason the Antichrist seeks to "take over" the Ark is because by this time in the Tribulation the Ark may have become a focal point of Israelite pilgrimage (Jeremiah 3:16). The Ark may have also been universally acknowledged as a superior Israelite "weapon" of war (especially if its reappearance coincides with an Israelite military victory; see chapter 16). Maybe the Antichrist will think the Ark can provide him with a strategic advantage that will enable him to attain and uphold his military domination over the world. In this light, the fearful declaration of the nations: "Who is like the beast, and who is able to wage war with him?" (Revelation 13:4) may echo the similar declaration of the nations when the Ark appeared in battle: "Woe to us! Who shall deliver us from the hand of these mighty gods?" (1 Samuel 4:8), or when the Ark destroyed the men of Beth-shemesh: "Who is able to stand before the LORD, this holy God?" (1 Samuel 6:20). Whatever the case, "taking over" the Ark would certainly appeal to the Antichrist's desire for recognition as deity.

These deductions may be valid, but we need more scriptural evidence to support such contentions. This case for the presence of the Ark in the Tribulation Temple and its desecration by Antichrist can perhaps be sustained from the unique terminology of Daniel 9:27.

On the Ark

In the text of Daniel 9:27 we read this: "On the wing of abominations will come one who makes desolate, even until a complete destruction, one that is decreed, is poured out on the one who makes desolate." The word "wing" literally translates the Hebrew term *kanaf* used in Daniel 9:27 and its construction has been such a problem for interpreters that almost every commentator has offered a different explanation. Interpretations that do not attempt to emend the text have ranged from poetic expressions of "rapid flight" (cf. "wings of the dawn," Psalm 139:9) to metaphorical ideas such as "shall rise up" (taking "wing" as figurative imagery of an eagle) or "overspreading" (as in the KJV). Others have taken "wing" literally to refer to the "pinnacle" of the Temple or the altar within the Temple since these had winglike projections and historically saw either idols or idolatrous sacrifices placed upon them.

I have already shown that it is likely that we have a wordplay on a foreign deity in the expression "abominations . . . who makes desolate" (Daniel 9:27). If this is so, then it would be consistent to see "wing" as having a similar association with idolatry. Along this line, several different proposals have been offered. One view is to understand "wing" as equivalent to the Hebrew word translated "horn." Since the Great Altar that received the sacrifices of all Israel at the Temple's entrance had "horns" at its four corners (to secure the sacrificial animals), it is thought that "wings" may have reference to this place. During the time of Antiochus IV Epiphanes (175 B.C.), this altar was desecrated by an unclean offering (1 Maccabees 1–6). It is suggested that the "horns" of this altar had to be demolished in order to install another "abominable" stage on it (cf. Judith 9.8).[22] A variation of this view proposes that "wing" is substituted for "horn" because "winged one" or "lord of wing" was a title of the foreign god *Ba'al Shamen*.[23]

Another view is that winged statues or emblems (like the Roman standards that bore images of the emperor)[24] may have been placed at the site of the altar. In my opinion, this line of evidence has the greater support. However, it is not necessary to limit the desecration to the outer altar on the basis of what the apocryphal references tell us about Antiochus' abomination. Rather, if the Antichrist is to take the progression of desecration a step *forward,* then the greater violation would have to proceed from the outside (area of lesser sanctity) to the inside (area of greater sanctity) of the Temple.

With that in mind, it may be that "wing" refers to the actual place where the abomination of desolation occurs—in this case, on the winged cherubim of the Ark itself.

The Ark Desecrated,
the Antichrist Doomed

In 2 Thessalonians 2:8 Paul predicted that the Antichrist ("that lawless one") will be destroyed at the coming of Christ. As we saw earlier, the term "lawlessness" in verse 3 is likely to be understood as "abomination." While Paul does not make a clear connection between the Antichrist's desecration of the Temple and his subsequent destruction, Daniel helps to make this plain.

The final phrase in Daniel 9:27, "that [which] is decreed, is poured out on the one who makes desolate," refers to the appointed destruction of the desolater.[25] This predicted judgment upon the one who desecrates the holy Temple is consistent with the Old Testament announcement of divine punishment on desecraters for their arrogance and intent to destroy what is holy. Such an end was decreed for the Assyrian invaders (Isaiah 10:23-26) and was repeated in more detail in Daniel 11:36, which describes both the arrogance (verses 36-38) and aggression (verse 39) of the Antichrist.[26] Therefore, the Antichrist's desecration of the Ark—an attempt to supplant God's presence with his own—will result in his complete destruction (Revelation 19:20).

Despite these supports for the appearance of the Ark in the end time, there is one text of Scripture that seems to deny any possibility of the Ark's existence beyond the time of the prophet Jeremiah. In the next chapter we must consider this passage—a text that implies the Ark would be forgotten in the future.

15

The Forgotten Ark

The Ark, which had been the seat of the special manifestation of Jehovah, shall be forgotten, because the whole city shall be filled with His presence.[1]

—Commentator A.W. Streane
on Jeremiah 3:16

In a timeworn joke about the encroachment of old age, one man asks another, "Do you know what the three signs of aging are?"

"No," replies the friend. "What?"

"Well, first your memory goes, and then... I *forget* the other two!"

One reason so few Christians know about the Ark is that somewhere down the course of history, the Ark has been forgotten. I do not mean that it has been forgotten as an ancient Israelite symbol, but that it has been relegated to a place of irrelevance and removed from any future role.

The explanation for this "forgotten Ark" phenomenon is a single Bible verse—Jeremiah 3:16—which has been interpreted almost exclusively as a statement of the Ark's disappearance in the past and its exclusion from the future. Consequently, it is typical in most Ark-related literature to read these kinds of comments about Jeremiah 3:16: "it was promised that Jerusalem would be the throne of the Lord, a fact that would render the Ark superfluous"[2] or, "this [is an] expression of antagonism to the Ark"[3] or, "the Ark will not be restored because it will no longer be necessary as a symbol of God's presence."[4] While some writers do caution that "the passage does not necessarily presuppose the disappearance of the Ark,"[5] they nevertheless join the camp of commentators who reject its future appearance.

Why is this verse viewed as proof that there will be no future restoration of the Ark? In this chapter I want to examine this passage and explain why I believe it *supports,* rather than denies, a future existence for the Ark.

Setting the Context

Jeremiah 3:16-17 has been variously translated based on the interpretation given it. While I will elaborate on the translation of crucial parts of the passage in the comments to follow, let us first begin by looking at the passage as it appears in the King James Version:

> It shall come to pass, when ye be multiplied and increased in the land, in those days, saith the LORD, they shall say no more, The ark of the covenant of the LORD: neither shall it come to mind: neither shall they remember it; neither shall they visit it; neither shall that be done any more. At that time they shall call Jerusalem the throne of the LORD; and all the nations shall be gathered unto it, to the name of the LORD, to Jerusalem: neither shall they walk any more after the imagination of their evil heart.

The opening words of verse 16 and the closing words of

verse 17 seem to indicate that the context of this passage is the millennial kingdom, when the focus is upon a regathered and regenerated national Israel. The author of the pseudepigraphal work the *Life of Jeremiah* (14–19) expected the Ark to stand at the center of the ingathered Jewish people in the last days after a period of persecution (the Tribulation). There it is stated that the tablets of the Law will be revealed at this time of restoration, and that prior to this age a fiery cloud will hover over the Ark, "for the glory of God will never cease from His Law" (14.18). If Jeremiah 3:16 taught that the Ark had no part in the future, the pseudepigraphal author would be contradicting this prophecy. It's unlikely he would have done that, however, because he would have claimed a continuity with Jeremiah's words in order to authenticate his own writings.

The Negative View

In contrast, many commentators have interpreted Jeremiah 3:16-17 in an opposite manner from *Life of Jeremiah*. They say Jeremiah teaches that all reliance upon material symbols, such as the Ark, will be abandoned in the future. Jeremiah, they claim, is holding out the prospect of a new "spiritual" worship superior to the old symbolic worship. Using Jeremiah 3:16 as a proof text, they then criticize any perceived "material" prophetic interpretation, especially one that accepts a restoration of Jewish worship in a future age. This is the usual Reformed interpretation, as articulated by Calvin, although he rejected it here:

> It has been thought by almost all Christians, that the prophet here teaches us, that when Christ should come, an end would be put to all the shadows of the law, so that there would be no more any Ark of the Covenant, as the fullness of the Godhead would dwell in Christ. This is indeed a view which

seems plausible, but the meaning of the prophet, I think, is wholly different.[6]

The typical Reformed interpretation makes Jeremiah's view of the future a negative one—the abandonment of the Ark and the rejection of the entire form of Israelite law that Jeremiah himself had so emphatically upheld (*see* Jeremiah 7:1–10:25). The Jewish commentator Abarbanel recognized this inconsistency and wondered how a promise that uprooted the Torah could possibly have been considered by the Scripture as good. But is the import of Jeremiah 3:16 really negative, or could the *reason* behind Jeremiah's negatives be positive?

The Positive View

One positive view, as espoused by Calvin, is that Jeremiah's purpose is to offer comfort for the future. Consider the context of Jeremiah 3: There was a division between the northern kingdom of Israel and the southern kingdom of Judah (verses 3-11). The spiritual forces that caused and perpetuated this split eventually led to the downfall of both kingdoms (verses 12-14). One of the chief contentions between them was that the north had the vast majority of territory, but the south retained possession of the Temple and the Ark. Thus the words "they will no longer say" (verse 16) may refer to the southern kingdom's one-time boast that they had the Ark. Jeremiah was saying that in the future, when the two kingdoms are once again reunited, there will no longer be such a boast. There will be a harmony between them that eliminates the use of the Ark as a matter of contention. This idea is confirmed by verse 18, which repeats the phrase "in those days" from verse 16 and continues, "Judah will walk with the house of Israel."

Such a reunion is indeed predicted during the millennial restoration (Ezekiel 37:15-22), and Jeremiah does have this in mind in chapter 3 of his book. This explanation, however, does not deal with the decisive question as to why the Ark would lose its significance. How can we explain Jeremiah's fourfold negation of the Ark?

One explanation offered for Jeremiah's seemingly negative statement is that Jeremiah, who lived in the time of King Josiah ben Amon, knew the Ark had been hidden 36 years prior to the Babylonian invasion, and thus inserted this prophetic statement to assure the Jewish people that the Ark would not reappear, nor should Israel bother looking for the Ark, until the last days. This is the viewpoint held by Rabbi Goren:

> Jeremiah gives us a hint of what happened to the Ark in the days of Josiah ben Amon. He [Josiah] became afraid that the Babylonians would take it into captivity. So he was interested in hiding it from the people altogether. . . . And I believe it is still hidden beneath the Temple Mount. Jeremiah said that the Ark would be taken out from our hearts, and that we would not visit it . . . [because] Jerusalem will become the throne of the Lord, which is more than the Holy of Holies. For this reason Jeremiah said that we would not need the Ark.[7]

The implication here is this: On the one hand, Jeremiah sought to discourage a search for the Ark—either by the Babylonians, since it had disappeared, or by the Israelites, since it had been removed by God to an unknown place. On the other hand, Jeremiah told the Jews that they did not need to be concerned for the future of the Ark because God had even bigger and better plans ahead. While this view may correctly interpret Jeremiah's intention, it still does not fully explain many of the particular statements in Jeremiah 3:16-17.

Let's move onward and see if we can discern Jeremiah's purpose behind the negative statements by taking a careful look at his precise wording.

A Powerful Overstatement

Notice that the opening phrase, "They shall say no more," is used repeatedly by Jeremiah to indicate that an earlier phase of divine revelation will progress to a later one (*see* Jeremiah 23:7; 31:29; 31:23). In each of these contexts it is clear that the progression does not invalidate the previous revelation. Jeremiah is preparing the Israelites for a period of transition without the Temple or Ark. He knew that divine judgment upon Israel was inevitable and that both of these focal points of the divine presence would be soon removed. Therefore, he assured the people—soon to be removed from their land to exile—that they, the Temple, and the Ark would one day be restored and that the day would come when their concern over these losses would end.

Jeremiah's statement is an example of a literary device called a *hyperbole,* or overstatement. The ideal future can best be pictured by a comparison to the past. Everything the past is not, the future will be. Disappointments will be reversed and fortunes restored. If the Ark was lost (or hidden), the natural longing was for its return. What Jeremiah says in hyperbolic fashion is that not only will the Ark be restored, but also that this restoration will be so great and extensive that no one will ever long for the Lord's presence again. The presence of the Lord, represented by the Ark, will be in Jerusalem, but it will not be limited to the Temple alone, for in that day His glory will encompass the entire city. Therefore, the Israelis will not say, "The Lord is enthroned above the cherubim," but rather they will say, "All Jerusalem is 'the Throne of the Lord'" (Jeremiah 3:17).

That the Ark is yet present in this enlarged setting may be seen in the expanded translation of Jeremiah 3:17a as found in *Targum Jonathan to the Prophets*: "Jerusalem shall be called the place of the house of the Lord's Shekinah." In contrast to the whole city being conceived of as God's earthly throne, the idea here is that Jerusalem houses the Temple that contains the divine presence, which was located at the Ark. If this was the intended meaning of Jeremiah's original text, it would strengthen, not diminish, the possibility that the Ark will return.

A Helpful Comparison

We can better understand the nature of Jeremiah's purposeful overstatement by comparing it to a similar statement in Isaiah 11:9, which was written in a millennial context: "They [wild beasts and reptiles] will not hurt or destroy in all My holy mountain [Jerusalem], for the earth will be full of the knowledge of the LORD as the waters cover the sea." So great will be the harmony in the created order because of God's presence that normally predatory and poisonous creatures will become tamed and harmless. This does not mean that these creatures will not exist or be present in the holy city, but that their function will be changed in the kingdom.

The same can be said of the Ark. Because the glory of God will fill the entire city (*see* Isaiah 4:5-6), there will be no need to focus on the Ark as the sole place of manifestation. This does not mean that the Ark will not exist or be present in the Temple, but merely that its function will be changed. Two functions that will cease will be that of the Ark as a witness to the Law and as a conduit of the divine power in warfare. This is because the Law will be internalized in that day (Jeremiah 31:33-34; Ezekiel 36:25-27) and the nations will no longer learn war (Isaiah 2:4). This interpretation is put forth in the textual notes of the standard-issue Bible used by the Israeli military:

> The Law of the Lord will be written in the heart,
> and there will be no need to keep it in the Ark.
> There will not be wars and there will be no need to

take the Ark from place to place on the battlefield as
it was in those former times.[8]

Some commentators argue that because Jerusalem is constituted as God's Throne (Jeremiah 3:17), it removes the need for
the Ark. In response, we could argue on these same grounds
that the Temple also would not be needed. In fact, most
commentators who say there will be no Ark also say that there
will be a Temple. Yet as we have seen, the Temple was rebuilt
after the return from exile and it is clear that a Temple will exist
again during the millennium when Israel's present exile is
ended (Ezekiel 40–48). In addition, as we have noted in chapter 13 of this book, it is stated by the prophets that God will
increase the glory of His glorious house (Isaiah 60:7c; Haggai
2:9). Therefore, it must be asked: If the Temple, which was
built to house the Ark, will be restored, then why not also the
Ark? If the Temple will receive greater glory, then why would
the Ark, which *brought* that glory to the First Temple, be
absent from the final Temple?

Another objection often raised is that Jeremiah 3:16 says,
"Nor shall it [the Ark] be made again." This seems to imply
that Jeremiah thought the Ark had been destroyed, and since
neither the divinely inscribed tablets nor the graven cherubim
can be remade, that rules out the Ark's existence in the future.
However, the translation "be made again" may not be a proper
rendering of the Hebrew word *'asah* in this context. This verb
generally means "to make" or "to do," but it also has secondary meanings. One of these meanings is "to use." It is perhaps
significant that one of the two instances in which the verb
appears with this nuance is in a text concerning the materials
"used" in the construction of the Ark (Exodus 38:24; cf. 1
Samuel 8:16).[9] Therefore, it is possible to translate this last
phrase in Jeremiah 3:16: "neither shall they *use* it again," in
which case the meaning is that the Ark would not be used as
before (for example, in warfare).

The Ark in the Tribulation

Jeremiah prophesied in Judah for 40 years. He began in the thirteenth year of King Josiah and continued until the time of the Judean exile. During that timespan he witnessed the reforms of Josiah and saw the repairs to the Temple and the Ark's return to the Holy of Holies. When Josiah was killed, Jeremiah realized that these reforms could not be maintained and that the final judgment of Judah by the nations was near. The Ark would most likely have been returned to its secret chamber at this time, and Jeremiah may have had a part in hiding it. The extrabiblical legends associated with his hiding the Ark trace their origin to this act, although the writers had no accurate knowledge of the location, which accounts for the various traditions. Since Jeremiah 3:16 is dated to Jeremiah's later oracles, the very time in which the Ark was supposedly hidden, it may bear an indirect testimony to this event.

What is significant is how Jeremiah describes the activity during the time just prior to "those days" (verses 16-17). "Those days" refer to the millennium, during which the Ark would not hold the same all-important place as in times past; its distinction as the glory-bearer would be shared with Jerusalem as a sanctuary-city. Jeremiah's words are that "they shall say no more . . . it shall not come to mind . . . nor shall they remember [the Ark]," implying that before this age of change the Israelites were actively doing all of these things. The period that precedes the millennium is the Tribulation; therefore the implication is that during the Tribulation the Ark will reappear and be the focal point of all Israel (and perhaps all the world).

The words Jeremiah uses in verse 16 describe the nature of this focus. The King James Version rightly translates the Hebrew text of one of the four negative phrases as "neither shall they visit it." This may mean that during the time of the Tribulation, the Ark's reappearance will lead to a worldwide

Jewish visitation to Jerusalem. Perhaps this will be in connection with the rebuilding of the Temple and the announcement that the messianic age of redemption has begun.

Another phrase in this verse, which the King James Version translates as "neither shall it come to mind," is better translated "neither shall it be taken to heart." This idiom means that the Jewish people should not worry about the Ark in the future as they have in the past. While this may include the 2,500 years of concern over the Ark's location, I believe Jeremiah is most likely talking about the concern that results from the Antichrist's desecration of the Ark when he seats himself in the Holy of Holies.

In summary, Jeremiah 3:16 does not teach that the Ark will not be restored in the future. Rather, it revises its future use among a spiritually restored people in a harmonious order under the rule of Messiah. The Ark will therefore no longer be needed in military action and the holiness of Jerusalem itself will characterize the city as an extended Holy of Holies. Rather than being a passage confirming the loss of the Ark, it is a passage that comforts the Jewish nation and promises the restoration of the Ark in the larger setting of Israel's future age of holiness and harmony.

"Forgotten," Yet Unforgettable

The Ark has not been forgotten by Judaism. For all its long history since the destruction and dispersion of A.D. 70, the nation of Israel has preserved the memory of the Ark. At the front of every synagogue an "ark," in the form of a decorative cabinet, takes center stage, holding the Torah scrolls used in the service. In this light, professor H.G. May therefore concludes:

> We may ask whether the Jews really ceased to have any sacred ark of their own after the fall of Jerusalem.... It would be surprising if these arks

did not preserve something of the form as well as of the function. . . . The ark in use in the early syna- gogues reflected a practice in the second temple which was, in turn, derived from the first temple.[10]

Such Torah-arks are always elaborately ornamented on the outside and hidden from public view by a heavy curtain bear- ing a rendition of the cherubim as two guardian lions. In some synagogues a lamp called the *ner tamid* ("eternal light") hangs before the Torah-ark, which symbolizes the Shekinah, the eternal presence of God. Since the Torah scrolls are the most expensive and important components of the synagogue, the Torah-ark remains the most prized possession of the Jewish community. It is the one object throughout centuries of po- groms and holocausts that they have labored and sacrificed to save. As such, it has borne a perpetual witness to the Jew of the "forgotten" but unforgettable Ark.

Even with this preservation of the Ark's centrality in Juda- ism, the Torah-ark could not replace the Ark any more than the synagogue could replace the Temple. The synagogue has no priesthood and no sacrifices. It is simply a meeting place for the people—a meeting place that originally began within the Temple precincts.[11] Therefore, just as the Jewish people expect a rebuilt Temple, so also can they anticipate a recovered Ark. It is this expectation of a future return that prompts us to draw closer to the Ark and look beyond the symbol to the substance that every eye shall one day behold.

16

The Ark Effect

Of all the treasures yet to be discovered, what could be more important, more fascinating, and more awe-inspiring than the Tablets of the Ten Commandments. No other archaeological find would have a greater impact on the destiny of man.[1]

—Rabbi Leibel Reznick, author,
The Holy Temple Revisited

The power of suggestion is great, and the suggestion that the Ark rests below the Temple Mount has been sufficient to restrict generations of observant Jews for nearly two millennia from the site of this Temple. The orthodox Jews have always restricted their entrance to this most holy site in Judaism because they do not know precisely where the Holy of Holies was located. They fear their own ritually impure status (a result attributed to their exile among the nations) will desecrate the site. Even though the Temple site is presently dominated by a pagan shrine (the Dome of the Rock) and daily trampled by foreigners (Arabs and Gentile tourists), it continues to be regarded as holy because of the supposed presence of the Ark hidden beneath.

Even today, rabbis who claim to possess a more exact knowledge of the precise location of the Holy of Holies still limit their access to the boundary area imposed around the raised platform. If the *tradition* of the Ark has been enough to govern the attitudes and actions of countless Jews, perhaps the *informed belief* that the Ark is actually present might bolster already zealous convictions and intentions of establishing a new religious rule in Israel.

That brings us to ask the ultimate question: What if the Ark were at last discovered? Undoubtedly such a find would have a profound impact on our world. There are at least four major consequences that could result. We might call these results "The Ark Effect."

Effect One: Instigate the Rebuilding of the Temple

Since the Ark is not simply a historic relic but a holy treasure, its presence would require the rebuilding of the Temple. As we have seen, the Tabernacle, and later the Temple, were designed for the very purpose of housing the Ark (Exodus 25:8; 2 Samuel 6:17; 7:2).

This result of the Ark's discovery is well understood by those in the Temple movement. As Gershon Salomon, leader of the Temple Mount Faithful, has observed:

> The Ark of the Covenant cannot be put in a museum, nor in a synagogue, but in only one place—the Temple. We know that the generation of the First Temple hid the Ark of the Covenant for the time of the Third Temple, the last and eternal Temple.[2]

If this view is correct, then the time of the Ark's appearance may set in motion those events that will lead to the rebuilding of the Temple. Gershon Salomon's sentiments are shared by most religious Jews, as the statement in *Bereshit Rabbah* 13:2

reveals: "All of Israel's prayers are only about the Temple." Disagreement exists, however, over how and when the Temple can be rebuilt. While traditionalist rabbis continue to believe that "the future Temple is in the hands of heaven" (Gemara, *Rosh HaShanah* 30a), the new generation of religious Jewish activists follow the alternate view that "the future Temple will certainly be built by man" (*Aruch l'Ner, Sukkah* 41a). A third position harmonizes these views and says that the spiritual Temple in heaven will descend and become fused with the rebuilt Temple on earth, just like a soul within a body (*see Midrash Tanhuma*).

However, the present movement to rebuild the Temple is motivated by the belief that if Jews will act upon the divine command to rebuild the Temple, heaven will respond and bring it to pass. The reemergence of the Ark would certainly serve as the catalyst that moves these activists to realize their goal of rebuilding the Temple.

In order to appreciate how the Ark could propel Temple activists toward their objective, let us consider one of the most prominent groups operating today in Israel.

The Current Activity

The Temple Mount and Land of Israel Faithful (TMF) has conducted activist operations in Israel since the temporary capture of the Temple Mount in 1967. The goal of this group is to accept the responsibility for fulfilling the biblical commandments to "possess the Land" (Joshua 1:6) and "to build My [God's] Temple" (Exodus 25:8). They believe that Israel will never be secure nor successful until this is accomplished.

While their activities presently center on demonstrations, they hope to establish a permanent physical presence near the Temple Mount. The purpose of this "presence" is to serve as a statement of Israel's right to the Temple Mount and to lay the Third Temple cornerstone, which they have already prepared.

My acquaintance with this organization began in October 1989 when I attended the group's first attempt to lay their cornerstone for the Third Temple on the Temple Mount. The details concerning this venture and the group in general have been covered in my earlier book *Ready to Rebuild* (Eugene, OR: Harvest House Publishers, 1992, pages 120-130). Since my initial encounters with the TMF I have had numerous occasions to visit with their leader, Gershon Salomon, and other key people in the group. Salomon is firmly convinced that as soon as the present government is ousted, the Arab presence removed, and access to the Temple Mount obtained, the Ark will be brought out and the Third Temple begun. Because he took part in the secret excavation to retrieve the Ark and other Temple vessels from beneath the Temple Mount, he is perhaps more strongly motivated by the prospect of its eventual discovery.

In January of 1994 I visited Salomon's newly opened TMF office in Jerusalem. Among the flags of Israel and the TMF was a banner with an embroidered picture of the Ark in the center (*see photo section*). Salomon sees the Arab presence on the Temple Mount as one of the reasons why the Ark has not yet been brought out. Just as the Ark has had to remain in hiding for 2,500 years because of foreign occupiers of the Temple Mount, so today is the Ark left unrecovered because of an outsider's presence:

> Only the Arab enemy is trying to make the last battle to stop the redemption of Israel, to stop the rebuilding of the Third Temple, to stop the wonderful day when the priests will take out from under the ground of the Temple the Ark of the Covenant, the Golden Altar from the wilderness, the seven-branched Menorah, and other vessels and put them in the right place in the Third Temple. . . . and our generation shall be the one to see these beautiful holy vessels.[3]

Yet, despite the entrenched Arab presence and the Labor government's efforts to thwart his cause, Salomon does not necessarily see the current situation on the Temple Mount as an obstacle. He believes that the compromising actions of the government and the expected treachery of the PLO will eventually so anger the pure hearts of Jews that they will instigate a national movement to restore the proper biblical order. He also believes it is certain that Israel will have to fight a war with the Arabs to regain their biblical borders and liberate the Temple Mount.

To this end the TMF continues to demonstrate several times a year (most notably, on Tisha B'Av, the Day of Atonement, the Feast of Tabernacles, and Passover). Depending on the occasion, the group will carry the four-and-a-half-ton cornerstone on a flatbed truck around the walls of the Old City, perform the ancient water-drawing ceremony at the Pool of Shiloah (which is connected with restoration of the Temple), and consecrate the cornerstone. They also dress in sackcloth and pray openly on the Temple Mount (usually at its gates) for the rebuilding of the Temple. On the day that the Declaration of Principles was signed, which the TMF calls "the false covenant," members of the group donned sackcloth, tore their shirts, and displayed other signs of mourning. On that occasion, Salomon said that "this false covenant between the Prime Minister of Israel and the evil one . . . cannot and will not exist . . . it is a revolt against God and the Land."[4]

Salomon had reasonably good relations with the former Likud government. Under that administration, Prime Minister Shamir had assured Salomon, "I am sure that many of your demands will be fulfilled in coming years."[5] Salomon also had received a letter from the former Speaker of the Knesset, Dov Shilansky, affirming that he followed the TMF's activities with "sympathy, affection, love and blessing."[6] But the relations changed radically under the new Labor government, with the

TMF being branded as extremists and Salomon forbidden entrance to the Temple Mount at any time.

A Look to the Future

Salomon has told me that most of the TMF's future plans must remain secret because in the past, early disclosure resulted in protests (such as the Temple Mount incident in 1990, during which 17 Palestinian Arabs were killed) and government restriction of demonstrations. Another reason that Salomon does not detail his activities is because his name is at the top of the radical Muslims' "hit list." However, Salomon did tell me of TMF's intentions to offer a *korban Pesach* ("Passover offering") on the Temple Mount at a future Passover celebration. This means offering a lamb as a blood sacrifice, and such an action would no doubt cause great controversy among both Arabs and Jews.[7] The act would have great significance because this kind of offering historically ceased with the destruction of the Second Temple in A.D. 70 (while other Passover rites were continued as before). With the first *korban Pesach* offered in 2,000 years on the Temple Mount, the TMF would be reminding the Jewish people of the absence of this ceremony—the heart of the Passover celebration—and in effect be announcing the imminent rebuilding of the Temple, which is required for the return of the sacrificial system.

Based on Theodore Herzl's Zionist model of seeking to fulfill God's will rather than waiting for Messiah to do everything, the TMF says that their human actions will influence God to respond.[8] If there is to be a restoration of the Passover in all its fullness from heaven, then perhaps this restoration can be hastened by taking the initiative on earth. If the TMF can act, they will act, and they expect the Ark to play a central role in what is to come. The imperative for the TMF is real, for they believe that the present desecration of the Temple Mount is the one obstacle that restrains the blessing of God and the advent of the messianic era.

Effect Two: Establish Religious Claim
over the Temple Mount

Defining the Controversy

Since the return of the Temple Mount to Islamic jurisdiction in 1967, Muslim revisionist historians have contended that the Jews maintained no presence on the Temple Mount before the coming of Islam in A.D. 637. The contemporary Islamic scholar Aref el Aref has stated that the only texts needed for a historical study of the structures on the Temple Mount are the buildings and Muslim inscriptions that adorn and explain them. For the Muslim, the history of the Temple Mount began with Mohammed's supposed vision of a night journey to Jerusalem. All the archaeological excavations of the last quarter century, even those adjacent to this very spot, have been considered irrelevant to the faithful of Islam. This viewpoint is exemplified by Bassam Abu-Lebdah, a spokesman for the administration of the Wakf and Islamic Affairs:

> The Al Aqsa mosque and the Dome of the Rock, together named the *Haram al-Sharif*, is the third most important place for the Muslim people. This area belonged to the Arabs 5,000 years ago and to Islam 1,400 years ago, and no Temple ever was there before in that area.[9]

As this statement reveals, to the faithful Muslim the Temple never existed. The Jewish people, who did not possess Jerusalem until modern times, are simply invaders on the historic Arab-Palestinian homeland. Refuting this claim, Rabbi Goren asserts that not only before the Muslim period, but also for centuries afterward, the Temple Mount was a place of Jewish presence:

> This [the Dome of the Rock and Al Aqsa mosque] was the Temple of King Solomon—who denies it?

> They [the Arabs] cannot deny it! The [Arab] Caliph
> Omar built the Dome of the Rock and the Al Aqsa
> mosque. He built the mosque on the southern side in
> the direction of Mecca for the Arabs. He did not
> build the Dome of the Rock for the Arabs—to them
> it was not holy. He built it to serve as a synagogue
> for the Jews. He was very friendly with the Jews
> because they had mobilized armies and participated
> with him in his battles. So he built the Dome of the
> Rock as a Jewish synagogue [which lasted] for 300
> years. He thought that it would become their Third
> Temple.[10]

According to other experts, the Dome of the Rock may have
been built as a "memorial" to the Jewish Temple, but it is
thought this favor toward the Jewish people lasted for only 20
years or so. It is also thought that a synagogue or a church
might have previously stood on the site, but no evidence of this
exists, although from time to time (when it was possible), a
Jewish synagogue was established at the northern corner of the
Temple Mount. Whatever Rabbi Goren's source, he, like the
Wakf official, believes firmly that history is on his side of the
Temple Mount controversy. Biblically and historically, the
facts unquestionably favor the Jewish claims—claims that
would become even more forceful if indeed the holy Ark is
found to occupy this sacred site.

Imagine what it would mean for Israel to possess the original 3,500-year-old title deed to the land of Israel (known as
the Abrahamic Covenant, recorded in the Torah that is thought
to be in the Ark), which includes 200,000 square miles of
Muslim-occupied territory from the wadi el-Arish in Egypt to
the Euphrates River near the Persian Gulf (Genesis 15:18-21)!
How would Muslims react, considering that Abraham is likewise their esteemed patriarch? Think what it would mean to
have, in Moses' own handwriting, the uncontestable word
from God that declared the Temple Mount was His choice for

the Jewish Temple (Exodus 15:17; cf. 2 Samuel 7:10, 13)! How would Muslims respond, since Moses is also one of their major prophets?

If the Jews could prove their claim that the Ark has existed beneath the Temple Mount for the past 3,000 years, it would confirm Israel's irrefutable historic right to sovereign jurisdiction of the site. Thus there is a great religious controversy over the site—a controversy that ultimately determines who has the right to control the land of Israel. This dispute can be observed in an exchange I had with Bassam Abu-Lebdah, a representative of the Muslim Wakf, and Gershon Salomon.

Bassam Abu-Lebdah, focusing on what he considers Israeli occupation of Palestinian lands, expressed his concern about Gershon Salomon's group and their attempt to return the Temple Mount to Jewish sovereignty:

> To the Gershon Salomon group I say: There was no Temple here, so stop fighting and stop preparing to break [sic—destroy] the mosque, because this area is first of all for the God [Allah] and after that it is . . . the place for Islam. . . . Jerusalem and the mosque are part of the Palestinian's land.[11]

Gershon Salomon responded by recounting the historical evidence that the Arabs are the real occupiers and that their attempt to prevent the rebuilding of the Jewish Temple is in fact opposition to God:

> This holy place became holy because of the decision of God and the linkage between God and the people of Israel. On this place started the history of the Jewish people 4,000 years ago, and without this biblical history there would be no Temple Mount. When the Moslems came to this place it was empty except for the remains of the destruction of the Second Jewish Temple. It was an unknown place to

Muslims before the seventh century [A.D.]. God decided when He started with Abraham, the first father of the Jewish people, that this place and all of this Land would be given to the Jewish people forever. This is an eternal decision, and we are back [in the Land] because it is the will of God. Jews are coming from the four corners of the world, exactly as all the prophets promised. . . . it is part of the process of redemption. And the climax of this redemption will be the rebuilding of the Third Temple, which you will see . . . on the Temple Mount. We will never build the Temple of God on another place—only on the rock which is today unfortunately under the Dome of the Rock. My goal, and the goal of our movement, is to make Jerusalem the Israeli capital and the city of God, and to rebuild the Temple on the rock.[12]

Exposing Muslim Myths

Salomon's words are ignored by Palestinians who were educated according to Arab revisionist history. Typical of this thinking is Palestinian writer Nasser Eddin Nashashibi, who has declared:

> For us, Jerusalem is Al Quds—the Holy. As a Moslem, I must believe what God told me in the Koran—that he had blessed Al Aqsa and the land around it, that we are commanded to care for this, and that we must not let it fall under foreign control. This we believe, and this we must obey.[13]

In fact, however, when the Muslims captured Jerusalem after Mohammed's death (A.D. 637), they did not call it Al Quds, but Ilya. Jerusalem is never mentioned in the Koran, and while the term Al Aqsa is used, it simply means "the endmost" or "farthest" and has nothing to do with Jerusalem. Originally, it probably referred to a remote place in Mecca, or at the extreme, Medina. In addition, while Palestinians will assert that the Al Aqsa mosque at the southern end of the Temple Mount is the third holiest site in Islam, other Muslim nations, such as Iran, Iraq, Turkey, and Syria, also claim to have "Islam's third-holiest shrine" on their soil. History further reveals that Jerusalem was never the focus of Arab national aspirations, nor was it ever a Muslim capital or cultural center. This was not even the case when all the West Bank was ruled by the Jordanians prior to 1967.

The reason the Dome of the Rock was placed on the Temple Mount was because Muslims were following the accepted practice of appropriating whatever lands they conquered. Early geographical and archaeological studies in the Holy Land reveal that the Arabs, in appropriating Jewish lands, simply Arabicized the Hebrew names of the cities they occupied.[14] The only place ever known to be built by the Muslims is the coastal plain city of Ramle. Because the Temple Mount had been the site of the Jews' holy sanctuary, the Arab (Ommayad) Caliph Abdul Malik ibn Marwan erected a wooden shrine over the rock (Arabic *es-Shakra*, "the Rock") some 50-60 years after the Arab conquest of Jerusalem, appropriating the place for Arab use. Since at that time no Muslim legend had been yet associated with the Rock, this shrine commemorated Solomon's Temple.

Even though the Jews had been driven out of their land by various conquerors, history attests that there has never been a time when there was not a Jewish remnant resident in Israel— especially in Jerusalem. Despite persecution and great deprivation, these Jews felt it was their sacred mission to preserve a Jewish presence in their land. Their challenge was made doubly difficult because the Islamic invasion of the seventh century was coupled with anti-Jewish sentiment. A fact largely forgotten nowadays, but clearly understood at the beginning of the modern Arab-Israeli conflict, was that the dominant Arab culture sought to completely eradicate every vestige of Jewish presence in what was then called Palestine. Only five years after the formation of the Jewish state, Carl Voss, then chairman of the executive council of the American Christian Palestine Committee, could write:

> The Palestine problem was and is a conflict of rights as well as a complex of wrongs. The establishment of Israel was and is a creative answer to the world problem of anti-Semitism—an answer which might not be absolutely just to Arab rights in Palestine, but which seemed just in view of the granting of sovereignty to so many Arab states throughout the Middle East.[15]

Facts such as these are unknown to the average Muslim and, unfortunately, to most Christians throughout the world. Secular media propaganda based on Arab revisionist history has caused Christians to assume that the Palestinian state is a historical entity. On the contrary, there has never existed such a thing. From the earliest days of "Palestine," both Jews and Arabs were called Palestinians.[16] For example, the *Jerusalem Post* used to be the *Palestine Post*. Only since 1948 when the State of Israel was created have Jews called themselves Israelis and left the resident Arab population to retain the name Palestinians.

If the Ark were discovered, it would force Arab historians to abandon their revisionist history, which could cause a massive religious and cultural reaction in the Muslim world. Islam has remained unchanged since the seventh century, and Muslims will do everything in their power to preserve their tradition. As in the past, and so in the future, whatever threatens the stability of Islam must be eliminated. (It was this mindset that ruled the actions of Iran's Ayatollah Khomeini.) Therefore, a Jewish claim to have the Ark might be sufficient provocation for an already frustrated Arab League to commence the *Jihad* ("holy war") upon Israel.

Effect Three: Usher in the Messianic Age for Israel

Jewish tradition has always held that the Ark would be discovered at the coming of the Messiah. Just as the Ark was historically considered a channel of divine blessing (2 Samuel 6:12), so also could the appearance of the Ark signal to world Jewry the beginning of the messianic era (a time of worldwide blessing emanating from Jerusalem). It could also kindle a national spiritual revival and a massive *aliyah* ("immigration") of Jews to the land of Israel. If thousands of Jews suddenly returned to Israel, additional land would be necessary for homes. This would necessitate a large-scale transfer of the resident Arab population and even the appropriation of Arab-occupied lands *outside* Israel—lands which were part of the boundaries in the Abrahamic Covenant. The Jewish nation may seek to justify their seizure of these lands based on the original land grant made to Abraham. Indeed, Rabbi Yisrael Ariel, founder of the Temple Institute, has already published a commentary on the biblical dimensions of the Promised Land in preparation for this moment.[17]

If the revival spurred by the recovery of the Ark takes place *before* the Islamic situation is resolved, then the sense of peace and security provided by the Ark's presence may prove to be false. Israel may become overconfident and think that it is safe to enter into a more permanent "peace" with its hostile neighbors. In fact, Ezekiel 38:11, 14 mentions the false security of the Israelites before the future invasion of Gog and Magog—a security that may result from the Ark's presence. Such a regathering of Jews is surprisingly welcomed by radical Muslims in light of their agenda, which may be seen in a speech by Hamas leader Sheikh Fathy Moussa, delivered at the Rahman mosque in Khan Yunis (Gaza Strip) on September 17, 1993:

The Koran says that before the Muslims can triumph, all Jews must be gathered in Palestine. This so-called "peace" will encourage many of them to come here now. And when they do, Muslims around the world will finally assemble and crush the Israeli state.

Effect Four: Provoke a War in the Middle East

The conflict in the Middle East stems from the imperialistic claims of Islam, which divides the world into two groups called *Dar Al Islam* ("the world of Islam," that is, the faithful) and *Dar Al Harb* ("the world of the sword," that is, the warriors until the judgment). There can be no compromise between these positions. Either a person belongs to Islam or he must perish. To Arabs, the problem with the State of Israel is not simply that it "occupies" Muslim land but *that it exists at all!* In 1994 the *Near East Report* quoted Libyan leader Muammar Qaddafi as saying, "The Western countries agreed among themselves to liquidate the Muslims of Bosnia, since they believe Bosnia must be Christian. We, on our side, must act this way in regard to Israel, which is a foreign stronghold within the Arab nation."[18]

Such statements reveal the intention of Islam to remove any "foreign" presence from its midst. Islam is primarily a religion of the sword and believes it is destined to fight a great end-time battle against all nations. Because of this belief, it is threatened by any power that appears to have superior might. Since there are legendary military powers associated with the Ark, the Muslim nations might fear that the delicate balance of power, already strained by the threat of Israel's nuclear arsenals, will have been compromised. In addition, the goal of the new world order is global unity among all nations. Israel's possession of the Ark might be considered a "tactical advantage" that threatens such unity and could provoke an international move against the country.

Additional Effects That Could Provoke Change

A Discovery of Temple Treasures

Some people have suggested that the recovery of the Ark or any of the Temple treasures, including the large amounts of buried gold and silver as indicated by the Copper Scroll, might provoke the Russian-Arab invasion of Israel predicted in Ezekiel 38–39. Dr. Gary Collett, who believes that his planned excavation at Qumran may unearth a portion of this wealth, offers a variation on this theory. He proposes that these riches could in turn finance the newly revived Med-Dead Project.

The Med-Dead Project's goal is to replace the rapidly receding waters of the Dead Sea with water from the Mediterranean Sea. Along the channel between the two seas would be hydroelectric power plants that could produce immense megawatts of electrical power as an alternative energy source.[19] Another goal of the project is to recover the great mineral and precious-metals resources that have accumulated undisturbed in the Dead Sea since its creation. The value of these resources is incalculable and would result in such phenomenal material prosperity for Israel that it would become the envy of the world. The expected recovery of valuable natural resources might be the enticement or "hooks" (Ezekiel 38:4) that lead to the end-time invasion.

Though it is impossible to predict what might happen, the Bible does tell us that changes will take place in the Dead Sea region during the last days (Ezekiel 47:8-12; Zechariah 14:8). Some people have also suggested that Isaiah 60:5 could apply: "You will see and be radiant, and your heart will thrill and rejoice; because the abundance of the sea will be turned to you, the wealth of the nations will come to you." This text, however, simply uses "sea" as a poetic parallel to "nations" and refers to the millennial promise that all the Gentile nations will bring their tribute to the future Temple (*see* Haggai 2:7; Zechariah 14:14).

A New Call to Action

While the TMF has provoked a significant reaction from both the Arabs and the Israeli government, some people in Israel believe that this organization has had its day and that new, more revolutionary action is needed. With the beginning of the New Jewish Year (Rosh Hashana 5754/September 1993) a new institution, the first of its kind in 2,000 years, began functioning on the Temple Mount with more than 20 active students. This new institution is the Temple Mount Yeshiva (*Yeshivat Har HaBayit*), organized in March of 1993 by Kach activist Baruch Ben Yosef. They are dedicated to studying the Talmud daily on the site of the Temple[20]—an action that is in direct opposition to the dictates of the Wakf. The Temple Mount Yeshiva students, who are also Kach activists, seek to agitate the Arabs and at the same time exercise their right as Jews to ascend to the Temple Mount. In a position paper distributed from their headquarters next to the Temple Institute, they state their purpose for organizing:

> The Yeshiva of the Temple Mount has been established as a prerequisite to the full liberation of Judaism's most holy cite [*sic*]. We, the founders of Yeshivat Har HaBayit, understand that the government of Israel has little, if any, concern regarding the future of what must become the center of Jewish thought and activity. We are also aware of the current overwhelming and tragic anxiety felt by most

Israelis over the willingness of the government to relinquish control of the liberated lands of 1967. Therefore, we have taken the burden upon ourselves to maintain and build upon the gifts given to our generation. That is to say, the Yeshiva of the Temple Mount intends to be the catalyst of change. We decided several months ago that the status quo on the Temple Mount cannot continue. The answer, we believed, was to put into operation the Yeshiva of the Temple Mount. We are training a generation of Jews that will know the laws of the Temple and prepare for its rebuilding. Our Yeshiva will not allow this pivotal issue to leave the agenda of the Jewish people. In spite of the harsh conditions imposed by the government and the Moslem Religious Council, we continue to work for the liberation of the Temple Mount, for we know that the disgrace of our Holy Mount is the source of our problems.[21]

The directors of the yeshiva do not agree with the widely held orthodox Jewish belief (currently represented by Sephardi Chief Rabbi Mordechai Eliahu) that the Third Temple will descend from heaven in fire. They would agree with Rabbi Yisrael Ariel of the Temple Institute, who has stated that this orthodox view comes from the Jewish apocryphal writings and the New Testament (*see* Revelation 21:2, 10) rather than from traditionally accepted Jewish texts.[22] Following the ancient Jewish legal expert Maimonides, the Temple Mount Yeshiva calls for the people of Israel to obey the biblical and rabbinic obligation to rebuild the Temple themselves. In fact, they believe that the divine punishment of *kareit* ("cutting off" [of the soul]) will result from the failure to rebuild the Temple and offer the Passover sacrifice. Thus they conclude their position paper with an imperative:

> There is but one way to redeem the Temple Mount and but one way to renew the sacrifices and build the Temple. "Action!" Just as we witnessed the destruction of six million Jews because of the inaction concerning the return to Zion, so will we endure terrible tragedy should we opt for the same inaction concerning the Temple Mount. . . . The fate and destiny of the Jewish people and their redemption are in the hands of each and every Jew. All that is required is the will and faith of Jews to enter the Temple Mount until we have the numbers to demand its return to its rightful owners. If everyone would make the commitment needed to redeem the Mount it will surely be speedily in our hands.[23]

In January of 1994 I spent some time with members of the Temple Mount Yeshiva and followed them during their daily circuits on the Temple Mount. During this walk they publicly point out archaeological remains and locations and relate them specifically to the Temple. This, of course, infuriates the Wakf. But it is an effective means of demonstrating their freedom as Jews to worship on the Mount, since their study is considered an act of worship.

The Israeli government opposes these "insensitive" actions toward the Arabs, but the activists insist that the present government's suppression of Jewish rights demonstrates the true lack of sensitivity. This ideology is evident in the following statement made by the yeshiva's American-born founder and leader, Rabbi Baruch Ben-Yosef:

> It is our purpose to clarify to the world that the State of Israel is not the Jewish state; [it] does not represent the Jewish people. It is one of the most anti-Semitic states that ever came into existence. And that is the reason why for 26 years the Temple Mount has been left in the hands of the enemy.

... The secular state has lost its legitimacy and its right to represent the Jewish people for denying us our natural rights to pray there, to serve God on the Temple Mount, and, of course, to rebuild the Temple. . . . The Arabs have no rights to the Temple Mount and one day they will find themselves out with their mosques off the Temple Mount in Mecca or somewhere else.[24]

The Temple Mount Yeshiva and other organizations like it are gaining ground each year. They represent a new generation of Israelis who are more religious and radically determined to see Israel return to its biblical heritage and purpose. Their zeal may well be one of the factors that not only invites the coming conflict with the Arabs but also motivates Israel to make a covenant with the European leader [the Antichrist] for the rebuilding of the Temple. And the recent government ban on such organizations and new restrictions on worship at the Western Wall have served to increase this zeal rather than lessen it.

The Most Important Effect

Much more could be said about what would happen if the Ark were recovered, yet these speculations may prove to be inaccurate when the actual biblical scenario comes to fruition. What we can know with certainty is that every event that takes place in the Middle East brings us one step closer to the prophetic fulfillment of future days. In view of the swift changes that have taken place in international affairs (the fall of the Iron Curtain, the collapse of communist rule in the former Soviet Union, the Persian Gulf War, and the Middle East peace process), such fulfillment may be realized sooner than many of us expect.

We would do well, then, to personally return to a careful scrutiny of the prophetic scriptures. In this way alone—

amongst all the competing and speculative theories about the lost Ark—will we find spiritual assurance in a confident relationship with the one whose presence once dwelt above the Ark.

17

The Middle East Conflict

Probably unwittingly, Rabin and his so-called government are speeding the arrival of Messiah. The Talmudic Sages give a list of experiences the Jewish people are to undergo before Messiah comes. One of them is a government that is no government.[1]

—Moshe Kohn

The conflict in the Middle East is set to explode. Yet even with all the warning signs that are present, some people blissfully continue to believe that peace may at last have come to this troubled region. But the facts of history and the nature of the conflict suggest otherwise. We need only to connect biblical prophecy with current events to see that the last days are drawing near. With that in mind, let's focus on what is happening in the Middle East and consider where we are along the prophetic time line.

Giving Up the Land

According to the self-rule pact signed between Israel and the PLO, Israel had to give up two areas of land in exchange for Palestinian recognition and an end to the Arab uprising. These two areas were Jericho and the Gaza Strip, both considered by the present government as no real loss to the Jewish nation. Prime Minister Yitzhak Rabin (a secular Jew) said he did not think religious Jews would be concerned about Jericho because the Bible stated that Joshua put a curse on it and that Jews could never live there.

The passage the prime minister had in mind was Joshua 6:26. But the curse related to *rebuilding* Jericho as a fortified city, not to *inhabiting* it (*see* the reference to "foundations" and "gates" in 1 Kings 16:34). Rabin also failed to remember that Jericho was included in the original land grant to Abraham (Genesis 15:18-21). God had stipulated that He was committing this territory to Israel's permanent care (Deuteronomy 11:21). As Rabbi Shlomo Riskin has pointed out, "The lands of 10 nations constitute Greater Israel, encompassing boundaries which will be realized only during the messianic period. But even if these areas do not yet fall under Israeli jurisdiction, they possess a potential for future sanctification."[2]

Not only do Jericho and the Gaza Strip fit within the promised boundaries, but they were also under Israeli jurisdiction. This gave them a present sanctity as well as that to be fulfilled in the future. Furthermore, the Jewish sages had said, "Jericho is the key to *HaEretz Yisrael* [The Land of Israel]. If Jericho is conquered, then immediately after, the country is conquered." It was the gateway to the Land—the first city the Israelites had to possess to inherit God's promise. As one religious leader put it to me, "The Ark conquered Jericho, but now Jericho will conquer the Ark!" By this he means that the control of Jericho will lead to the control of Jerusalem, and with it the Temple Mount . . . where the Ark is hidden.

The prospect of losing Jericho is most disconcerting to Israelis who know their history. When the PLO was established in the 1950s, the Gaza Strip Jericho, and even the West Bank belonged to the Arabs. The PLO's charter, based on the Arab League Charter of 1948, did not call for "liberating" these areas but rather the whole of Palestine, which by definition is everything west of the Jordan River. Many Israelis therefore contend that it is not a *piece* of Israel that Rabin has given up, but the *peace* of Israel. Former president George Bush, on July 30, 1986, commented on the concerns over concessions Israel had made to the Arabs: "Radical forces don't respect weakness. They prey on it. History certainly teaches us that much." Many Jews view the concessions of land, returned Palestinian prisoners, and other "guarantees" as the selling out of Israel and the sending of a signal to its Arab enemies that the country is ripe for conquest.

The PLO's intentions were revealed when it requested 140 square miles of land "around Jericho" in addition to the town itself.[3] They also called for a total transfer of all archaeological sites and findings excavated by Israel in the West Bank and Gaza since 1967. This includes the Dead Sea region and Jerusalem.[4] While the Israeli government has not yet agreed to this demand, it did agree to a lesser amount of territory around Jericho (some 21 miles), which deal still includes the region where the Dead Sea Scroll caves are located. As we have seen, this is also where some Temple treasure hunters believe the Ark, the Tabernacle, or at least the ashes of the red heifer are located. If the Copper Scroll is correct, then Israel has given up not only undiscovered biblical and historical documents, but perhaps also Temple treasures necessary for the future Temple. Because Islam's own historical claims would be threatened by any discovery of such items, their fate in Muslim hands can be predicted.

The True Obstacle to Peace

The political concessions and territorial compromises being made today will not secure a lasting peace in the Middle East; the solution to the ages-old conflict must be settled on strictly religious grounds. In biblical terms, we cannot separate the religion and politics of Israel; whenever her faith failed, the political entity perished (2 Kings 21:11-15; cf. Proverbs 14:34).

The same holds true for Israel's prophetic destiny. There cannot be a separation between Israel's political kingdom and Israel's Promised Land, because the one requires the other for fulfillment (Ezekiel 37:24-25). For this reason, the guarantee of Israel's future political stability is linked to the reestablishment of ancient religious worship (2 Chronicles 7:14; Ezekiel 37:26).

This religious factor is the one obstacle to obtaining peace in the Middle East. And the most irreconcilable problem with the greatest potential for conflict centers squarely on the status of Jerusalem—the proclaimed capital of two opposing states and the sacred center of two conflicting religions. In order to understand why the present Middle East conflict *and* all the biblical end-time events center on Jerusalem, we need to appreciate the Jewish view of the sanctity of this city.

An Undying Passion

Jerusalem means everything to a Jew. The famous Rabbi Nachman once expressed this proverbially when he said, "Wherever I go, I go to Jerusalem." The truth of this statement is exemplified by the life of the observant Jew. He prays for Jerusalem, "the mother of Israel," every day in his morning and evening prayers and when thanks is given for meals. On every Sabbath and on all holy days Jerusalem is especially remembered. At two of these celebrations, Passover and Yom Kippur, the services conclude with a unified expression for national redemption with the words *Leshana Haba B'yerushalayim* ("Next year in Jerusalem!"). When houses are plastered and painted, an empty spot on the wall is always left to recall Jerusalem. In Jewish wedding ceremonies, ashes are put on the head of the bridegroom and a glass is broken in solemn remembrance of Jerusalem (that is, the Temple's destruction). And at death, a Jewish person's coffin is packed with a little earth from Jerusalem. "More than a city, Jerusalem is a basic and eternal concept that has affected the heart of Jewish life in every age."[5]

It is the sanctity of Jerusalem that produces such passion. This sanctity is based on the belief that God's name dwells there eternally. Bound together in this idea is God's election of Jerusalem as the site for the holy Temple and the Shekinah, the divine presence that once attended the Ark. While today many political, sociological, and religious concerns are the focal points of the strife in Jerusalem, perhaps tomorrow the issue of the Ark—particularly as it concerns the rebuilding of the Temple—will serve to intensify the conflict. Such a prospect is quite possible; we have already seen how Arab riots forced a closure of the only Jewish access to the tunnels beneath the Temple Mount. Tension is high because of the Muslim prohibitions that restrict Jewish religious access to the Temple Mount.

To see how a renewed search for (or the discovery of) the Ark might provoke the Middle East situation, we need to examine the present struggle between Jew and Muslim over both Jerusalem and the Temple Mount.

The Battle for Jerusalem

The struggle for possession of the land in the territories west of the Jordan River has one ultimate focus. Until this goal is attained, no short-term solution will be satisfactory. This goal, of course, is Jerusalem. That Jerusalem was and is the ultimate objective for the Arab countries may be seen in a nationally circulated *Washington Post* service article:

> The return of Jerusalem, one of Islam's holiest cities after Mecca, is a sacred call to battle by Iran's Islamic revolutionary government and by increasingly militant Muslim organizations in Arab nations across North Africa, the Middle East and Asia. . . . Jordan's King Hussein says, "Jerusalem is the

essence of peace between us." . . . [and] PLO Chairman Yasser Arafat . . . continues to speak of Jerusalem as the capital of an independent Palestine.[6]

The signing of the Declaration of Principles on September 13, 1993, began the final countdown for resolving the status of Jerusalem. The terms of that agreement set 1996 as the target year for coming up with a solution—a date that coincidentally marks the 3,000-year anniversary of King David's original capture of Jerusalem and establishment of the city as Israel's capital. For the first time since the unification of Jerusalem in 1967, the Rabin government is considering dividing the city once again, although in some way promising to maintain Jewish rule over the eastern (PLO) division.

Such a division already exists at the Temple Mount, where Israel claims sovereignty but allows the Muslim Wakf complete jurisdiction. Under this compromise, Jews (and Christians) are not permitted to conduct any religious activities in the area. Even the mere act of carrying a Bible or bowing the head to pray invites immediate removal from the site by Muslim officials. This situation would be greatly exacerbated if East Jerusalem became the capital of a Palestinian state. Jerusalem's former mayor Teddy Kollek once proposed that the current arrangement at the Temple Mount be made into a law. This would have guaranteed the Muslims permanent jurisdiction of the Mount even under sustained Israeli control. Kollek would not have been opposed to a Palestinian flag of state or a Muslim flag being flown over the Temple Mount.[7] His permissive attitude is representative of the Labor party. However, a study of the actual intentions of the PLO will reveal that even these compromises would never have been acceptable to the Palestinians.

PLO Means "Palestinian Lands Only"

When the PLO was established, the Gaza Strip and the West

Bank belonged to the Arabs. The PLO was not set up to "liberate" these territories but rather the *rest* of the land, including all Jewish settlements in Haifa, Acre, Jaffa, and Tel-Aviv. The Arab League Charter, as well as the Intafada, are based on the liberation of land "occupied" in 1948—that is, from the founding of the State of Israel. In other words, PLO really means "Palestinian Lands Only." This fact seems to be unknown or to have been forgotten by the American media, and therefore few people are aware of the PLO's actual intentions in the agreement signed with the Israeli Labor government.

For instance, George Habash, leader of the Popular Front for the Liberation of Palestine, the second-largest PLO faction, has asserted the real intentions behind accepting limited land grants from Israel. In the Popular Front's newspaper, *Al-Hadaf*, he declared, "We seek to establish a state which we can use in order to liberate the other part of the Palestinian soil."[8] The PLO plan, then, is the gradual acquisition of *all* Israeli territory. This will be accomplished through what Salah Khalaf Abu Iyad, Arafat's principal deputy, once called the dual means of "rifle and diplomacy." He stated this plan plainly at a Fatah Day celebration in Amman on January 1, 1991: "Now we accept the formation of the Palestinian state in part of Palestine, in the Gaza Strip and West Bank. We will start from that part and we will liberate Palestine, inch by inch."

This "phased program" was originally adopted at the twelfth session of the Palestinian National Council in June of 1974 and was reconfirmed in 1988. It was again reaffirmed to 19 Arab ministers assembled in Cairo by none other than PLO chairman Arafat on September 19, 1993:

> Our first goal is the liberation of all occupied territories . . . and the establishment of a Palestinian state whose capital is Jerusalem. The agreement we arrived at is not a complete solution. . . . it is

only the basis for an interim solution and the forerunner to a final settlement, which must be based on
complete withdrawal from all occupied Palestinian
lands, especially holy Jerusalem.[9]

Interestingly, Arafat said this less than a week after the
Declaration of Principles was signed. In effect, he was reassur-
ing these Arab ministers of the original PLO commitment.

Should there be any question as to what is meant by a
"Palestinian state," one needs only to look at the logos of all
seven major branches of the PLO. At the center of each logo is
the outline of the Palestinian state, which clearly includes all
the territory west of the Jordan River—that is, *all* of Israel!
The PLO's goal of taking all the land has been affirmed by
Nayef Hawatmeh, leader of the Democratic Front for the
Liberation of Palestine, the third-largest PLO organization:
"The popular revolution in Palestine will continue the struggle
to expel the Zionist occupation from all Palestinian Arab soil,
from the [Jordan] River to the [Mediterranean] Sea."[10]

The Palestinians have never concealed that their ultimate
objective is to control Jerusalem. Shortly after the Peace
Accord was signed, an election held at the Muslim Bir Zeit
University in Ramallah gave all nine student council seats to
Hamas members. They won on the platform slogan "Jerusalem first."[11] Ziad Yaish, editor of the local Arabic daily newspaper *A-Sha'ab*, stated the Palestinian perspective plainly:
"Most Palestinians here regard East Jerusalem as the capital
of a coming Palestinian state; that Jerusalem is not united."[12]

Arafat himself has openly boasted, "The Palestinian state is
within our grasp. Soon the Palestinian flag will fly on the
walls, the minarets, and the cathedrals of Jerusalem."[13] He
made clear his intention toward the Temple Mount when he
later added, "I will design my own house—not in Jericho but
in Jerusalem. I remember living there with my uncle near the
Wailing Wall."[14]

Arafat's memory is apparently tainted with thoughts of vengeance. His uncle's house, like all Arab homes in the Mograhabi district, was bulldozed by order of Teddy Kollek immediately after the Six-Day War. This was done to widen the Western Wall plaza and make room for the huge crowd of Jewish worshipers returning to the site after more than 20 years' absence. Arafat's dream of returning to the Temple Mount may also be evident from the huge photographic mural that covers the wall behind his office desk at the PLO headquarters in Tunis, Tunisia. The scene? The Dome of the Rock.

Most Israelis have completely rejected Prime Minister Rabin's proposal to redivide Jerusalem and create a dual status for it as both the Israeli and Palestinian capital. Yet this is the goal that the Palestinians have worked toward in all past and present negotiations. In response, Jerusalem has sent its own signal.

Jerusalem Sends a Signal

In November 1993, for the first time in 28 years—in fact, since before the existence of a united Jewish Jerusalem—a new mayor took control of the city. One writer clearly understood the significance of this election:

> Ordinarily, we Americans don't pay much attention to a mayor's election . . . but the election of a new mayor in Jerusalem is an exception. It may not make any difference to us who gets to be mayor of Tokyo, London or Rome. The world probably won't change no matter who wins. But it might in the case of Jerusalem.[15]

The man deposed in this election was Teddy Kollek, a staunch Labor supporter who had been building a relationship with the Arab population of East Jerusalem for a quarter century. The winner, an equally staunch supporter of the Likud party, was Ehud Olmert, who had formerly served in the right-wing Shamir government. Whereas Kollek had always spoken of Jews and Arabs coexisting and had enforced policies restricting religious Jews from settling in Arab areas, Olmert began his administration by announcing that he would *not* permit a division of the capital and that he *would* encourage the Jewish settlements.[16] Joining Olmert in a demonstration of solidarity were the right-wing religious parties who gained control of the Jerusalem council and Ronni Milo, a conservative Likud member, who won the mayorship of Tel-Aviv.

Under the Labor government, Israelis could not buy Arab houses in specially designated areas.[17] But the *Ateret Cohanim*, Beit Orot, and Eldad were ready when Kollek was voted out. All had raised private foreign funds to purchase Arab houses in the Wadi Hilweh, the City of David section of the Silwan village, and the Muslim Quarter adjacent to the Temple Mount. They already own more than 40 houses in the City of David and expect to purchase the remaining 60 houses by 1996.[18]

The first of these groups, *Ateret Cohanim* ("Crown of the Priests"), is also a yeshiva (seminary) founded in 1979 to train priestly descendants for future ritual service in the rebuilt Third Temple. Students from this yeshiva had taken part in Rabbis Goren and Getz's excavations under the Temple Mount,[19] and their home-buying activity may therefore be connected to other purposes. Certainly their control of property adjacent to the Temple Mount would permit further excavation for the Ark.

Ehud Olmert's recent victory signalled the rejection of the Labor government by the religious community and the secular right. Their message was that dealing with the PLO and land-for-peace policies threatens Jerusalem's future and will not be tolerated. They were afraid that if the "peace" process continued under Kollek, the future of the city would next be negotiated and that Israeli sovereignty over the Temple Mount would be lost. Olmert's political stance will at least allow some local measure of resistance to this compromise and may even facilitate the rise of reactionary groups that want to remove the Arabs from the Temple Mount and reassert a Jewish presence there. Olmert has already made all contributions to the East Jerusalem settlements tax-deductible and has offered his full support to every effort to revive the rights of Jews to live and build in all parts of the Holy City. With the current Israeli government now under pressure from the PLO to evacuate all Jewish settlements within the "territories," Jerusalem will literally be standing alone against the world.

Reuven Rivlin, a moderate Likud party member who at one time was thought to be a contender for mayor of Jerusalem, has said that Jerusalem is a microcosm for Jewish-Arab relations in general. He insists that whatever works in that city can work anywhere.[20] The reverse is also true: If it does not work in Jerusalem, then it cannot work anywhere else. Jerusalem will, therefore, become the death knell to any proposed peace process. And in fact, it has already sent a clear signal to the world.

Fanning the Flames

In March 1994 an unprecedented closing of the Western Wall (the only remnant of the Temple Mount accessible to Jews) followed an Arab stoning at the wall. The latter event was in response to the Hebron mosque shooting that took place on February 25, 1994. This closure was the first-ever attempt by the government to restrict the religious rights of all Israelis at the Temple Mount. This action was viewed by religious Jews as more symbolic than security-oriented. It was seen as a clear indication of the Israeli government's attitude toward the future of the Temple Mount. Rabbi Benny Alon, who is the head of a movement attempting to establish a Jewish presence throughout Judea and Samaria, said this in response to the government's action:

> We [Israel] do not impose sovereignty over the Temple Mount, and as a result we are afraid of rocks thrown over to the Western Wall. We have already conceded the Temple Mount [to the Palestinians] so the Western Wall also must be evacuated because it is dangerous.[21]

After closing the wall, the government restricted the right of Jewish worshipers to carry arms. Perhaps the final blow came when the government later declared that "all Arab-hating groups" were illegal and placed them on par with militant Islamic groups. These Jewish religious groups were branded as "terrorists" because their objectives "include the establishment of a theocracy in the biblical Land of Israel and the violent expulsion of Arabs from that Land."[22] Under this definition, such groups as Kach, Kahane Chai, the Jewish Defense League, the Temple Mount Yeshiva, and the Temple Mount Faithful are now illegal terrorist organizations.

This ruling means that the leaders and members of these organizations must forfeit their firearms, even though most of them are on Islamic "hit-lists." Faced with the prospect of imprisonment, groups such as Kach have officially disbanded, but most have simply gone underground or disregarded the government's threat. They have also threatened—as have the settlers in the Golan Heights and in Hebron—to foment a civil war in Israel. David Axelrod, a Kahane Chai spokesman, confirmed this with his declaration, "They're paving the way for a bloody civil war." Moshe Belogordosky, a leader in the West Bank settlement Kfar Tapua, also added his sentiments: "The government in essence declared war on a large part of its citizens. God willing, there will be a revolution and another government."[23] These groups see the Israeli government holding to an arrogant and dangerous double standard: calling them terrorists while at the same time negotiating with a terrorist organization, the PLO.

The Muslim Reaction

It is possible that the Muslim Wakf may have influenced the Israeli government's decision. In January 1994 I met briefly with Adnan Husseini, executive director of the Wakf. I learned that no mention of the Jewish Temple or of anything other than Islamic sites was permitted on the Temple Mount. While I was allowed to film within the Dome of the Rock, and even to ascend the outer Dome via the scaffolding in place at that time during the Dome's restoration, I had to be accompanied by a Wakf representative who alone could speak about the buildings on the site. This censure of any reference to anything Jewish is a reaction against the government of Israel, which the Wakf says is responsible for the actions of Jewish Temple movement groups. In a previous interview, Mr. Husseini revealed the Wakf's feelings about groups like the *Ateret Cohanim* and the Temple Mount Faithful:

> We see no difference between these two groups and the government. We consider the government and these two groups as one body. The government leaves these persons working. . . . What the Jews want there is a pure Jewish country. If they want to fight us, they will have to fight Islam. . . . They [the TMF] want to convert the Haram [Temple Mount] into another place. The stone [cornerstone] symbolizes that they have started to build the Third Temple. The stone is pointing forward to something more—that is, the Temple. That is why everybody wanted to protect the Haram last year [the 1990 Temple Mount riot]. And the government says, "We are a democracy; we can't shut his [Gershon Salomon's] mouth."[24]

Mr. Husseini also has gone on record concerning the digging of the Western Wall Tunnel, including the clandestine excavations of Rabbis Goren and Getz, and the Wakf's perspective of these actions:

> They [the government] have done four or five attacks on the mosque from their diggings under it. What they found under the Haram is 90 percent Islamic and 10 percent pre-Islamic. Now they are digging a long tunnel along the wall [of the Al-Aqsa compound] under the Moslem Quarter. Already, seven buildings owned by Moslems have collapsed due to these diggings.[25]

Clearly we can see that the Muslim authorities will hold the Israeli government responsible for whatever group acts against Islamic control of the Temple Mount. This was the case in 1969 when the government was blamed for the fire set in the Al-Aqsa mosque by the crazed Australian "Christian" cultist Dennis Rohan. It happened again when Arab delegates obtained a United Nations censure against Israel for the Temple Mount riot of October 1990, which some people think was instigated by the TMF. And in 1994, the Israeli army was blamed for Goldstein's shooting spree in the Hebron mosque. In turn, both Gershon Salomon on behalf of the TMF and Baruch ben-Yosef on behalf of the Jewish Defense League have filed petitions to the Israeli Supreme Court against the restrictions and actions of the Wakf.

As long as Jewish religious groups continue to assert their cause for the Temple Mount, retaliation against Israel will be the result. The present Israeli government, aware of the Islamic perspective, seeks to demonstrate its control over such groups as a gesture of peace.[26] But the Muslim world rejects such attempts, and with each incursion moves closer to the threat of war.

Awaiting the Inevitable

The possibility that war may be imminent can be seen from the irreconcilable religious and nationalistic convictions held by Israelis and Arabs. For example, Abu Alli, an Hamas Brigade spokesman, gave this reason for continuing terrorist attacks against Israelis: "We in Hamas see the killing of Jews as an act that brings us closer to Allah."[27] Similar impassioned rhetoric has come from no less a figure than former Ashkenazi Chief Rabbi Shlomo Goren: "Arafat is responsible for thousands of murders. Therefore, everyone in Israel who meets him in the streets has the right to kill him."[28] Recently, Rabbi Goren was threatened with court-martial by the Labor government for telling the West Bank and Gaza Strip settlers that it would be a sin to move and that they must resist the government's orders as being against God. Many of the settlers side with Goren; they say the government is insane to order them to evacuate their homes and Israeli land and turn in their army-issued rifles. Rabbi Meir Kahane's son, Benjamin Ze'ev Kahane, went further, calling the government's orders "illegal" and "criminal."[29]

One of the fundamental demands of the PLO has been for an autonomous Palestianian police force to protect the new Palestinian settlements from nearby Israeli settlers. And what would Palestinians do with their own police force? An unusually unambiguous answer was given by the rather moderate head of the Gaza bar association, Freih Abu Middain. He stated this in response to the February 1994 shooting of Muslims in the Hebron mosque: "Had this massacre happened after we had a Palestinian police force, we would be going into the Jewish settlements and killing at least 100 people there. Our people will not remain silent."[30]

Just as the Koran requires the avenging of "family honor" by such acts, militant Jews share much the same viewpoint with respect to atrocities committed against them. This is what motivated Dr. Goldstein to "settle the score" in the mosque. He was well aware that in 1929, Hebron's Arabs murdered 67 Jewish men, women, and children and burned their synagogues. He was also aware that Arafat had masterminded the 1972 murder of the Israeli Olympic team in Munich, the 1974 murder of schoolchildren at Ma'alot, and infirmed Jewish passengers of the *Achille Lauro* cruise ship. He was also aware that PLO and Hamas groups had killed 30 Israelis since the "White House handshake" and that two of his friends, Mordechai Lapid and his 19-year-old son (a yeshiva student), had been murdered outside Hebron by Palestinians. In the latter event, his friend is said to have died in his arms. One week later, he killed 29 Muslim worshipers at Hebron. Just before his shooting spree, during the Jewish celebration of Purim, Dr. Goldstein read to his son the Purim text in Esther 9:5: "Thus the Jews struck all their enemies . . . killing and destroying; and they did what they pleased to those who hated them."

Many of the settlers in the nearby Israeli settlement of Kiryat Arba now regard Goldstein as a patriot and hero (after the fashion of Mordecai in Esther 9:4) and have been equally forthcoming in their rage. As evidence of the community's viewpoint, when the news went out that 50 Arabs had been shot, one woman's outcry matched that of Abu Middain's: "We should kill 500, not 50!"[31] Given these volatile ultranationalist tempers, the government's ban on Jewish religious organizations, and the instability of Israel's own political powers, our next steps on the prophetic time line may well move us rapidly toward Gog and Magog and the Tribulation.

Will the "peace" process continue, only to be crowned by treachery as the PLO leads an Arab army against Jewish "occupiers" and forces a final showdown in Israel? Will the ban on "extremist" Jewish religious groups force a civil war in Israel that will have to be resolved on an international scale? Will the Labor government be overthrown and a new reactionary right-wing government take its place, forcing the Arab world to go to war or face expulsion from the Land? The specific catalyst for the final conflict is uncertain; but it is clear that such a conflict will come.

Oliver Wendell Holmes, Jr. once pronounced the only possible outcome for Israel and the Arabs when at the beginning of Zionist realization in 1919 he observed, "Between two groups of people who want to make inconsistent kinds of worlds, I see no remedy but force."

And as the Middle East conflict lurches away from the prospect of peace, will the Ark be recovered and move onto the stage of these final days? If our understanding of the prophets and their prophecies is correct, it is likely. When that day appears, just as all eyes are now turned to the Middle East, so also will everyone's attention turn to the Ark. Is the world prepared for that day?

18

All Eyes on the Ark

*I have no doubt that you and I shall see the Ark of
the Covenant in the middle of the Third Temple on the
Temple Mount in Jerusalem, very soon—in our life.*[1]

—Gershon Salomon, leader,
the Temple Mount Faithful

When the Israelites came around the second time to the
border of the Promised Land, they bore a tremendous
burden from their forefathers. They were a generation who
had not seen the great miracles associated with the exodus
(Numbers 14:22-23, 31). Instead, they had spent 40 years
remembering the lesson of failure inherited from their fathers
(Numbers 14:33-34). The day finally came when they returned
to the very spot where their parents had disbelieved the report
that God was able to fulfill His promise and bring them into the
Land (Numbers 14:8, 11). Their lack of faith gave way to fear
and they rebelled against God's appointed leaders, Moses and
Aaron (Numbers 14:2-4, 10). And now, the children of that
former generation were facing the same test of belief and
obedience.

However, crossing over into the new land was no easy
matter. It was flood season and the Jordan River, normally a

small muddy brook, had overflowed its high banks and become an impassable, torrential flood (Joshua 3:15-16). How would this band of untested and doubtful Jews cross this seemingly insurmountable obstacle so that they might face the foe on the other side as confident soldiers of faith? The answer was found in a single command: They were to set their eyes on the Ark (Joshua 3:3). Joshua later explained this command to the people: "By this you shall know that the living God is among you. . . . Behold, the ark of the covenant of the Lord of all the earth is crossing over ahead of you into the Jordan" (verses 10-11).

An Ancient Time Capsule

Long after the Israelites crossed the Jordan, the Ark continued to serve as a focal point for the nation in times of doubt and distress. Its presence among the people served as an ancient time capsule that evidenced the providence of God in the history of His people. No other nation on the face of the earth had a God who performed miracles (Exodus 15:11; 34:10), and the power demonstrated by the Ark was proof positive that the God of Israel had supreme control over all of His creation.

We have seen in this book that the Lord's prior use of something as a sacred symbol does not prevent His future use of it. The Temple treasures and most notably the Ark are predicted to be returned to their original places within a revived sacrificial system in a rebuilt Jewish Temple. As men in times past looked to the Ark, so also at the present time are men looking for the Ark. In both cases it is not because they want to *replace* reverence for God with an object. Rather, it is out of reverence *for* God that they seek to restore an object essential to God's program of future worship. Unfortunately, there is a teaching today that misunderstands this and claims that the Ark and everything with it has been replaced forever.

A Regrettable Confusion

This teaching is called *replacement theology* because it advocates that Israel and its symbolic system of worship (presented in the Old Testament) was replaced by the church and its spiritual system of worship (presented in the New Testament). This means that the Temple and everything connected with it, including the Ark, were irreversibly replaced by the church as the new (spiritual) Temple. Likewise, the nation of Israel was superseded and replaced by the Christian community, the New Israel.

This perspective is a radical departure from that of traditional Judaism and those Christians throughout time who have held to a literal interpretation of the Old Testament. They have always maintained, to one degree or another, that the Old Testament offers Israel the hope of restoration (complete with a functioning Temple and service) and that the New Testament reaffirms this hope (*see* Romans 9–11).

Replacement theology has resulted from a regrettable confusion over the use of typology, especially in cases in which a material object has been thought to foreshadow a future spiritual reality. The opinion has been that when the *reality* of a type appeared, its *shadow* (the type itself) would disappear. The Ark of the Covenant is considered just such a shadow—a shadow that gave way to substance in the coming of Christ.

In their attempt to find Christ foreshadowed in every aspect of the Old Testament worship system, Christian typologists have identified Jesus as the Ark of the New Covenant even though the New Testament does not use the Ark in such a comparison (even where it would be expected—*see* Hebrews 9:4-5). These typologists take every detail of the Ark and reinterpret it symbolically in light of this association.

The wood of the Ark is seen as symbolizing Christ's humanity and the gold is seen as His deity. Others say the outer gold is a type of the Father; the wood in the center is a type of the Son (the cross); and the gold within is a type of the Holy Spirit.[2] In addition, the crown about the lid of the Ark has been thought to symbolize the kingship of Christ; the four rings at its corners supposedly represent the gospel of Christ going to the four corners of the world; and the two cherubim and the mercy seat are said to indicate the Trinity (cherubim = Father and Holy Spirit; mercy seat = Christ).

However, there is no scriptural precedent for such extreme typology. While in general the Ark, and especially the mercy seat, may symbolize the atoning work of Christ in verses like Matthew 27:51 (where the Temple's veil was torn in two) and Romans 3:25 (where some translate "propitiation" as "mercy seat"), this association is made only indirectly and certainly not in terms of replacement. Nowhere do we see any indication that a type like the Ark must lose its meaning or cease to exist. Nor do we see that its association with Christ must end at the cross and not follow Him into the future as a perpetual memorial and witness or as a functional part of the restored worship of the theocratic kingdom.

Interestingly this theological position is set in stone (literally) in Israel at the site of Kiriath-jearim, where the Ark once rested in the days of Samuel. Today the Sisters of Saint Joseph of the Apparition maintain the Our Lady Ark of the Covenant Church on the top of the hill where, according to tradition, Abinadab's house was located (he was the priest who tended the Ark). On top of this church is a huge stone statue that makes a striking statement: The Ark of the Covenant is present, but standing on top of the Ark (between the cherubim) is Mary, who is holding the baby Jesus in one arm. In Jesus' hands are two objects: the tablets of Moses (the Old Covenant) and the manna. One of the sisters explained the statue in this way: Mary is the true Ark of the Covenant. Just as the Ark of old was a repository for the presence of God, so also Mary's womb was for Jesus. Jesus is both the manna, the bread which came from heaven, and the New Covenant. Since both represent the new revelation of God, they stand above the old revelation (the Ark), now passed away.

A Look to the Future

There is reason to believe the Ark will have a role in the future because its purpose is connected to that of the Temple and therefore to Christ's second coming (Ezekiel 43:1-12; Haggai 2:6-9; Zechariah 6:12-13; Malachi 3:1; 4:5). If it helps to think in terms of comparison, then think in terms of the Ark of the Lord versus the Lord of the Ark, since in the past the focal point of God's presence was restricted to the Ark, while in the future the divine presence will fill all Jerusalem (although it may emanate from the Ark).

This great and imminent event is awaited by Gershon Salomon and others like him. While Salomon's expectation of the Ark is not necessarily representative of most Israelis today, he speaks for those who believe that a day is soon coming when the Ark and the other Temple treasures will take center stage in the affairs of the world:

> The bringing of the Ark of the Covenant and all the holy vessels to the Third Temple will be by the will of God. We shall see it whether or not we want to see it because God [has already] decided it. And if God has decided it, it is [as good as] fulfilled. We shall be the generation of the complete redemption—we shall see again as a reality the Ark of the Covenant here on the hill of God, and nations and peoples will come from all the world to see the glory of God.[3]

A Promise of What Is to Come

One day, and perhaps soon, the Lord will complete His promise for the Jewish people and return personally to establish His kingdom on earth. Until that time, He has instructed His people—whether Jews or Gentiles—to never forget what

He has promised or His power to bring it to pass. In Exodus 34:10, God said:

> Behold, I am going to make a covenant. Before all your people I will perform miracles which have not been produced in all the earth, nor among any of the nations; and all the people among whom you live will see the working of the LORD, for it is a fearful thing that I am going to perform with you.

This covenant that God made, the Mosaic Covenant, was designed to create a distinguishably holy nation among all the nations of the earth. Central to this demonstration were the Tabernacle, the Temple, and their accompanying treasures. This covenant was made with the Jews, not the Gentiles, and remains to be fulfilled by means of a future covenant that will enable Israelites to finally experience the righteousness that the Mosaic Covenant could only require, not provide (Jeremiah 31:33-34). This future covenant describes the presence of God dwelling with a restored national Israel in a rebuilt Temple (Ezekiel 37:26-28). And, as we have seen, this coming restoration should properly include the Ark.

The events that will lead Israel to recover her blessings in a new covenant were foretold in Deuteronomy 4. There, God predicted Israel's dispersion under the dominion of Gentile idolaters (verses 27-28), a condition that has existed until this day. He then promised that He would not forget His original covenant but return His people spiritually and nationally after the Tribulation period. This promise is explicitly detailed in verses 30-31:

> When you are in distress and all these things have come upon you, in the latter days, you will return to the LORD your God and listen to His voice. For the LORD your God is a compassionate God; He will not fail you nor destroy you nor forget the covenant with your fathers which He swore to them.

ALL EYES ON THE ARK ✦ 319

God confirmed the reality of His promise by giving Israel the distinct privilege of knowing His presence. This privilege set them apart both for discipline and for restoration, since they were forever tied to God as His chosen people (*see* Jeremiah 31:35-37). In Deuteronomy 4:36-39 this confirmation is recalled in terms that imply the presence of the Ark:

> Out of the heavens He let you hear His voice
> . . . and on earth He let you see His great fire, and
> you heard His words from the midst of the fire.
> . . . And He personally brought you from Egypt
> by His great power, driving out from before you
> nations greater and mightier than you. . . . He is
> God in heaven above and on the earth below; there
> is no other.

On earth, the Ark was the place where God's glory was displayed as a pillar of fire by night; where Moses, Aaron, and Joshua heard God's voice; and which served as the symbol of God's power in warfare. If these divine deeds were associated with the Ark in Israel's early days, then perhaps the call to remember them in the latter days when Israel once again becomes a nation may imply the Ark's reappearance at that time. Whatever the case, the command for the future is the same as the command in the past: Look to the Lord—which in Joshua's time, at least, required that all eyes be on the Ark.

Looking Beyond the Ark

In the Old Testament, the command to look to the Ark of the Lord was tantamount to looking to the Lord of the Ark. That command, with its attendant blessings, remains the same today. Those who will look to the Lord of the Ark will find that His powerful presence is there to guide them and to deliver them from sin's destruction. The New Testament has declared that the day is fast approaching when God will gloriously appear to His own once again. The call at the present hour is to look to the Lord and live with anticipation, "looking for the blessed hope and the appearing of the glory of our great God and Savior, Christ Jesus" (Titus 2:13).

An Israeli pastor, the son of a Holocaust survivor whose life has spanned most of Israel's modern history (including its searches for the Ark), puts this matter in proper perspective:

> Long ago God taught His nation that the Ark of the Covenant represented His presence among [them]. For so many years now we [Jews] have had no knowledge as to [the location] of the Ark of the Covenant. But believers in the Messiah—those who put their trust in Jesus—are looking for the original [presence of God]. Many people even today are looking for the Ark of the Covenant, and they think that if they find the Ark it will solve all of their problems. [While] it would be very nice to find the Ark of the Covenant and to see what the people saw in the desert, to find the presence of God is a matter of faith, of looking for the right Messiah—Jesus.[4]

My friend, as you have read of what God is doing to prepare this world for His coming, have you made certain that *you* are prepared for that coming? When I speak in seminars and conferences across the country, I always ask this question at the end of my meetings: "Christ is coming—are you going?" If you do not enjoy that certainty, you can find it at this moment no matter where you are. Simply acknowledge to God that you are a sinner, look to Jesus as your Savior from sin, and trust God to save you from your sin for Jesus' sake.

Perhaps you have already done this, but your life has slipped away from the Savior and has too long been lived for yourself. Perhaps you have been distracted by misplaced priorities. Ask God to help you renew your focus. And take time to prepare for Christ's coming by looking to Him each day, by recommitting yourself to His service, and by studying His Word—the best preparation of all!

The Greatest Treasure of All

In this book we have talked about Temple treasures that existed in the past and may be restored to a role in Israel's future. But there are also treasures beyond time. Jesus Himself said, "Where your treasure is, there will your heart be also" (Matthew 6:21). He therefore commanded His disciples, "Lay up for yourselves *treasures in heaven*, where neither moth nor rust destroys, and where thieves do not break in and steal" (Matthew 6:20, emphasis added). As wonderful as it is to join in a search for hidden treasure on earth, the treasure that is in heaven can readily be found. The Bible is the map to this treasure and it clearly marks the spot for all to see.

It has been said that there are last things, and things that last. Perhaps the Ark of the Lord will be recovered in these last days; but beyond that, we know with absolute certainty the Lord of the Ark will soon appear. He is truly the lasting treasure at the end of every man's search!

Conclusion

In Edgar Allen Poe's detective story *The Purloined Letter*, the plot turns on an elaborate and lengthy search for a stolen letter whose hiding place has eluded even the prefect of the Paris police. The irony in the story is revealed when the letter is finally discovered by a scholarly detective who explains that everyone had been looking for the letter only in obscure hiding places, while in truth, it was always in the most obvious place.

Would it not prove ironic if, after all the centuries of pursuit around the globe, we happened to find that the Temple treasures and especially the Ark never left their home on the Temple Mount? The evidence I have presented in this book seems to point in that direction.

However, our purpose in searching for Temple treasures has not only been to find evidence for the *Ark* of the Lord, but also to discover the *Lord* of the Ark. The Bible itself affirms that this discovery is the very purpose for which we were made: "that [we] should seek God, if perhaps [we] might grope for Him and find Him, though He is not far from each one of us" (Acts 17:27).

Perhaps this is a discovery that you have not yet made, although you may have pursued it all your life in every realm of religion. Could it be that you have conducted your search for the Savior in all the obscure places, while all the time He has been "not far from each one of us"? Among Moses' last words

323

to the Israelites was the encouragement that God's revelation of Himself was not hidden: "For this commandment . . . is not too difficult for you, nor is it out of reach. . . . But the word is very near you, in your mouth and in your heart, that you may observe it. . . . to love the LORD your God, to walk in His ways and to keep His commandments" (Deuteronomy 30:11, 14, 16).

In the New Testament, Paul applies this verse to the search for the Messiah (Romans 10:6-8). There he says that the word which is near is the word of faith, which promises "that if you confess with your mouth Jesus as Lord, and believe in your heart that God raised Him from the dead, you shall be saved" (verse 9). It is my personal prayer that your search for this greatest of all treasures would end with Jesus, the Messiah of Israel, "in whom are hidden all the treasures of wisdom and knowledge" (Colossians 2:3). And when you have found Him you will discover the greater truth that He has in fact found you, and that your own search was always a part of His seeking you.

> *Treasures seeking, here I find*
> *Wealth of more than worldly kind,*
> *Life eternal—full and free*
> *All from the Lord, who sought for me.*

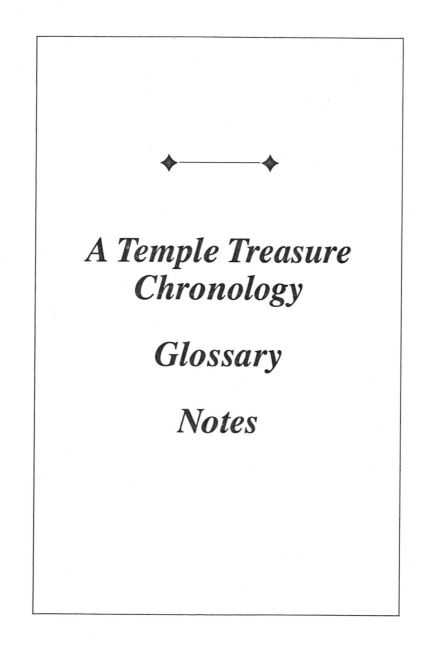

A Temple Treasure
Chronology

Glossary

Notes

A Temple Treasure
Chronology

Major Events Connected
with the Ark of the Covenant

The Exodus

c. 1446 B.C.   Moses receives the earthly pattern for
the Ark based on a divine revelation on
Mount Sinai. This Ark is patterned
after the heavenly archetype (Exodus
24:15-18; 25:8-22, 40).

Moses makes the acacia wood box and
deposits the second set of tablets (along
with the broken pieces of the first set)
within it (Deuteronomy 10:1-5). This
was most likely set within the golden
boxes (or overlaid) when Bezalel later
constructed the Tabernacle vessels (*see*
Ibn Ezra; *Yoma* 3b, 72b).

Moses' craftsmen Bezalel (and
Oholiab?) construct the Ark and the
other Temple treasures according to the
divine design over a six-month period
(Ark: Exodus 31:1-7; 38:1-9; table of
showbread: Exodus 25:23-30; Menorah:

Exodus 25:31-40; Altar of Incense: Exodus 30:1-10).

Moses inspects the finished parts of the Ark (Exodus 39:35) and the Ark is anointed (Exodus 30:26; 40:9; cf. Leviticus 8:10). Instructions are given concerning its care by the Kohathite Levites (Numbers 3:31).

The Ark is assembled and installed in the Holy of Holies in the Tabernacle (Exodus 26:34; 40:3, 20-21).

c. 1446-1406 B.C.	The covered Ark (Numbers 4:5-6) travels throughout the wilderness with the Kohathite Levites in the midst of the Israelite tribes (Numbers 10:21).
c. 1445 B.C.	The Ark travels three days ahead of the Israelite tribes, "seeking a place of settlement" on their three-day, 100-mile journey to Kibhroth ha-Taavah in Paran (Numbers 10:33-36). [This verse is marked by inverted Hebrew letters (*nuns*) in the synagogue Torah scroll and is recited whenever the "Ark" is brought out and returned to the modern Torah-ark.]

The Ark remains in the camp with Moses as the rebellious Israelites at Kadesh-barnea are defeated in their unaided attempt to conquer the Promised Land (Numbers 14:44-45).

c. 1444 B.C.	Aaron's rod miraculously sprouts blossoms, in validation of the Aaronic priesthood, when placed before the Ark (Numbers 17:7-10).

c. 1407 B.C.   The Ark goes out to war against the
Midianites with Phinehas the priest
(Numbers 31:6-7).

Moses orders the Levites to place the
Torat Moshe (autograph of the
Pentateuch) beside the Ark within the
Holy of Holies, to be removed and read
at the festival of *Sukkot* (Deuteronomy
31:9-11, 24-26).

The Conquest Settlement

c. 1406 B.C.   The Ark crosses the Jordan River ahead
of the Israelites. The river divides,
duplicating the miraculous parting of
the Red Sea (Joshua 3:3–4:11).

The Ark leads the army of Israel during
its march around the walls of Jericho.
On the seventh day, the city was
destroyed (Joshua 6:4-20).

Joshua and the elders of Israel come
before the Ark to seek divine guidance
after the defeat at Ai (Joshua 7:6-15).

c. 1400 B.C.   The Ark is set between Mounts Ebal
and Gerizim as the Israelite tribes,
divided between the mountains,
rehearse the conditional provisions of
the Mosaic Covenant (Joshua 8:33).

c. 1399-1385 B.C.   The Ark is stationed with the
Tabernacle at Gilgal for 14 years, going
out from there into battles with Joshua
(Joshua 5:10; 10:9-15).

c. 1385-1371 B.C.   The Ark and Tabernacle are moved to
Shiloh (Joshua 18:1).

c. 1371 B.C.   The Ark is temporarily brought to
Shechem for a ceremony during which
Israel reaffirms her commitment to the
Abrahamic and Mosaic Covenants
(Joshua 24:1-26).

c. 1371-1370 B.C.   The Ark is temporarily housed at
Bethel during the civil war between
Israel and Benjamin (Judges 20:18,
26-28; cf. Joshua 22:13).

The Judges

c. 1385-1050 B.C.   The Ark is housed with the Tabernacle
at Shiloh (1 Samuel 3:3; cf. *Seder Olam
Rabbah*, chapter 11) for 369 years. The
high priest Eli receives no word from
God in the presence of the Ark during
his 40-year judgeship; however, Samuel,
as a boy, slept near the Ark and was
given a revelation by God (1 Samuel
3:3-21). Shiloh was destroyed sometime
after the battle at Aphek around 1050
B.C. (1 Samuel 4; cf. Jeremiah 7:14;
26:9) while the Ark was in the
possession of the Philistines (see
below).

c. 1050 B.C.   The Ark is captured by the Philistines.
For seven months it is moved around
throughout their territory, bringing
plagues wherever it went (1 Samuel
4:1–6:1).

c. 1049 B.C.   The Philistines return the Ark with a
peace offering in the form of golden
tumors, and the Ark is miraculously
transported into the Israelite city of
Beth-shemesh on a cart (1 Samuel
6:4-18).

The men of Beth-shemesh presumptuously peer into the Ark and are struck dead to serve as a witness against the Ark's desecration (1 Samuel 6:19-20; cf. Numbers 4:20).

c. 1048-1028 B.C.   The Ark is transferred to Kiriath-jearim and the priestly family of Abinadab, where Eleazar the priest cares for it for 20 years during the judgeship of Samuel (1 Samuel 6:21; 7:1-2). During this period, the Tabernacle was located at Nob (1 Samuel 21:1; 22:9-11), and Israel lamented this separation (1 Samuel 7:2).

The Monarchy

c. 1000 B.C.   The Ark, which was ignored during the reign of Saul, is hastily moved by David without regard to the biblical prescription for transport (see Exodus 25:14-15; Numbers 3:30-31; 4:15; 7:9), and Uzzah is struck dead for touching the Ark (2 Samuel 6:1-7; 1 Chronicles 13:5-10).

The Ark is transferred to the house of Obed-edom for three months. During that time God's blessing is evidenced on his household (2 Samuel 6:10-12; 1 Chronicles 13:13-14).

c. 999 B.C.   David transfers the Ark to Jerusalem. He leads the procession, wearing the priestly ephod (2 Samuel 6:1-23; 1 Chronicles 15:1–16:43). During this period, the Tabernacle was located in Gibeon (1 Kings 3:4).

c. 999-960 B.C.   David determines to build a Temple in Jerusalem that will permanently house the Ark, but is only allowed to make preparation for building (2 Samuel 7:1-7; 1 Chronicles 17:1-6; 22:1–23:1; 29:2-9).

990 B.C.   David purchases the threshing floor of Araunah (Ornan) the Jebusite as the site for the Holy of Holies and the Ark (2 Samuel 24:18-25; 1 Chronicles 21:18-26).

980 B.C.   David and Bathsheba commit adultery. Despite David's urgings, Bathsheba's husband, Uriah, will not stay at his own house because the Ark, Israel, and Judah were all in temporary shelters (2 Samuel 11:4, 11).

c. 970 B.C.   David flees Jerusalem for 9 months during Absalom's usurpation of the throne. The high priest Zadok and all the Levites follow David, bringing the Ark with them, but are commanded by David to return it to Jerusalem (2 Samuel 15:24-29).

c. 965 B.C.   David gives Solomon the plans for the Temple, the Temple treasures, and the new vessels—plans based on the heavenly archetype (2 Chronicles 28:11-19).

960 B.C.   Solomon abandons the high place at Gibeon and offers sacrifices before the Ark in Jerusalem (1 Kings 3:15).

957 B.C.   Solomon commissions the building of

two 15-foot olive wood cherubim, overlaid with gold, under whose overspreading wings the Ark will be placed in the newly built Holy of Holies (1 Kings 6:19-28; 2 Chronicles 3:8-13).

950 B.C. Solomon installs the Ark, Tabernacle, and Temple vessels in the First Temple, and the Shekinah glory returns to the Ark within the Holy of Holies (1 Kings 8:4-11; 2 Chronicles 5:7-14).

926 B.C. Pharaoh Shishak plunders the Temple treasuries and the treasury of the king's house (1 Kings 14:25-28; 2 Chronicles 12:2-9).

752 B.C. King Jehoash of Israel defeats King Amaziah of Judah and plunders the treasuries of the Temple and the king's house, including those items stored with Obed-edom (2 Kings 14:14; 2 Chronicles 25:24).

701 B.C. King Hezekiah of Judah gives the wealth of the Temple treasuries and the king's house to the Assyrians as tribute (2 Kings 18:15).

King Hezekiah sets the letter from Assyrian Rabshakeh before the Ark and prays to the "LORD, the God of Israel, who art enthroned above the cherubim" (2 Kings 19:14-15; Isaiah 37:14-16).

700 B.C. King Hezekiah foolishly shows the treasures of the Temple treasury and the king's house to Berodach-baladan, a

prince of Babylon, and his envoys. The prophet Isaiah predicted this would lead to the eventual plunder of the Temple by the Babylonians (2 Kings 20:12-21; 2 Chronicles 32:31).

695-642 B.C. King Manasseh of Judah places idols within the Temple, including the Holy Place and the Holy of Holies. The Ark and the other Temple treasures were probably removed by the faithful Levites (whom Manasseh deposed) to prevent their defilement. Manasseh repents, but does not restore these treasures to the Temple (2 Kings 21:4-7; 2 Chronicles 33:7-9, 15).

622 B.C. King Josiah of Judah, grandson of Manasseh, restores the Temple and recovers one of the Temple treasures, the *Torat Moshe* (autograph of the Pentateuch), which once was placed beside the Ark and apparently was hidden in the Temple in the time of Manasseh (2 Kings 22:8; 2 Chronicles 34:14-18).

Josiah commands the Levites to return the Ark to the restored Temple (2 Chronicles 35:3). Evidently, the Ark had been hidden in the subterranean chamber under the Holy of Holies by the Levites. After the death of Josiah (2 Kings 23:29; 2 Chronicles 35:23-24), the Levites returned the Ark to this hiding place in view of the impending (and prophesied) Babylonian invasion (*see Yoma* 52b; *Tosefta Yoma* 2:13;

Horiot 12a; Talmud Babli *Shekalim* 6:2; Talmud Yerushalmi *Shekalim* 6:1; *Keritot* 5b; *Yad, Bet Ha-Bechirah* 4:1; *Tosefta Sotah* 13:2; *Seder Olam Rabbah* 24; *Yalkut* 2:247; *Kuzari* 3:39 [48b]; Rashi, Radak, Ralbag on 2 Chronicles 35:3).

605 B.C.–A.D. 1994   According to tradition, the Temple treasures under the Temple Mount have remained hidden throughout the time of the Babylonian invasions, the Judean exile, the entire Second Temple period (during which time Jerusalem was under foreign occupation and the Temple and its treasures were subject to defilement, capture, or destruction), and the present day.

169 B.C.   Antiochus Epiphanes IV removes Temple vessels (1 Maccabees 1:21), and new vessels are made and purified in the restoration under Judah Maccabeus (1 Maccabees 4:49-50; 2 Maccabees 10:3).

163 B.C.–A.D. 73   The Jewish apocryphal, apocalyptic, and pseudepigraphal writings, including the Dead Sea Scrolls, are written. They include prophecies about the restoration of the Temple treasures in the end times. In particular, the Copper Scroll lists the hiding places of Temple taxation money or some of the Temple treasures themselves.

A.D. 70   The Romans destroy the Herodian Temple. They plunder the Temple treasury and the Temple proper, removing, according to the Arch of Titus' Triumph, the menorah, the table of showbread, and the two silver trumpets. These treasures were then deposited by Emperor Vespasian in a special "Peace Temple" (Josephus, *Wars* 7:148-150). It is suspected that of these, at least the menorah was a duplicate and not an original Temple treasure (*see* Josephus, *Wars* 6:388).

A.D. 455   The sixth-century Byzantine historian Procopius of Caesarea, in his history of the Gothic Wars, reports that Belisarius paraded the duplicate Temple vessels during his triumphal procession in Carthage.

A.D. 527-565   According to Procopius, a Jew in Justinian's court had warned against keeping the Temple vessels at Constantinople (Byzantium), so they were transferred to the crypts beneath the Nea Church in Jerusalem.

A.D. 1119-1126   The Knights Templar establish their headquarters on the Temple Mount adjacent to the Dome of the Rock and are suspected to have tunneled beneath the *'Even Shetiyyah* in search of the Holy Grail, which Graham Hancock, *The Sign and the Seal* (1992), has argued is identified with the Ark.

A.D. 1204   Any Temple vessels stored in the treasury of Constantinople are thought to be lost or destroyed when the town is sacked in the course of the Fourth Crusade.

Modern-Day Events

1867   Charles Warren, under the auspices of the Palestine Exploration Fund, conducts explorations and excavations on and under the Temple Mount. While his goal was not to recover Temple treasure, his excavation records are an important source of information for present-day researchers. Later, in 1981, Rabbis Goren and Getz rediscover Warren's Gate and use it as an access point to excavate for the Ark.

1906   Finnish mystic Valter Juvelius claims to know the precise location of the Ark in relation to the Temple Mount.

1910-1911   Montagu Parker, based on Juvelius' ideas, heads a British excavation team that sets out to recover the Ark. His clandestine excavations under the Dome of the Rock discover early Bronze-age tombs, but he is interrupted by the Muslim authorities and never completes his search.

1927-1929   Antonia T. Futterer claims he discovered a secret passageway under Mount Nebo in Jordan that supposedly leads to the cave of the hidden Ark. He is never able to raise funds to conduct a full-scale search.

1952   The Copper Scroll is discovered in Cave III above the Wadi Jafet Zaben, north of the Qumran settlement. The Aramaic text described 64 separate hiding places of treasure connected to the Jerusalem Temple. The original copy is now in the Citadel Museum in

Amman, Jordan. This document has
become the "treasure map" of those
searching for Temple treasure and the
Ark in the Dead Sea region.

June 7–July 7, 1967   Rabbi Shlomo Goren presides over the
Temple Mount and sends out a corps of
Israeli army engineers to map the
sacred area. Based on this information,
Rabbi Goren believes he can identify
the site of the Holy of Holies, under
which he believes lies the Ark in a
subterranean chamber.

1968   Vendyl Jones begins his search for the
ashes of the red heifer and the lost Ark
at the Wadi Jafet Zaben. He also
believes he has located the "Cave of
the Column" supposedly indicated in
the Copper Scroll. Accompanied
initially by archaeologist Dr. Pesach
Bar-Adon, and encouraged by Rabbi
Shlomo Goren, he claims that his finds
will contribute to the future rebuilding
of the Temple.

1977   Larry Blaser secures an excavation
permit from the Israeli Antiquities
Authority to dig for the Ark within a
sealed cave located in the cliffs of Ein-
Gedi, which overlook the Dead Sea.
The cave proves to be a naturally
sealed structure, ending the possibility
of a manmade object being contained
within.

1979   Ron Wyatt receives a "revelation" that
the Protestant site of Calvary (next to
the present Arab bus station) is

Jeremiah's Grotto, in which he believes the Ark is hidden. Excavation of the site begins.

June 1981   Paramount Pictures releases the fantasy film *Raiders of the Lost Ark* in movie theaters around the world. Overnight, a new public interest in the search for the Ark is generated.

July 1981–1982   Rabbis Shlomo Goren and Yehuda Getz rediscover the Warren Gate entrance and begin a highly secretive year-and-a-half excavation under the Temple Mount in the direction of the Holy of Holies, based on Rabbi Goren's 1967 survey. While the excavation was discovered and stopped by the Muslim and Israeli authorities, the rabbis believe they know exactly where the Ark lies buried beneath the Mount.

October 31, 1981   Tom Crotser claims to have discovered the Ark under Mount Pisgah, in Jordan, using the map originally made by A.T. Futterer. Although he shows a slide of a metal object, professional analysis of the object contends that it is of modern origin.

January 6, 1982   Ron Wyatt claims to have discovered the Ark within a stone case, along with the table of showbread, inside a cavern in Jerusalem at a site identified by General Gordon as Mount Calvary.

1988   The Temple Institute, founded by Rabbi Yisrael Ariel, opens in the Jewish Quarter of Jerusalem's Old City. One of its purposes is to restore the vessels of the Temple in preparation for the rebuilding of the Third Temple. Some of the completed or projected items include the Temple menorah, the table of showbread, the altar of incense, the silver trumpets, the breastplate and golden crown of the high priest, and the stone vessels for the red heifer purification process. The institute says there is no need to make another Ark, since the original is only meters away under the Temple Mount.

1992   Journalist Graham Hancock publishes a large volume on the search for the Ark, advancing the theory that it is hidden in the lowest level of the Church of Saint Mary of Zion in Axum, Ethiopia.

January 1992   Professors Zvi ben-Avraham and Uri Basson of Tel-Aviv University's Department of Geophysics and Planetary Sciences release a report of their geophysical investigation of the Qumran plateau using ground-penetrating radar and seismic-reflection profiles. A separate report by Dr. Gary Collett and Aubrey Richardson claims that this site is the Wadi Ha-Kippah of the Copper Scroll and that their research reveals the presence of possible Temple treasure.

March 15, 1992   Dr. Randall Price makes public the excavation and claims of Rabbis Shlomo Goren and Yehuda Getz on the nationally aired CBS TV special "Ancient Secrets of the Bible."

April 1992   Vendyl Jones reasserts his claim that he is on the trail of the Ark as he discovers 900 pounds of a reddish substance he identifies as the Temple incense. An earlier discovery near his site, a juglet of "anointing oil," is claimed by Jones to connect his cave with the Copper Scroll's Temple treasure.

Spring 1993   The Temple Institute in Jerusalem displays Israeli craftsman Chaim Odem's model of the Ark in its newly refurbished visitor's center. Lecturers for the Institute explain to audiences that according to traditional Jewish sources, the Ark is under the Temple Mount and has been located by Rabbis Goren and Getz.

October 1993   Rabbis Yisrael Ariel and Chaim Richman of The Temple Institute publish *The Odyssey of the Third Temple*, a 170-page book with illustrations describing their work of restoring the Temple vessels. The jacket of the book prominently displays their model of the Ark.

December 1993   The Israeli Antiquities Authority, under Dr. Amir Drori, launch "Operation Scroll," a massive search and retrieval operation in caves along the Dead Sea. They employ over 200 archaeologists and even use backhoes to locate artifacts in light of the September 13, 1993, signing of the Declaration of Principles between the PLO and Israel. Excavations at Dr. Collett's site confirm the presence of stone-lined storage bins. The full results of these excavations have not yet been revealed.

January 1994

Dr. Gershon Salomon, founder and director of the Temple Mount and Land of Israel Faithful, announces on national television (in the United States) that he believes the Third Temple and the Ark of the Covenant will be seen by the world within his lifetime.

April 1994

National Geographic Explorer series airs program entitled "The Search for the Lost Ark." Sites in Ethiopia and Qumran are featured.

Spring-summer 1994

Vendyl Jones renews his excavations at the Wadi Jaffet Zaben, claiming that "new discoveries" will be uncovered.

Summer 1994

Dr. Gary Collett and Aubrey Richardson, in conjunction with archaeologist Dr. James Strange, pursue the excavation of the Qumran plateau in hopes of locating anomalies that may have Temple treasures within them.

Glossary

Abomination of Desolation (Hebrew, *hashiqutz meshomem*, "the abomination that makes desolate"): The expression used to describe the act of setting up an idolatrous image in the Holy Place, thus defiling or "making desolate" the Temple, and ending the offering of all sacrifices. This was done in the past by Antiochus Epiphanes (Daniel 11:31), whose act reflects the future defilement by the Antichrist (Daniel 9:27). Both Daniel and Jesus indicated that this future act would signal the start of the Great Tribulation (Daniel 12:11; Matthew 24:15; Mark 13:14).

'Acharit ha-yamim (Hebrew, "end of the days"): The Hebrew term used to designate that period of the end time described by the biblical prophets. It includes *Yom YHWH* ("the day of the Lord") in which God's judgment falls upon Israel's adversaries, as well as *Yemot ha-Mashiach* ("the days of Messiah"), the period preceding the judgment. It is followed by *'olam ha-ba* ("the world to come"), the eschatological future world.

Aliyah (Hebrew, "to go up, ascend"): The Jewish expression used for the act of returning or making immigration to the land of Israel.

Amillennialism (Latin, "no millennium"): The theological view that Christ and His saints will *not* reign for a thousand years in connection with His final return.

Anti-Semitism: The term applied to the hostile attitude toward Jews, individually and collectively. The consequences of this viewpoint have ranged from restrictive laws against Jews and the social isolation of Jewish groups to pogroms and attempted genocide in the Nazi Holocaust. Christian anti-Semitism has historically resulted from an adoption of *replacement theology*.

Apocalyptic Literature (Greek, *apocalypsis*, "unveiling"): Prophetic writings concerning the end of the world and/or God's final judgment, both in and outside the canon of Scripture. In particular it has reference to that body of Jewish prophetic writing that developed between the sixth century B.C. and the first century A.D.

Aqsa or *Aksa* (Arabic, "the farther"): Term used for the farther mosque in the Koran (Surah 17). It probably originally indicated a mosque located in the northern corner of Mecca, but the tradition was later moved to Jerusalem, hence the Al Aqsa Mosque.

'Aron (Hebrew, "box, chest"): The distinctive term used for the lower portion of the Ark, that is, the gold-covered wooden container holding the sacred items. It is also used in compound form for the Ark with its lid, for example, *'Aron Ha-Brit* ("Ark of the Covenant").

Ashkenazi (Yiddish: pl. *Ashkenazim*): Those Jews and their descendants who came from Germany or parts of Europe as contrasted with *Sephardi[m]* (Jews from Spain or Portugal).

Atara L'yoshna (Hebrew, "crown to its original [form]"): The name of an activist organization in the Temple movement that seeks to restore Jewish life to its former state, that is, biblical Judaism with complete Jewish sovereignty and a rebuilt Temple. It is involved primarily with Jewish settlement in the Muslim Quarter.

Ateret Cohanim (Hebrew, "crown of the priests"): The name of an activist organization in the Temple movement that maintains a yeshiva for the training of priests for future Temple service. It is affiliated with Atara L'yoshna in settlement activities.

Azarah (Hebrew, "enclosure"): The term for the sacred precinct of the Jerusalem Temple or its outer court.

Ba'al (Hebrew, "lord"): Generally, a Canaanite deity, but specifically the epithet of the fertility and storm god. The *Ba'al* cult was an idolatrous influence during the biblical period that corrupted Israel and brought about the destruction of the First Temple.

Basilica (Latin, "portico, colonnaded building"): A long rectangular building with two rows of pillars or columns dividing it into a central nave and two aisles. Common to Roman administrative architecture, its design influenced both that of the royal portico on the Temple Mount and that of synagogues and churches of the period.

Byzantine: The period of Roman Christian rule in Jerusalem (A.D. 313-638) during which Christianity was made the official religion of the Roman Empire, and the center of imperial power was moved to Byzantium. The Byzantine period is divided into the early period (313-491), the great Christian architectural period, and the late period (491-638), which saw a temporary conquest by the Persians, and ended with the Islamic invasion under Caliph Omar Ibn el-Khattab.

Byzantium (*see* Constantinople).

Caliph (Arabic, "succeed"): The title of an official successor to Mohammed. Wherever a caliph prayed a mosque had to be built by his followers.

Chabad: The initials of the three Hebrew words *chokmah* ("wisdom"), *binah* ("understanding"), *da'at* ("knowledge"), which are used as the name of the Hasidic movement founded in White Russia by Shneur Zalman of Lyady. Chabad Lubavitch is a specific organization of Chabad, headquartered in Brooklyn, New York, whose spiritual leader is Rabbi Menachem M. Schneerson.

Chronology (Greek, "study of time"): A study of the time sequence of important events. A biblical chronology is an attempt to order the various dates preserved in Scripture to arrive at a complete list of events without gaps in time.

Cohen (Hebrew, "priest," pl. *cohanim*): An Israelite descendant of the family of Aaron, which was designated as a priestly line (Exodus 28:1, 41). Because this family belonged to the tribe of Levi, they are referred to as the Levitical priesthood. Their functions were ritualistic in nature and revolved around service in the Temple during Temple times.

Constantinople: The capital of the Byzantine (Christian) Empire, named after its Roman conqueror, Emperor Constantine I (c. A.D. 324), and located on the European shore at the southern end of the narrow straits of the Bosporus, which connect the Black Sea with the Sea of Mamara (or present-day Istanbul, Turkey). Because legend attributes its founding to a Megarian captain by the name of Byzas (c. 667 B.C.), it was later called Byzantium.

Devir (Hebrew, "sanctuary," though derived from word meaning "the back part of a room"): The third division of the Temple, namely, the innermost chamber, the Holy of Holies, where the Ark of the Covenant was housed.

Diaspora (Greek, "dispersion"): The term used to describe the area of Jewish settlement outside the land of Israel. Jews today are said to be either "in the Land" (Israel) or "in the Diaspora" (everywhere else).

Dispensationalism: The view of biblical history that maintains one plan of salvation in which God reveals Himself to man and deals with man in different ways in each successive period of their relationship or economy (dispensation) of time.

Eastern Gate: The gate of Second Temple times that served as the eastern entrance into the Temple. The original name of this gate during that period was the Shushan Gate, which may exist today beneath the present sealed double gate called the Golden Gate or just south of it. The term "golden" was mistakenly applied to this gate because the reference in Acts 3:2 to another inner Temple gate used the Greek word *horaia* ("beautiful"), which was misunderstood as *aurea* ("golden"). It is thought that this Eastern Gate might also be the Double Gate mentioned in the Copper Scroll, in which are hidden the red heifer urn and a scroll describing the red heifer ceremony.

Ephod: The two-piece, sleeveless linen garment of the priests, and especially of the high priest, whose ephod was attached to the body by a woven band and joined at the shoulders by straps (*see* Exodus 28:6-14). Because the two stones (called Urim and Thummim), used for discerning God's will, were located next to it inside the pouch of the breastplate (Exodus 28:30-31), the ephod may have been thought to possess divining powers (*see* Judges 8:27; 17:5; 18:14-20). Some people have erroneously thought it identified with the Ark in some Bible passages.

'Eretz Israel (Hebrew, "Land of Israel"): The Hebrew term used by Jews to designate the biblical Promised Land, the historical homeland of the Jewish people.

Eschatology (Greek, "study of last things"): The study of things relating to the end of the world, the final judgment, and the life and world to come.

es-Sakhra (*see* Sakhra).

'Even Shetiyyah (Hebrew, "Foundation Stone"): The stone, that according to ancient Jewish sources existed within the Holy of Holies in the Temple and upon which the Ark of the Covenant rested in First Temple times. According to tradition this stone is identified with the rock inside the Muslim Dome of the Rock.

Falasha: Ethiopian Jews who claim descent from Israel through Menelik I, an offspring of a supposed liaison between King Solomon and the Queen of Sheba. While their Jewish identity is still disputed by some, the State of Israel has recognized them as "black Jews" and has aided in their immigration to Israel in two operations, Operation Moses and Operation Solomon.

Gemara (Hebrew, "study"): The commentary material included in the Talmud from Jewish tradition, as opposed to material from the Bible or logical reasoning.

Gihon (Hebrew, "gush" or "burst forth"): The spring on the eastern slope of the Ophel that served as the chief water source for Jerusalem in the days during the biblical period.

Gush Emunim (Hebrew, "Bloc of the Faithful"): The movement to foster Jewish settlements in the West Bank in order to continue the national stream of Zionism. Activist by definition, members of this movement have been involved with attempting to blow up the Dome of the Rock and participating in anti-Arab attacks and demonstrations.

Halakah (Hebrew, "walk," pl. *halakot*): The official or lawful way according to which a Jew ought to conduct his life. The Jewish *Halakah* contains various moral laws and ritual prescriptions, based on the Bible, that embrace all the teachings of Judaism. It also refers to those parts of the Talmud which deal with legal matters.

Haram (Arabic, "enclosure"): The present platform upon which the Dome of the Rock is built and which is thought to approximate the original Herodian Temple platform. The full title used by the Muslims is *Haram es-Sharif* ("The Noble Enclosure").

Hasidism (Hebrew, "righteous, pious"): A religious movement founded by Israel ben Eliezer Ba'al Shem Tov in the first half of the eighteenth century. Originally it was a religious revivalist movement of popular mysticism that began in West Germany in the Middle Ages.

Hechal (Hebrew, originally from Sumerian *e-gal,* "great house," and Assyrian *ekallu,* "palace, temple"): The second division of the Temple, namely, the main room or sanctuary.

Hendiadys (Greek, *hen dia duoin* = "*one through two*"): The rhetorical use of two words connected by a conjunction to express the same idea as a single word with a qualifier.

Holocaust (Literally meaning "a burnt offering or sacrifice): The term applied to the attempted genocide of European Jewry in the ovens of the Nazi death camps during the Second World War. More than six million men, women, and children were systematically exterminated in this sacrifice of Jewish lives.

Intafada (Arabic, "uprising, strike"): The Palestinian revolt against Israeli rule in the so-called "occupied territories" that began in 1987 and was abated temporarily after the signing of the Declaration of Principles on September 13, 1993, between Israel and the PLO.

Islam: A monotheistic religion whose only deity is *'Allah* ("God") and whose prophet is Mohammed. It venerates certain Old Testament figures and traditions and accepts some traditions about Jesus, who is considered a lesser prophet. Its primary religious text is the Koran, a set of divine revelations made to Mohammed.

Jebusites: The original Canaanite inhabitants of Jerusalem at the first conquest of the city by Joshua (Joshua 10:23; 12:10) and the second, and complete, conquest of the city by David (2 Samuel 5:6-8; 1 Chronicles 11:4-9). The water shaft entered by David and his men to breach the walls, which was later connected by Solomon and others to reach the upper city by tunnels, was of Jebusite origin.

Jihad (Arabic, "holy war"): The term used in Muslim religious law for the holy war waged against all infidels until the end of time.

Josephus, Flavius: The Roman name of a Jewish historian and military leader known in Hebrew as *Yosef ben Mattiyahu* (Mattathias). His many historical writings, apparently intended for a Roman audience, constitute the best extrabiblical source for the study of Jewish life during the period of the Second Temple.

Kabbalah: The Jewish mystical tradition; *Kabbalist:* A Jewish mystic or student of the Kabbalah.

Kach (Hebrew, "thus"): The name of the Israeli party created by the late Rabbi Meir Kahane, advocating the deportation of all Arabs from the land of Israel after due compensation. Members of the Kach party have attempted to take over the Temple Mount in the past. They were forced to disband in April 1994, and have since gone underground.

Kebra Nagast (lit., "Glory of Kings"): The thirteenth-century A.D. Ethiopian royal chronicles, which gives the etiology of Ethiopian Judaism. Originally compiled in Ethiopia and written in *Ge'ez*, it records the legend of the Queen of Sheba's visit to King Solomon and the return of their son Menelik I to Ethiopia with the Ark of the Covenant.

Knesset (Hebrew from Aramaic, "assembly"): The parliament of the State of Israel.

Knights Templar (full title: the "Poor Knights of Christ and of the Temple of Solomon"): A mystic religious order of European (Crusader) warrior monks headquartered in Jerusalem during the twelfth century A.D., which maintained a strict code of secrecy among its members, engaged in a quest for the Holy Grail, and have been theoretically linked to the search for the Ark in Ethiopia (by Graham Hancock).

Koran (also *Qur'an,* Arabic, "recitation"): The most holy book in Islam, believed by Muslims to be 114 chapters dictated by the archangel Gabriel to the prophet Mohammed at Mecca and Medina.

Kotel (Hebrew, "wall," from *kathal*, "to join together, make into blocks"): The Western or Wailing Wall, popularly called *Ha-Kotel*, "The Wall." This section of wall after the destruction of the

Second Temple was the only remnant of the Temple (a retaining wall) accessible to the Jewish people. It first became accessible to Jews for worship in modern times on June 7, 1967.

Likud (Hebrew, "union, alignment"): The right-wing bloc or political party in the Israeli system of representation. The present representative of Likud is Prime Minister Yitzhaq Shamir.

Lubavitch (lit., "town of love"): The town in White Russia which served as the center of *Habad* Hasidism from 1813 to 1915 and whose name has become synonymous with the movement.

Maimonides (*see also* Rambam): Rabbi Moshe ben Maimon (A.D. 1135-1204). One of the foremost Jewish scholars of the Middle Ages. His *Misheh Torah* is one of the classic texts of Jewish law and his *Guide to the Perplexed* is one of the classics of Jewish philosophy. In the former work, of special interest are his treatises: "The Laws of the King Messiah" and "The Laws of the Temple."

Mashiah (Hebrew, "anointed [one]"): Equivalent to the Greek term *Christos* from which is derived the English "Christ." In traditional orthodox Jewish definition this is a human political-military deliverer who is sent by God to usher in the age of redemption for Israel promised by the biblical prophets. In historic orthodox Christian definition the Jewish concept is further developed by God the Son being sent to fulfill this role. Thus, Christians accept a divine Messiah whom they identify with the Jewish man Jesus of Nazareth.

Mekilta: The earliest commentary on the book of Exodus (c. A.D. 120), which is often quoted in the Talmud. It was written by the school of Rabbi Yishmael.

Menorah (Hebrew, "lamp"; pl. *menorot*): A term used for the seven-branched oil lamps, or candelabrum, used in both the Tabernacle and the Temple.

Messianic Age (or messianic era): The era of redemption, that period that spans the beginning of redemption for the Jewish people in the land of Israel (interpreted by some as 1948) through the coming and rule of King Messiah at the end of the 6,000 years of history to bring a reign of universal peace, moral justice, and spiritual life.

Messianic Jews: Orthodox Jews who believe the messianic times are imminent. Most messianic Jews in Israel are actively preparing for the Messiah's coming through the adoption of more biblical lifestyles and in research and activism toward rebuilding the Temple. In the United States, the term is used of Jewish Christians, or Jews who believe Jesus is the Messiah.

Middot (Hebrew, "measurements"): A tractate of the Jewish Mishnah that deals specifically with the measurements of the Temple.

Midrash (Hebrew, "interpretation"): A written collection of rabbinical interpretation of the Bible compiled by the *Soferim* ("scribes") in the fourth century A.D. The midrashic method of interpreting Scripture was employed to clarify legal points or to bring out lessons by the use of stories.

Mishnah (Hebrew, "learning, repetition"): The earliest written collection of Jewish oral law (that is, Jewish religious and legal teachings handed down orally). It was compiled about A.D. 200 by Rabbi Judah ha-Nasi ("the Prince"). It comprises the first part of the Talmud and appears in the form of homiletical discourses by the Jewish sages.

Mitzvah (Hebrew, "commandment," pl. *mitzvot*): The term for a religious and moral obligation, whether one of the 613 biblical commandments or any other traditional ordinance, observance, teaching, or statute.

Mohammed (from Arabic *hmd*, "to praise," also *Muhammed*): The founder and prophet of Islam, who was born in A.D. 570 and died at Medina in A.D. 632.

Moshiach (Ashkenazi-accented Hebrew spelling of Messiah, literally "anointed one"): The Messiah, in contemporary orthodox Judaism, is envisioned as a human political and military leader who will usher in the Day of Redemption for the Jewish people. Christians are more familiar with the term through the Greek *Christos*, translated "Christ."

Moslem (*see* Muslim).

Muslim (from Arabic *'aslama*, "to submit, convert to Islam"): A believer or follower of Islam.

'Ophel (Hebrew, "hill, mound"): The southeastern spur north of the City of David that is the oldest known part of Jerusalem. It is the section of Jebusite territory captured by King David and was the site of the Tabernacle during his days.

Orthodox (Greek, "straight"): Those holding to religious views that have been traditionally accepted and taught. Orthodox Jews are those accepting the Tanakh (Old Testament) as divine revelation, and the Talmud as divine direction for the interpretation of the Tanakh, and are observant (practitioners) of Jewish law. There are many different divisions within orthodox Judaism today.

Palestine: A pejorative term for the country west of the Jordan River, first coined by the Greeks and Romans after the word *Philistine*, the enemies of Israel who inhabited the Mediterranean coastal plain. The Bible refers to the same territory as *Canaan*, after its pre-Israelite inhabitants, though Jews have always called it *'Eretz Yisrael* ("Land of Israel").

Pesach (Hebrew, "Passover"): The Hebrew term for the festival of Passover, which commemorates the Israelite exodus from Egypt (Exodus 12:1-36) and was celebrated at the last great reform of the Second Temple, during which the Ark was reinstalled (2 Chronicles 35:1-3). Prophetically, it looks toward the final exodus of God's people under Messiah (*see* 1 Corinthians 5:7; Revelation 15:3-4; cf. Exodus 15).

Postmillennialism (Latin, "after millennium"): The theological view that Christ and/or His saints will reign on the earth *before* His final return.

Premillennialism (Latin, "before millennium"): The theological view that Christ and His saints will reign on the earth for a thousand years *after* His final return.

Pseudepigrapha (Greek, "false writings"): A collection of non-canonical works of mystical Jewish-Hellenistic origin, generally composed after the sixth century B.C. These writings were influenced by Persian cosmology (view of the universe) and are highly apocalyptic in nature.

Qetz (Hebrew, "end"): A time designation which, in the prophets, and especially as interpreted by the later rabbis, is the auspicious or determined time for the Messiah to bring an end to the Jewish exile or Diaspora.

Quds (Arabic, "holy"): Arabic term used for both Jerusalem and the Temple Mount area (the sanctuary), as in *Al Quds*, "the Holy City."

Rabbi (Hebrew, "master"): Derived from the Hebrew verb *rabab*, "to be great," the term is an honorable title for an ordained Jewish teacher of the Law or a leader of a Jewish community. Roughly equivalent to Christian "pastor" or "bishop."

Rambam: Acronym for *R*abbi *M*oshe *b*en *M*aimon (A.D. 1135-1204), or Maimonides. One of Judaism's leading Torah authorities and philosophers who wrote a commentary on the Mishnah in Arabic known as the *Book of Illumination*.

Rashi: Acronym for *R*abbi *Sh*lomo (ben Yitzkak) *Y*archi (A.D. 1040-1105), the medieval author of the most important commentary on the Bible and Talmud. His commentary on the Torah was the first known Hebrew book to be printed.

Replacement Theology: A theological view among both Catholics and Protestants that the Jews have been rejected and replaced by "the true Israel," the church. Those who espouse this view disavow any distinct ethnic future for the Jewish people in connection with the biblical covenants, believing that their only spiritual destiny is either to perish or become a part of the Christian church.

Rosh Hashanah (Hebrew, "head of the year"): The Jewish festival of the civil New Year celebrated on the first and second days of the month Tishri (equivalent to September/October on the Julian [Christian] calendar).

Sakhra (Arabic, "rock"): Arabic term for the sacred rock within the Islamic shrine on the Temple Mount, hence: *Qubbet es-Sakhra*, "Dome of the Rock."

Sanhedrin: The assembly of ordained Jewish scholars that functioned both as a supreme court and as a legislature in Israel before A.D. 70. With the destruction of the Temple and the end of Jewish independence, the Sanhedrin ceased to function.

Sheikh (Arabic, "elder, chief"): A Muslim high priest, ruler, or head of an Arab tribe or family.

Shekinah (Hebrew, "dwelling, resting"): A term used for the divine presence of God that was manifested by "dwelling" between the wings of the cherubim above the Ark (*see* 1 Chronicles 13:6). It represented the immanence of God with the Israelites, first in the Tabernacle and later in the First Temple.

Shiloah (Hebrew, "the one sent"): Hebrew term for the Greek (New Testament) *Siloam*, the pool located at the end of the water tunnel of King Hezekiah that collected water from the Gihon Spring on the eastern slope of the *'Ophel*. During the ancient *Hoshana Rabba* water was drawn from this source for the libation poured on the altar in the Temple.

Six-Day War: The war that occurred June 5-10, 1967, when Israel reacted to Arab threats and blockade by defeating the Egyptian, Jordanian, and Syrian forces. The Sinai Peninsula, the West Bank, and the Golan Heights fell to Israel in this conflict. The Sinai was returned to Egypt in 1979 as a condition of the Camp David Peace Treaty. For Jerusalem the war was a three-day conflict, June 5-7, that resulted in the liberation of East Jerusalem and the Temple Mount from Jordan.

Soreg (Hebrew, "partition"): The partition dividing the inner court of the Jews from the outer court of the Gentiles in the Second Temple precinct. A sign was placed on this partition warning Gentiles not to enter on pain of death.

Stoa (Greek, "porch"): A covered colonnade or portico in Greek and Roman architecture, like the portico of Solomon (John 10:23; Acts 3:11; 5:12), which surrounded the southern end of the Temple complex and included the Court of the Gentiles. After the destruction of the Temple, pillars from this structure were used in Byzantine, and later Arab, buildings.

Sukkot (Hebrew, "booths"): The Hebrew term for the one-week Feast of Tabernacles; the last of the three pilgrim festivals that begins on the fifteenth of Tishri (approximately September/ October on the Julian [Christian] calendar). The word *sukkot* is the plural of *sukkah*, a booth or tabernacle that the Israelites dwelt in during their time of wandering in the wilderness (Leviticus 23:42).

Synagogue (Greek, "gathering together"): An institution that was developed by Jews in the Diaspora, after the destruction of the First Temple, for worship and study of the Bible.

Tabot (pl. *tabatot*): An Amharic word derived from the Hebrew *tebah* (a "container," usually used of a boat). A ritual object used in Ethiopian orthodox Christianity and housed within every orthodox church. According to one theory, the Tabota Zion in the Church of Saint Mary of Zion in Axum is the Ark of the Covenant.

Talmud (Hebrew, "teaching"): The entire corpus of Jewish oral law including the Mishnah together with a written compendium of discussions and commentary on the Mishnah called *Gemara*. Its teachings and rulings span a period between Ezra in the Old Testament (c. 450 B.C.) and the middle of the Roman period (c. A.D. 550). Because it includes rulings made by generations of scholars and jurists in many academies in both Palestine and Babylon it exists in two versions: the *Jerusalem* (discussions in the Jerusalem academies) and the *Babylonian* (discussions in the Babylonian academies).

Tanakh or *Tanach*: Term used for the Jewish Bible made up of the Hebrew initials for the words *T*orah ("law"), *N*eveim ("prophets"), *K*etubim ("writings"), the three divisions of the Old Testament.

Targum (Hebrew, "translation"): The authorized translation of the Torah by the proselyte Onkelos (c. A.D. 90). In Talmudic times, it was read along with the Torah, so that the congregation could understand what was being read (cf. Nehemiah 8:7-8). In many cases, the Targum renders the text homiletically rather than literally.

Tel (Hebrew, "mound, hill"; Arabic *tell*): A technical term in archaeology referring to an artificial elevation of earth that consists of ancient occupational layers buried within.

Tisha B'Av (Hebrew, "ninth of Av"): A fast day commemorating the destruction of the First and Second Temples that occurs on the ninth day of Av, the first month of the Jewish religious year, approximating July/August on the Julian (Christian) calendar.

Topography (Greek, "study of place"): The description of a particular place, including its physical structures and elevation.

Torah (Hebrew, "law"): Used either of the first five books of the Old Testament (the Pentateuch), or of the entire body of traditional Jewish teaching and literature.

Torat Moshe (Hebrew, "Law of Moses"): The original autograph of the first five books of the Tanakh (Old Testament) called the Torah (Hebrew) or Pentateuch (Greek), written by Moses and deposited either in or beside the Ark (Deuteronomy 31:24-26).

Tosefta (Hebrew, "additions"): Additions to the Mishnah by Rabbi Chiyya and Rabbi Oshia (c. A.D. 230). These additions are often cited by the Talmud and published as a supplement to it with most editions.

Tribulation: That period of time, according to the premillennial interpretation of prophecy, which follows the rapture of the church. Lasting for seven years, the first three-and-one-half years are a time of peace that witness the rise of Antichrist and the rebuilding of the Jewish Temple. The last three-and-one-half years are a time of divine judgment known in the Old Testament as "the time of Jacob's trouble." At the end of this period, climaxed by the battle of Armageddon, Christ returns to rescue Israel and set up His millennial kingdom.

Tsuvah (Hebrew, "turning"): The act or condition of spiritual repentance, that is, a turning to God from self, sin, or idols. Prophetically, the term refers to the spiritual regeneration of the Jewish remnant (Isaiah 59:20-21; Romans 11:26-27) at the end of the Tribulation period with the coming of the Messiah (Zechariah 12:10–13:2).

Typology (Greek, *tupos*, "type"): The study of the various types in the Bible that foreshadowed later, more developed revelations of characters or figures (the antitypes), whether positive or negative. A positive example is David as a type of Christ (Psalm 22:1 and Matthew 27:46). A negative example is Antiochus as a type of Antichrist (Daniel 11:21-35 and 36-45).

Ulam (Hebrew, from Akkadian *ellamu*, "front [porch]"): The first division of the Temple, namely, the forecourt or main entrance porch.

Wakf (also *Waqf*): The Supreme Muslim Council, which maintains religious jurisdiction over Islamic holy places, and in particular the Temple Mount.

Yeshiva (Hebrew, "sitting"): A Jewish traditional academy, or school, devoted primarily to the advanced study of the Talmud and rabbinic literature; roughly equivalent to a Christian seminary.

Yom Kippur (Hebrew, "Day of Atonement"): The most solemn day of the Jewish year, celebrated on the ninth day of Tishri (September/October on the Julian [Christian] calendar). Considered the day of judgment and reckoning, it is a time when Jews individually and as a nation are cleansed of sin and granted atonement. It was on this day alone that the high priest was permitted to enter the Holy of Holies in the Temple.

Zion (Hebrew meaning disputed): Originally the hill area north of Jerusalem, the *'Ophel*, where the Tabernacle resided. Through poetic usage it became a synonym for the city of Jerusalem and Israel itself, and spiritually as the eschatological ideal of God's chosen place on earth.

Notes

Preface

1. *The Baptist Standard* (Southern Baptist Convention), September 22, 1993, p. 3. In this article, however, two Southern Baptist theologians—Dr. Paige Patterson, president of Southeastern Seminary in Wake Forest, North Carolina, and James DeLoach, former senior associate pastor at Second Baptist, Houston, Texas—were highlighted as defending the position of prophetic significance.
2. *See* Ezekiel 37:15-22, which has seen fulfillment by the modern return of Jews to the Promised Land; Ezekiel 37:23-28 awaits fulfillment with the future return of the Davidic Messiah (verses 24-25), who will rule in the promised millennial Temple (verse 28).
3. Leith Anderson, "The Church at History's Hinge," *Bibliotheca Sacra* 151 (January-March 1994): 3.
4. Ibid.

Chapter 1—Sign of the End Times

1. The Jeremiah-Baruch traditions are complex yet very similar. However, rather than arguing for a dependence of one upon the other, it appears that both go back to an earlier common source. *See* George W.E. Nickelsburg, Jr., "Narrative Traditions in the Paralipomena of Jeremiah and 2 Baruch," *Catholic Biblical Quarterly* 35 (1973): 65.
2. For this argument, *see* B.Z. Watcholder, "The Letter from Judah Maccabee to Aristobulus: Is 2 Maccabees 1:10b–2:18 Authentic?" *Hebrew Union College Annual* 49 (1978): 89-133.
3. *See also* the Tannaitic idea of all things remaining "undecided" until Elijah comes (T'duyyot 8:7; Menahot 45a).
4. For a thorough discussion of the Samaritan version, *see* Marilyn F. Collins, "The Hidden Vessels in Samaritan Traditions," *Journal for the Study of Judaism* 3 (1972): 97-116.
5. In the Jewish Midrash (commentary) on this text (Bereshit Rabbah 81:4 on Genesis 35:4), the story is told of a religious quarrel between a Jewish rabbi and a Samaritan. In the story the rabbi brings up this verse and claims that the only reason the Samaritan worships on Mount Gerizim is because he is eager to get to the idols hidden beneath this site.
6. In the Dead Sea Scrolls (4Q Testimonia, 4Q 158, and 1QS IX, 11), a prophet like Moses also appears in a messianic function in the last days.
7. Note the association of the captured vessels to the fall of Jerusalem made by the use of the word *then*.
8. Questions and Answers on Exodus 2.53 (which exists only in an Armenian version).
9. For complete details on this subject see my book *The Desecration and Restoration of the Temple as an Eschatological Motif in the Old Testament, Jewish Apocalyptic Literature, and the New Testament* (Ann Arbor, MI: UMI Publications, 1994).
10. For details concerning these vessels, *see* Rabbis Yisrael Ariel and Chaim Richman, *The Odyssey of the Third Temple* (Jerusalem: 1993).

Chapter 2—The Ark Affair

1. Interview with Gershon Salomon, TMF office, January 23, 1994.
2. Rabbi Leibel Reznick, *The Holy Temple Revisited* (New Jersey: Jason Aronson, Inc., 1990), pp. 146-147.
3. Ibid.

Chapter 3—God in a Box

1. Should you want a more precise measurement based on a standard cubit, the dimensions were: 3'9" x 2'3" x 2'3". Or if the cubit was only five handbreadths (15 inches): 3'1.5" x 1'10.5" x 1'10.5". According to Rabbi Getz, who made a measurement of the inner gates within the Warren Gate, a cubit equals 57.8 centimeters. If this later cubit used for the Second Temple was the same as that used for the Ark, then the measurements would be 3'7" x 2'2" x 2'2".
2. It is a cognate with Akkadian aranu, which also means "box" or "chest." The Hebrew word was used in reference to the Temple money chest (2 Kings 12:9; 2 Chronicles 24:8-11).
3. The term was also used for the ark of papyrus that carried Moses as an infant. The word means "box" or "container," but in these cases the specific connotation is "vessel."
4. This "ark" of Tutankhamen is about 32 inches long and has transport poles that slide through brass rings underneath the chest. It is on display at the Cairo Museum, Cairo, Egypt.
5. However, this would not have applied to the cherubim, since Egyptian sphinxes were religious symbols.
6. Jerusalem Talmud, tractate Shekalim 6:1. Other sources say that this layer was only as thick as a gold dinar coin (Eruvin 19a; Mikdash Aharon; Kreiti u'Fleiti, Yoreh De'ah 43). Others say it was either a handbreadth or three inches, *Yoma* 72b; Rabbi Chananel; Abarbanel (Maaseh Choshev 8:2); one-half handbreadth (1.5 inches), or a fingerbreadth (.75 inches): Baba Bathra 14a; Bareitha Melekheth HaMishkan 6. While three inches would require far too much gold for the amount actually employed, the amount must have been sufficient to ensure the preservation of the Ark with the passage of time.
7. *See Yoma* 72b; Rashi; Ralbag.
8. Flavius Josephus, *Antiquities of the Jews* 8:3, 3.
9. However, *Yoma* 54a records that the Second Temple did contain pictorial reproductions of the cherubim. If this were so, it is difficult to understand how Josephus could not know of this detail when he includes so many other details—even from the Holy of Holies itself.
10. From Rabbeinu Bachya's statement based on Rambam.
11. The singular *cherub* is rarely used, since one feature noted about these creatures is that they never appear alone (hence the usual plural reference *cherubim*).
12. *See* 1 Kings 6:23-28; 1 Chronicles 28:18; 2 Chronicles 3:10-13; 5:7.
13. Nevertheless, the motion of the cherubim is recalled in the Chronicler's use of the term "chariot" to describe the Ark (1 Chronicles 28:18). This term has in view the throne of God (as in Ezekiel 1), which, due to its ability to move rapidly, is not limited by location or time.
14. *See* Menahem Haran, "The Ark and the Cherubim," *Israel Exploration Journal* 9:1 (1959): 36, and Rabbi Dov Shalom Steinberg, *The Mishkan and the Holy Garments*, translated by R. Moshe Miller (Jerusalem: Torah Chaim Institute, 1992), p. 17.
15. For a discussion of these evidences, *see* Roland de Vaux, *Les chrubins et l'arche d'alliance, les sphinx gardiens et les trnes divins dans l'Ancien Orient*, Mlanges de

l'Universit Saint-Joseph 37 (1960-1961): 91-124; and in English, his *Ancient Israel* 1:298-301.

16. For an example of this type, *see* the illustration of King Hiram of Byblus seated on his cherub-throne (tenth century B.C.) in W.F. Albright, "What Were the Cherubim?" *The Biblical Archaeologist Reader* 1 (Scholars Press, 1975), pp. 95-97.

17. Rabbi Saadia Gaon, as cited in Ibn Ezra, Perush HaKitzur.

18. The Babylonian Talmud, *Yoma* 52b, adds the following items: a vial of anointing oil and the chest in which the Philistines sent a gift to the God of Israel (probably the golden models of the tumors and mice, which were connected with the Philistine plagues). However, the accounts of the Ark's contents in Deuteronomy 10:5 and especially 1 Kings 8:9 explicitly state that at this time only the tablets of the Law were present.

19. The Old Testament, Josephus, and Philo are all unanimous in their verdict that the only items in the Ark were the tablets. The other two standard items—the jar of manna and Aaron's rod—were said to have been kept in front of the Ark (Exodus 16:33-34; Numbers 17:10; 1 Kings 8:9; 2 Chronicles 5:10; *see* Philo, De Vita Mosis 2.97; Josephus, *Antiquities* 3.6.5 ¶138; 8.4.1 ¶104.

20. Interview with Rabbi Shlomo Goren, Tel-Aviv, January 25, 1994.

21. *See* Alan R. Millard, "Re-Creating the Tablets of the Law," *Bible Review* 10:1 (February 1994): 49-53.

22. *See* Baba Batra 14a for this debate.

23. That Israel adopted practices identical with other pagan cultures is no problem to the uniqueness of God's special revelation to them as the chosen people. Some explain this by showing the reasonableness of God to accommodate His people to local customs, but with a distinct theological meaning that magnified the God of Israel by contrast. I am of the opinion that the "cultic" (ritual) system was revealed to man from the Garden of Eden onward, and so was a part of the practice of all the separate cultures that developed after the division of the nations at Babel. Thus, even pagan cultures retained a trace of the original divine structure, though perverted and altered with the intrusion of false deities. God's purpose for Israel is to return to the original pure worship introduced in Eden, and therefore His commands concerning the establishment of the sanctuary are in accordance with this original design.

24. Henry Soltau, *The Holy Vessels and Furniture of the Tabernacle* (Grand Rapids: Kregel Publishing Co., 1971), p. 28.

25. *The International Standard Bible Encyclopedia* (Revised), s.v. "Ark of the Covenant," by W. Lotz, M.G. Kyle, and C.E. Armerding, 1:294.

26. *See Interpreter's Dictionary of the Bible*, s.v. "Ark of the Covenant," by G. Henton Davies 1 (1962): 223, which notes that with the study of the symbolism of the Ark we are "in the presence of several parallel ancient ideas which largely overlap."

27. *See* H.G. May, "The Ark—A Miniature Temple," *The American Journal of Semitic Languages and Literatures* 52:4 (July, 1936): 225, 346; *Encyclopedia Judaica*, s.v. "Divination (in the Bible)," by Shimeon Amir 6:112-114.

28. The tenses of the verbs here are imperfects with *waw* consecutives and do not denote habitual or repeated action, but rather something that occurred at a specific point in time.

Chapter 4—The Hinge of History

1. *Raiders of the Lost Ark* (Paramount Pictures, 1981).

2. The biblical text of 1 Samuel 6:19 gives the number slain as 50,070; however, this is generally conceded by conservative scholars as a copyist's error. The Greek

translation of the Hebrew Old Testament (LXX) reads 70 people, as does the account given by Josephus, the first-century Jewish-Roman historian (*Antiquities of the Jews* 6.1.4).

3. *See* the discussion of this in Terence Fretheim, "The Cultic Use of the Ark of the Covenant in the Monarchial Period" (Ph.D. dissertation, Princeton Theological Seminary, 1967), p. 119.

4. The Ark had wandered through Sinai, Kadesh-Barnea, Shiloh in Ephraim, and Eben-Ezer (where it was captured) to a series of cities at the Benjaminite borders: Gilgal and Jericho (east), Kiriath-jearim and Beth-shemesh (west), Bethel (north), and possibly Mizpah. It had also traveled for seven months through the Philistine cities of Ashdod, Gath, and Ekron, which were located on the coastal plain.

5. I owe this insight to Eduard Nielsen, "Some Reflections on the History of the Ark," *Supplements to Vetus Testamentum* 7 (1959): 68, n. 2. However, Nielsen, following Galling, thought that the reason was because the Lord first dwelt between the cherubim at the Davidic inauguration and Solomonic installation. They believed that before this time the Lord was not attached to the Ark in any permanent manner.

6. This argument was first advanced in full form by Menahem Haran, "The Disappearance of the Ark," *Israel Exploration Journal* 13 (1963): 46-58.

7. Ferdinand Gregorovius, *The Ghetto & the Jews of Rome*, translated by Moses Hadas (New York: Schocken Books, 1966), pp. 19-20. The reference to the Ark in his poem (available in the same volume, p. 15, and translated by Randall Jarrell) reads: "No more from the Arch of Titus,/Can the marble pictures grieve us:/Candlesticks, the Temple's tablets I/But Jehovah's holy emblems/Shine forth after a thousand years."

Chapter 5—What Happened to the Ark?

1. Richard Elliot Friedman, *Who Wrote the Bible?* (London: Jonathan Cape Publishers, 1988), p. 156.

2. "The Disappearance of the Ark," *Israel Exploration Journal* 13 (1963), p. 46. Haran's book *Temples and Temple Service in Ancient Israel* (Oxford: Claredon Press, 1978) is a classic sourcebook in Temple study (although based on an assumption of the Documentary Hypothesis) and contains valuable material about the Ark.

3. Terence E. Fretheim, "The Cultic Use of the Ark of the Covenant in the Monarchial Period" (Ph.D. dissertation, Princeton Theological Seminary, 1967), p. 1.

4. *See* Benjamin Mazar, "The Campaign of Pharaoh Shishak to Palestine," *Supplements to Vetus Testamentum* 4 (1957): 57-66.

5. Menahem Haran, *Temples and Temple Services in Ancient Israel*, p. 285.

Chapter 6—Lost in Legends

1. Tanhuma, Va-Yakhel, 7.

2. Erich Von Daniken, *Chariots of the Gods?* (New York: Bantam Books, 1971), p. 40.

3. Yelammedenu in Yalkut 1, 739; Wayekullu in Likkutim 2. 17a-b.

4. Ibid.; Sifre, Num. 85; Sifre, Zech. 79; 193.

5. Translation from E.A. Wallis Budge, *The Queen of Sheba and Her Only Son Menelik*, based on the "Book of the Glory of Kings" (Oxford: University Press, 1932), p. 29.

6. For details, see Cyril C. Dobson, *The Mystery of the Fate of the Ark of the Covenant* (Haverhill, MA: Anglo-Saxon Federation of America, 1939), pp. 59-96.

7. J.R. Church, *The Ark of the Covenant—We Have Found It* (Oklahoma City: Prophecy Publications, 1993), pp. 13-15.
8. However, J.R. Church abandoned this theory in a later presentation about the location of the Ark. *See* video *What Really Happened to the Ark of the Covenant* (Oklahoma City: Prophecy Publications, 1993).
9. As recorded in the seventh-century Jewish apocalypse *War of the King Messiah.*
10. Meir Ben-Dov, *Jerusalem Man and Stone* (Tel-Aviv: Modan Publishing House, 1990), p. 140.
11. Interview with Dan Bahat in the Western Wall Tunnel, January 21, 1994.
12. *Yoma* 52b; Tosefta Sotah 13:2; Rav; Yer.
13. *See* Shekalim 6:1. Rabbi Hananiah was the last deputy high priest before the destruction of the Second Temple, and lived sometime afterwards. He is regarded by the Talmud as one who could give reliable testimony concerning the Temple practices (*see* Pesahim 14a; Zevahim 103b; Eduyyot 2:1-3).
14. *See* Shoshanim L'David; Yer; Tosefta Sotah 13:2; Rambam, Hil. Beit HaBechirah 4:1; Song of Songs Rabbah 3:3; Tifereth Yisrael; Radak (Kimchi) on 2 Chronicles 35:3; Rav; Yer.
15. *See* Mikra Massores and arguments based on Chullin 24a.
16. As recorded by the Roman historian Tacitus, *Historiae* 5. 9. 1.
17. Aryeh Kaplan, *Jerusalem: The Eye of the Universe* (New York: The National Conference of Synagogue Youth/Union of Orthodox Jewish Congregations of America, 1984), p. 23.

Chapter 7—Do All Arks Go to Heaven?

1. Henry Morris, *The Revelation Record: A Scientific and Devotional Commentary on the Prophetic Book of the End Times* (Wheaton, IL: Tyndale House, 1983), p. 211.
2. From a letter to the editor by the Reverend Spencer Brien, Immanuel Evangelical Lutheran Church, Compton, Illinois, in *Biblical Archaeology Review* (July/August 1983), p. 31.
3. For a listing and discussion of all the relevant texts, *see* Niels-Erik Andreasen, "The Heavenly Sanctuary in the Old Testament," *The Sanctuary and the Atonement*, edited by A.V. Wallenkampf and W. Richard Lesher (Washington, D.C.: 1981), pp. 67-86.
4. For a more detailed discussion of these interpretations, *see* Richard M. Davidson, *Typology in Scripture* (Berrien Springs, MI: 1981), pp. 372-374.
5. *See* 1 Kings 16:10, where the *tabnit* sent by King Ahaz to Urijah the priest is a depiction of the *original altar* seen by the king on a trip to Damascus, which is at the same time a *model* for the duplicate altar to be built and installed in the Jerusalem Temple (that is, the original object that is to be imitated). For further arguments on this view, *see* Victor Hurowitz, "I Have Built for You an Exalted House: Temple Building in the Bible in the Light of Mesopotamian and Northwest Semitic Writings," *Journal for the Study of the Old Testament (Supplement)*, series 115 (Sheffield, England: JSOT Press, 1992), pp. 168-170.
6. Angel Manuel Rodriguez, "Sanctuary Theology in the Book of Exodus," *Andrews University Seminary Studies* 24:2 (Summer 1986): 142. From this understanding of the term, the *tabnit*, as a solid, three-dimensional object, could be either a miniature model or the real archetypal sanctuary.
7. *See* J. Coert Rylaarsdam, "The Book of Exodus," *Interpreter's Bible*, edited by George Buttrick (Nashville, TN: Abingdon Press, 1962) 1:1021. The primary source for the presentation of the ancient Near Eastern parallels to the *tabnit* is Richard Clifford, "The Cosmic Mountain in Canaan and in the Old Testament,"

Harvard Semitic Monographs 4 (Cambridge: Harvard University Press, 1972). *See also* Hurowitz, "I Have Built for You," pp. 169-170, which cites various Babylonian inscriptions that give examples of revelations of models involving cult objects and includes a Hittite text in which a dreamer sees a god and is commanded to make a statue exactly according to what he has seen and dedicate it to the deity.

8. The description in Ezekiel 1 is more of a throne room than a temple; however, in the context, it appears that God has revealed Himself to Ezekiel in His heavenly Temple—as a dramatic contrast—while He pronounces judgment upon the desecration of His earthly Temple (chapters 4–8).

9. David Noel Freedman, "Temple Without Hands," *Temples and High Places in Biblical Times: Proceedings of the Colloquium in Honor of the Centennial of Hebrew Union College—Jewish Institute of Religion* (Jerusalem: The Nelson Glueck School of Biblical Archaeology of Hebrew Union College, 1981), p. 26.

10. Revelation 15:5 combines all the earthly sanctuaries into one as typifying the ideal heavenly model: "After these things I looked, and the temple of the tabernacle of testimony in heaven was opened." From the other mentions of the heavenly Temple in Revelation we learn that it houses an altar (6:9; 8:3, 5; 9:13; 14:18; 16:7), God's throne (16:17), and the Ark (11:19). Some people also believe the veil which separated the Holy Place from the Holy of Holies is present in those texts. The veil depicts an "opening" to the heavenly throne room (or Temple) through which angelic beings or John himself passes immediately into the divine presence (*see* Revelation 4:1-3; 6:14-17; 15:5; 16:1, 17); for example, J. Webb Mealy, "After the Thousand Years: Resurrection and Judgment in Revelation 20," *Journal for the Study of the New Testament (Supplement)*, series 70 (Sheffield, England: JSOT Press, 1993), pp. 143-162, 196-197.

11. Catholic theologians teach this position in conjunction with their concept of the perpetual offering of Christ. Protestant theologians usually hold this position out of a desire to maintain a closer correspondence in analogy with the Old Testament Day of Atonement ritual presented in the book of Hebrews.

Chapter 8—The Great Treasure Hunt Outside Israel

1. Ephraim Isaac, "Is the Ark of the Covenant in Ethiopia?" *Biblical Archaeology Review* 19:4 (July–August 1993), p. 60.

2. Naomi Shepherd, *The Zealous Intruders: The Western Recovery of Palestine* (San Francisco: Harper & Row, 1987), p. 193.

3. Interview with Rabbi Shlomo Goren, Tel-Aviv office, January 24, 1994.

4. "Real Lost Ark May Be Lying with Relics in Museum Cellar," *The San Antonio Star* (August 2, 1981), p. 12. Ms. Love's claim to fame is that she supposedly discovered the head of Aphrodite among such museum collections.

5. One source for these accounts, along with the work of Silberman listed below, is *The Zealous Intruders* by Hebrew University instructor Naomi Shepherd.

6. Interview with Dan Bahat, Western Wall Tunnels, January 20, 1994.

7. Cyril C. Dobson, *The Mystery of the Fate of the Ark of the Covenant* (Haverhill, MA: Anglo-Saxon Federation of America, 1939), p. 27.

8. Neil Asher Silberman, *Digging for God and Country: Exploration, Archaeology and the Secret Struggle for the Holy Land, 1799-1917* (New York: Knopf Publishing Co., 1982), pp. 180-188; *see also* Richard Halliburton, *Complete Book of Marvels* (Indianapolis, IN: The Babbs-Merrill Co., Inc., 1960), pp. 422-424.

9. Interview with Tom Crotser by Dr. Anis Shorrosh as reported in his book, *The Exciting Discovery of the Ark of the Covenant* (Winona, MN: Justin Books, 1984), p. 27.

10. Access to this information was provided to Crotser by a former student of Futterer, the Reverend Clinton Locy, who had been made custodian of his private papers.
11. For details of Futterer's expedition, see the author's privately printed report published under the title *Palestine Speaks* (Los Angeles, 1931), pp. 535-545.
12. *Biblical Archaeology Review* (May-June 1983), p. 67 (note); cf. A.F. Futterer, *Search Is on for Lost Ark of the Covenant* (published by the author, 1927).
13. The only official permission they received was from the Jordanian military commander and the director of the Terra Santa Monastery located on top of Mount Nebo. They were requested to limit their activity to picture-taking.
14. "Tom Crotser Has Found the Ark of the Covenant—Or Has He?" *Biblical Archaeology Review* (May-June 1983), p. 69. Dr. Horn also mentioned that he saw what appeared to be modern-looking nails protruding from the corners of the box. Others who have examined the photo (as well as several of the poorer-quality pictures) believe that what appear to be nails are actually distortions caused by the camera flash.
15. As cited by staff writer Joyce Turner in her article "Religious Group Says It Located Ark of Covenant," *Longview Morning Journal* (July 11, 1982) section H.
16. Tom Crotser, *The Ark of the Covenant* (Winfield, KS: Institute for Restoring Ancient History International, 1983).
17. Anis A. Shorrosh, *The Exciting Discovery of the Ark.*
18. Conversation with Anis Shorrosh in Philadelphia, October 3, 1992.
19. Crotser's photograph of Noah's Ark, a copy of which I still possess, was presented as part of the evidence for the discovery of Noah's Ark in a film and book for Sun International Pictures, entitled *The Search for Noah's Ark* (written by David Balsiger).
20. Turner, "Religious Group Located Ark." Crotser's claim that the Vatican has complete knowledge of the Ark's presence at this location is also implied by his reference to a plaque inside the monastery chapel, which apparently stated that the Ark of the Covenant was buried there (that is, on Mount Nebo). However, this statement was based on Catholic scripture (the apocryphal book of Maccabees, which records the Ark tradition) and not some hidden agenda to guard the Ark from the outside world.
21. Shorrosh, p. 29. Originally quoted in *The Wichita Eagle-Beacon* and cited in *Longview Morning Journal* article, July 11, 1982.
22. Ibid.
23. Ephraim Isaac, "Is the Ark of the Covenant in Ethiopia?" *Biblical Archaeology Review* 19:4 (July-August 1993): 60-63.
24. Ibid., p. 61.
25. *See* Arthur Bloomfield, *Where Is the Ark of the Covenant and What Is Its Role in Bible Prophecy?* (Minneapolis: Dimension Books, 1976); Grant Jeffrey, *Armageddon: Appointment with Destiny* (New York: Bantam Books, 1989) and *Heaven* (New York: Bantam Books, 1990).
26. This includes his alternate tradition that places the Ethiopian Jewish entrance into Ethiopia around the time of Manasseh. It says that those Ethiopians with Menelik I first settled in Egypt and later built the Jewish temple in Elephantine, eventually coming to Ethiopia in the time of Manasseh. This view agrees chronologically with the time during which Manasseh committed his atrocities, which is also the same time the Ark supposedly disappeared.
27. A description of this ceremony is given by Edna Mason Kaula, *The Land and People of Ethiopia* (New York, 1965), pp. 136-137.
28. As reported in the *Jerusalem Post* (international edition) (October 3, 1992), p. 9. The purpose of Kaplan's book is to "demythologize" the history of Ethiopian

tradition, since the 20 sacred apocryphal books of the Ethiopian community were only translated into Ge'ez (the community's liturgical language) from Arabic in the Middle Ages.

29. Harry R. Atkins, "Ark of the Covenant: Not in Ethiopia," *Biblical Archaeology Review* (November–December 1993), p. 78.

30. Graham Hancock, *The Sign and the Seal: Quest for the Lost Ark of the Covenant* (New York: Crown Publishers, 1992), p. 128.

31. Interview with Rabbi Shlomo Goren, Tel-Aviv office, January 24, 1994.

32. Alfred Edersheim, *The Temple: Its Ministry and Services as They Were at the Time of Christ* (Grand Rapids: William B. Eerdmans Publishing Co., reprint 1972), pp. 146-150.

33. Hancock, pp. 409-411.

34. In addition, the Chronicler's pattern, especially with regard to the Davidic dynasty, is to portray positive virtues in exclusion to negative in order to validate the Judean monarchy and Temple worship as God's only legitimate agents.

35. Interview with Fantahune Melaku, translated by Maru Asmare, Ethiopian village, Jerusalem, January 27, 1994.

36. So strong was this tradition of the broken and complete tablets in the one Ark that it was used as the basis for the moral principle that a scholar who has forgotten his learning is still entitled to respect.

37. Hancock, pp. 37-38.

38. Interview with Rabbi Shlomo Goren, Tel-Aviv office, January 24, 1994.

39. Conversation with Grant Jeffrey in Dallas, June 24, 1992. Jeffrey believes that a $42 million surplus allotment for Operation Solomon, the last Ethiopian aliyah (immigration), went to secure the transport of the Ark to Israel. If Jeffrey knew the rabbis who were allegedly in possession of the Ark, he could not be persuaded to reveal it.

Chapter 9—The Great Treasure Hunt Inside Israel

1. Interview with Dan Bahat, Western Wall Tunnel, January 21, 1994.

2. This entire affair was reported in an article entitled "The Ark That Wasn't There," *Biblical Archaeology Review* (July-August 1983), pp. 58-61.

3. The spokesman for the Weizman Institute who performed the chemical test was Marvin Antelman, a chemical consultant in Rehovot. He confirmed the presence of myrrh, saffron, and galbanum and said that the bulk density, pH, ash content, and reaction with acid all compare favorably with what would be expected of *pitum haketoret*; *see* Dell Griffin, "Christian Group May Have Found Temple Incense," *The Jerusalem Post* (international edition), May 9, 1992, p. 28; and "Incense from the Temple Found in Dig Near Kumran, Texas Bible Scholar Claims," *Jerusalem Post*, May 10, 1992.

4. Reuters News Service article, "Man Says He's Close to Finding Lost Ark," *San Antonio Express-News*, May 16, 1992.

5. Interview of Jones by Mark Seal, "Masquerader of the Lost Ark," *Texas Monthly* (August 1992), p. 163.

6. Ibid., p. 117.

7. This new emphasis since the release of the film in 1981 is evident in the front-page news story from Jones's hometown newspaper, the *Tyler Morning Telegraph*. The article contained a photo of Jones with the movie poster and was entitled "Tylerite Hunts Ark of Covenant." Ever since, Jones has regularly appeared sporting a T-shirt with the movie-poster illustration; *see* photo in "Still in Search of the Lost Ark," *Christianity Today* (July 20, 1992), p. 49.

8. Mark Seal, "Masquerader of the Lost Ark," p. 140.

9. My own knowledge of Jones's religious beliefs comes from personal interaction with him in Israel while on tour and from a mutual Jewish friend, Yitzhak Oked, who has been working with Jones to further his *B'nai Noach* organization.

10. Aubrey L. Richardson, Sr. and Garold R. Collett, "Qumran: Summary Excerpts of Research and Reports from 1988 thru 1990" (updated edition, November-December 1990), p. 7.

11. Ibid., p. 10.

12. Excavation and ministry report, November 1993, p. 2.

13. Excavation and ministry report, January 1994, p. 2.

14. Zvi ben-Avraham and Uri Basson, "Geophysical Investigation of the Qumran Plateau Using Ground-Penetrating Radar and Seismic-Reflection Profiles" (Tel-Aviv University: Department of Geophysics and Planetary Sciences, 1992), pp. 3-5.

15. Richardson and Collett, p. 12 (attachment B).

16. Correspondence with Gordon Franz, February 18, 1994, p. 3.

17. Dr. Strange was also present when Larry Blaser attempted to find the Ark at Ein-Gedi. His willingness to lend his credentials for Collett's dig may reveal his long-standing interest in uncovering such treasure, surely every archaeologist's dream.

1.8 The only published details of this report are found in Dr. Lewis, *Prophecy 2000* (Green Forest, AR: New Leaf Press, 1993), pp. 178-181.

19. Video report of Wyatt Archaeological Research Organization, privately circulated.

20. Ibid.

21. "Discovered," newsletter of Wyatt Archaeological Research Organization, July 1993, p. 2.

22. Bill Crouse, "Ron Wyatt: Are His Claims Bonafide?" *Ararat Report* 17 (May-June 1988): 8.

23. Ibid.

24. Letter to Gordon Franz from Reverend John Woods, Executive Director, The Gospel Mission of Washington, D.C., February 4, 1994.

Chapter 10—The Secret Beneath the Stone

1. Excerpted from *Zohar*, a collection of mystical Jewish writings, p. 480.

2. Interview with Rabbi Shlomo Goren, Tel-Aviv office, January 24, 1994.

3. Interview with Rabbi Meir Yehuda Getz, January 25, 1994. Interview with Rabbi Getz in his office, June 23, 1993.

4. *See* Rabbi Goren, *The Temple Mount* (Tel-Aviv, 1992), pp. 258-268 [Hebrew].

5. Interview with Dan Bahat at the Western Wall Tunnel, January 21, 1994.

6. Introductory statement in an interview conducted at Warren's Gate, January 21, 1994.

7. Interview with Dan Bahat (by Jimmy DeYoung), July 19, 1991.

8. Interview with Rabbi Goren, Tel-Aviv office, January 24, 1994.

9. This account is a composite based on two separate interviews conducted with Rabbi Getz in his office June 23, 1993, and at Warren's Gate, January 25, 1994.

10. Interview with Rabbi Goren (by Jimmy DeYoung), June 18, 1991.

11. Interview with Rabbi Getz, January 25, 1994.

12. Interview with Rabbi Goren, Tel-Aviv office, January 24, 1994.

13. Interview with Rabbi Goren (by Jimmy DeYoung), June 22, 1991.

14. Interview with Rabbi Goren, Tel-Aviv office, January 24, 1994.

15. Ibid.

16. Interview with Rabbi Chaim Richman, June 23, 1991.
17. Interview with Rabbi Goren, Tel-Aviv office, January 24, 1994.
18. Interview with Gershon Salomon, TMF office, January 23, 1994.
19. Interview with Rabbi Goren, Tel-Aviv office, January 24, 1994.
20. This two-hour program produced by Desperado Films and Sun International Pictures, Inc. was hosted by actor William Devane and aired on Saturday, March 15, 1992. It is now available on video from Sun Home Video. I presented the story about Rabbis Goren and Getz, and the film footage of their interviews was done by Jimmy DeYoung. These original interviews are also available on DeYoung's video version of my first book, *Ready to Rebuild*.
21. The success of the program compelled CBS to produce a sequel, "Ancient Secrets of the Bible II."
22. Louis Rapoport, "The Mystery of the Real Lost Ark," *Jewish Digest* (September 1982), p. 29.
23. Interview with Dan Bahat, Western Wall Tunnel, January 21, 1994.
24. Interview with Rabbi Goren, Tel-Aviv office, January 24, 1994.
25. Interview with Rabbi Getz, office of the Western Wall, June 17, 1993.
26. Interview with Gershon Salomon, TMF office, January 23, 1994.
27. Interview with Rabbi Getz, Western Wall Tunnel, January 21, 1994.
28. Ibid.
29. Interview with Gershon Salomon, TMF office, January 23, 1994.
30. Interview with Dan Bahat, Western Wall Tunnel, January 21, 1994.
31. Interview with Gershon Salomon, TMF office, January 23, 1994.
32. For stories documented by the British explorers, see Neil A. Silberman, *Digging for God and Country: Exploration, Archaeology and the Secret Struggle for the Holy Land 1799-1917* (New York: Knopf Publishers, 1982), p. 186; and for the Arab legends in particular, see Zev Vilnay, *Legends of the Holy Land* (Jerusalem: "Daf-Chen" Press, 1978), p. 123.
33. David Allen Lewis, *Prophecy 2000* (Green Forest, AR: New Leaf Press, 1993), p. 176.
34. Interview with Rabbi Goren, office of the Western Wall, June 17, 1993.
35. Quoted from a court brief cited in the official newsletter of the Temple Mount and Land of Israel Faithful organization, issued from Jerusalem, Winter 1993.
36. David Allen Lewis, *Prophecy 2000*, p. 176.
37. Interview with Rabbi Goren, Tel-Aviv office, January 24, 1994.
38. Interview with Rabbi Getz, January 25, 1994.
39. Ibid.
40. Interview with Gershon Salomon, TMF office, January 26, 1994.
41. Interview with Rabbi Goren, January 25, 1994.

Chapter 11—The Ark and the Temple

1. Interview with Gershon Salomon (by John Ankerberg), Chattanooga, Tennessee, spring 1993. Printed with permission of The John Ankerberg Show.
2. Herbert G. May, "The Ark—A Miniature Temple," *The American Journal of Semitic Languages and Literatures* 52:4 (July 1936): 224. While it might be argued that temples existed before the Ark was made, we may resort to the sanctuary concept with its attendant cherubim. In this case, all pre-Israelite temples must be considered a pagan corruption of this original ideal, which found its proper expression only with God's command to build the Ark and its house—a command given to Moses at Mount Sinai.
3. An example of a higher-critical scholar who does not believe the Tabernacle was a fictionalized projection of the Temple is Hebrew University professor Menahem

Haran, *The Temple and Temple-Service in Ancient Israel* (Oxford: Oxford University Press, 1978), pp. 195ff.

4. Richard E. Friedman, "The Tabernacle in the Temple," *Biblical Archaeologist* (Fall 1980): 241-242; Anchor Bible Dictionary, s.v. "Tabernacle," ed. Noel David Freedman (New York: Doubleday & Co., 1992), 6:292-300. It should be noted that the exact measurements of the Tabernacle are never stated as such in these texts, but are derived from Friedman's interpretive analysis of the materials and structure listed.

5. In opposition to this view, especially as articulated by Friedman (above) is that of Victor Hurowitz, "The Form and Fate of the Priestly Tabernacle—Remarks on a Recent Proposal," *Jewish Quarterly Review.*

6. For a study of this device, *see* Shemaryahu Talmon, "The Textual Study of the Bible—A New Outlook," *Qumran and the History of the Biblical Text,* eds. F.M. Cross and S. Talmon (Cambridge: Harvard University Press, 1975), pp. 321-400.

7. For a study of the psalmist's view of the relationship between the Tabernacle and the Temple, *see* V. Rabe, "The Temple as Tabernacle" (Ph.D. dissertation, Harvard University, 1963), pp. 35ff. Some of the Psalms suggested for this comparison are 15:1-2; 27:4-6; 43:3; 46:4; 76:2-3; 84:10; and also Lamentations 2:6-7.

8. Richard E. Friedman, "The Tabernacle in the Temple," p. 246.

9. For more on the exegetical support for interpreting Daniel 9:27 as having a reference to the future, see my "Prophetic Postponement in Daniel 9 and Other Texts," chapter 7 in *Current Issues in Dispensationalism,* eds. C.C. Ryrie, John Master, and W. Willis (Chicago: Moody Press, 1994).

10. Although some rabbis attempted to make a historical correlation, such a view was unconvincing to the majority of rabbinic commentators, who were decidedly for a future interpretation (*see* Scherman and Zlotowitz, *Daniel,* The Artscroll Tanach Series, 259-262. Abarbanel noted that the return to Jerusalem and even the rebuilding of the Second Temple did not bring the expected redemption nor atone for past sins, since it was itself a part of the exile and atonement. He held that the real and complete redemption was still far off in history, and thus not yet fulfilled according to Daniel's prophecy.

11. For example, we read this in G.V. Caird, *A Commentary on the Revelation of St. John the Divine,* Harper New Testament Commentaries (New York: Harper & Row, 1966), p. 131: "In a book of symbols such as Revelation the last thing that the temple and the holy city could refer to was the physical temple and the earthly Jerusalem. A literal meaning would be inconsistent with his symbolism elsewhere." Caird, in order to maintain his idea of consistency, here makes the outer court represent the members of the church who have compromised with the world, and the holy city represent the world outside the church (p. 132). However, there is no textual or hermeneutical control to justify this identification, and any such interpretation as this must therefore be arbitrary.

12. For an example of this thinking, see M. Kiddle, *The Revelation of St. John,* Moffatt New Testament Commentary (New York: Harper & Row, 1940), pp. 178-179.

13. *See* Albert Barnes, *The Book of Revelation* (New York: Harper, 1851), pp. 268-269; Kiddle, *The Revelation of St. John,* p. 179; R.C.H. Lenski, *The Interpretation of St. John's Revelation* (Columbus, OH: Luther Book Concern, 1935), p. 328; Homer Hailey, *Revelation, an Introduction and Commentary* (Grand Rapids: Baker Book House, 1979), p. 250; G.R. Beasley-Murray, *The Book of Revelation* (Grand Rapids: William B. Eerdmans Publishing Co., 1978), p. 182.

14. John F. Walvoord, *The Revelation of Jesus Christ* (Chicago: Moody Press, 1966), p. 176.

15. *See* Isbon T. Beckwith, *The Apocalypse of John* (New York: Macmillan Publishing Co., 1919), p. 586. Even when the reference is to the church, such as in 1 Corinthians 3:17, it is clear that the Temple in Jerusalem is in view by analogy.

16. George E. Ladd, *A Commentary on the Revelation* (Grand Rapids: William B. Eerdmans Publishing Co., 1972), p. 152.

17. J.B. Smith, *A Revelation of Jesus Christ* (Scottsdale, PA: Herald Publishing House, 1961), p. 164.

18. Alan F. Johnson, *Revelation*, Expositor's Bible Commentary, vol. 12 (Grand Rapids: Zondervan Publishing Co., 1981), p. 500.

19. J.A. Seiss, *The Apocalypse*, 3 vols. (New York: Charles C. Cook, 1909), 2:159. This is the brazen altar of burnt offering in the outer court rather than the golden altar of incense in the Holy Place. That's because the worshipers seem to be in proximity to it (and only priests could go into the Holy Place), and it may be observed that when an altar is spoken of in the text without further qualification it always refers to the brazen altar (*see* Beckwith, *The Apocalypse of John*, p. 597.

20. Ladd, p. 152.

21. M. Kiddle, pp. 179-180.

22. Robert L. Thomas, *The Argument of the Book of Revelation* (Th.D. dissertation, Dallas Theological Seminary, 1959), pp. 187-188; cf. A.T. Robertson, "Revelation," *Word Pictures in the New Testament*, 6 vols. (Nashville, TN: Broadman Press, 1933), 6:384.

23. Robert L. Thomas, *Exegetical Digest of Revelation 8–14* (Sun Valley, CA: 1993), p. 155.

24. E.W. Bullinger, *The Apocalypse or "The Day of the Lord"* (London: Eyre and Spottiswoode, n.d.), 347.

25. Ladd, p. 152.

26. A.T. Robertson, 6:376.

27. In Daniel 12:11 the 1,290 days = 42 months based on a 360-day lunar calendar.

28. *Encyclopedia Biblica*, s.v. "Ark of the Covenant," by T.K. Cheyne, eds. T.K. Cheyne and J. Sutherland Black (Edinburgh: T. & T. Clark, 1909), pp. 309-310.

29. Interview with Gershon Salomon by John Ankerberg, Chattanooga, Tennessee, spring 1993. Printed with permission of The John Ankerberg Show.

Chapter 12—The Messiah Connection

1. *Catholic Encyclopedia*, s.v. "Ark," by Charles Souray, eds. C. Herbermann, E. Pace, et al. (New York: Robert Appleton Co., 1907), 1:724.

2. Interview with Rabbi Meyer Yehuda Getz, Western Wall office, June 21, 1993.

3. Interview with Gershon Salomon, TMF office, January 23, 1994.

4. Lisa Beyer, "Expecting the Messiah," *Time* (March 23, 1992), p. 49; Kenneth Woodward and Hannah Brown, "Doth My Redeemer Live?" *Newsweek* (April 27, 1992), p. 53.

5. Two of the most widely circulated are Rabbi Abraham Stone's *Highlights of Moshiach Based upon the Talmud, Midrash, and Classical Rabbinic Sources* and Rabbi Jacob Immanuel Schochet's *Mashiach: The Principle of Mashiach and the Messianic Era in Jewish Law and Tradition*.

6. While Hasidic magazines such as *Chai Today, Wellsprings*, and *L'Chaim* all carry articles relating to the present messianic expectation, a newsletter devoted entirely to the subject, called *Moshiach Matters*, has recently been published by the International Campaign to Help Bring Moshiach.

7. For example, full-page ads in the *New York Times* announced "The Time of Your Redemption Has Arrived."

8. An introduction to the Jewish concept of the Messiah is available by dialing 1-800-4-MOSHIACH in the United States and 1-800-2-MASHIACH in Canada. The four-minute message (in English) is changed weekly. A more detailed daily message can be heard by dialing (718) 953-6168 (in English, Hebrew, or Yiddish). With all three hotlines, questions can be left for return calls. For those who are interested in contacting the international campaign headquarters in New York, call (718) 778-6000.

9. Throughout this article the term *Jewish messianist* will be used rather than *Messianic Jew*, although the latter is most used in Israel. The substitution is made to avoid confusion with Jews who believe in Jesus as Messiah; in the United States, they are commonly known as Messianic Jews.

10. As cited by Elwood McQuaid in the article "Messianic Moods," *Moody* (October 1989).

11. The name *Habad* is actually an acronym for H = *chokmah* ("wisdom"), b = *binah* ("understanding"), d = *da'at* ("knowledge"). The *a* vowels are supplied only for readability; the Hebrew consonants alone make the word.

12. Ten of the signs are that 1) the world is either righteous or guilty, 2) truth is in short supply, 3) inflation will skyrocket, 4) Israel will have begun to be repopulated according to Ezekiel 36:8-12, 5) wise people will be scarce, 6) the Jews will have despaired of redemption, 7) the young will be contemptuous of the old, 8) scholarship will be poor, 9) piety will be disgusting, and 10) a growing number of Jews will turn on their own people. For a discussion of these signs, see Moshe Kohn, "The Do-Gooders Are Holding Up Messiah," *Jerusalem Post* (international edition), August 15, 1992, p. 13.

13. *Jerusalem Post* (international edition), August 31, 1991.

14. "Debate Splits Lubavitcher Hasidim: Is the Messiah Now Among Them?" *New York Times*, January 29, 1993, p. A14.

15. *Jerusalem Post* (weekend magazine), October 5, 1991, p. 13.

16. As cited in *Endtime* magazine (July-August 1992), p. 17.

17. *Newsweek*, April 27, 1992, p. 53 (top of third column).

18. Menachem Brod, cited in "Announcing the Days of Redemption," by Carl Schraz, *Jerusalem Post* (international edition), October 5, 1991, p. 23.

19. Ibid.

20. *Wellsprings* (Winter 1992), pp. 20-28. This entire issue is devoted exclusively to articles dealing with the Messiah.

21. Ibid., p. 20. The citation referred to by Maimonides reads, "The King Messiah will arise and return the kingship of the House of David to its former power. He will build the Temple, and gather the Jews scattered in exile. In his time all (Jewish) laws will come back into force."

22. Ibid., p. 17.

23. R. Menachem M. Schneerson, "A Changing Reality," *Lubavitch International* (Winter 1993): 3.

24. *Wellsprings* (December 1992), p. 27.

25. Ibid., p. 24.

26. *Jerusalem Post*, October 5, 1991, p. 13.

27. Ibid., p. 22.

28. Reported by Jimmy DeYoung after a phone conversation with Rabbi Kahane on October 16, 1992.

29. Personal correspondence with Reuven Prager, November 1993. The original statement was excerpted by Prager from a *Jerusalem Post* article of that same year.

Chapter 13—The Last Days' Ark

1. *The Lives of the Prophets*, translated by D.R.A. Hare in *The Old Testament Pseudepigraph*, ed. James Charlesworth (New York: Doubleday & Co., 1985), 2:388.

2. I have taken the Hebrew term translated "precious things" as "wealth," in harmony with Zechariah 14:14. The term can also be translated as "desire" and could refer to the Messiah, according to both Jewish tradition and early Christian interpretation. If it is "the Messiah" that is "the desire of all nations," then the "coming" here must be the second coming rather than the first, because the nations do not acknowledge Messiah or give glory to God until the latter demonstrates His glory through Israel (*see* Ezekiel 36:23, 36; 37:27-28; 38:16; 39:7, 21; Revelation 15:4; 20:3). This interpretation would also support the identification of the "latter Temple" as the millennial Temple.

3. As cited by Rabbi Shalom Dov Steinberg, *The Third Beis HaMikdash*, translated by Rabbi Moshe Leib Miller (Jerusalem: Moznaim Publications, 1993).

4. For those who wish to study this matter further, *see* Jerry M. Hullinger, "A Proposed Solution to the Problem of Animal Sacrifices in Ezekiel 40–48 (Ph.D. dissertation, Dallas Theological Seminary, 1993) and John Whitcomb, "Christ's Atonement and Animal Sacrifices in Israel, *Grace Theological Journal* 6:2 (1985): 201-217.

5. *Encyclopedia Judaica*, s.v. "Eschatology," by Louis Hartman 6:873-874.

6. *Houston Chronicle*, May 5, 1994, p. 16A.

7. William Rusher, "No Peace in Store for Israel," *San Antonio Express-News*, September 21, 1993, p. 11-A.

8. Grant Livingstone, "Israel's Integrity and the SLA," *Jerusalem Post* (international edition).

9. Associated Press article, "Weapons Still Pouring into the Middle East," *Houston Chronicle*, August 12, 1993.

10. James Hackett, "Moslem Bomb: Not If, But When," *Jerusalem Post* (international edition), May 23, 1992.

11. Dan Izenberg, "Eitan: Uranium Sites Revealed to Egypt," *Jerusalem Post* (international edition), November 1994.

12. For recent arguments for a pretribulation invasion, see Zola Levit and Tom McCall, *The Coming Russian Invasion of Israel* (Chicago: Moody Press, 1992), and Hal Lindsey and Chuck Misler, *The Magog Factor* (Hal Lindsey Ministries, 1992), and "Magog Updates," *Personal Update: A Newsletter of Koinonia House* (Coeur d'Alene, ID 83816-0347). A good survey of this position is also provided by Arnold Fructenbaum, *The Footprints of the Messiah* (Tustin, CA: Ariel Press, 1978), pp. 69-83.

13. Richard W. Judy, "From Anarchy to Zhirinovsky?" *National Review* (March 21, 1994), p. 49.

14. Ibid.

15. Dean Fischer, "This Is a Step Toward a Palestinian State," *Time* (September 27, 1993), p. 32.

16. This was so interpreted because the Vatican had previously stood with Arab sympathies against Israel (the Vatican takes a replacement theology stance that dictates a non-Jewish control of the Holy Land). However, Pope John Paul II's recent call for the faithful of the Roman Catholic church to "combat anti-Semitism wherever it is found" was considered a direct opposition to basic Muslim purpose. *U.S. News & World Report* (January 10, 1994), p. 9.

17. Austin Bay (researcher and writer on military and intelligence issues), "Violent Fringe Threatening Mideast," *San Antonio Express-News*, March 3, 1994, p. 4-B.

Chapter 14—The Ark and the Antichrist

1. This application is understood of Gentiles if we accept that John's first epistle was written against the heresy of gnosticism. While it is possible that Jews were among the members of this cult, it was primarily a Gentile aberration drawn from Greek wisdom teaching. Furthermore, the reference to the Antichrist "coming up out of the sea" in Revelation 13:1 indicates that he is a Gentile because in the book of Revelation, the term "sea" usually refers to the nations.
2. *Encyclopedia Judaica*, s.v. "Antichrist," by Michael Stone, 3:59.
3. David Flusser, "The Hubris of the Antichrist in a Fragment from Qumran," *Immanuel 10* (Spring 1980): 31.
4. *Encyclopedia Judaica*, s.v. "Armilus," by Jacob Klatzkin, 3:476-477.
5. Hermann J. Austel, "shomem," Theological Workbook of the Old Testament 2, eds. L. Harris, G. Archer, B.K. Waltke (Chicago: Moody Press, 1980): 936-937.
6. David Daube, *The New Testament and Rabbinic Judaism* (London, 1956), p. 420, cites the rabbinic tradition of attaching significance to expressions in the original text that hint at mystery by irregularity of form, and suggests that the article had been used early as an intentional device to distinguish something or someone special. He points out that the unusual form of this expression in the Greek text of Mark 13 must be explained by a dependence on Daniel 9:27, "with the article in Midrashic fashion interpreted as singling out a particular individual—the Antichrist, a heathen god, the Emperor or his statue."
7. For example, such deliberate vocalic alteration is found in 2 Samuel 4:1, 4 and Jeremiah 7:31-32 (cf. 32:35), where the Aramaic term *tephat* ("fireplace"), referring to the site of ritual child sacrifice in the Hinnom Valley, is *tophet* in Hebrew, apparently after the pattern of *boshet* ("shame"). The same vocalic substitution was also made for Tashterat as Tashtaroth. Micah 1:10-16 also offers an example of assonance wordplay. For other examples, see 2 Samuel 2:8; 1 Chronicles 7:33; Jeremiah 3:24; Hosea 9:10. This method of parody substitution was used not only for foreign deities, but also for people who were detestable because of ethical or covenantal violations; for example, the close relative of Boaz and Ruth is not referred to by name, but is called *peloni Talmoni* ("such a one") because he refused to honor his obligation to serve as a "kinsman redeemer" in marriage (Ruth 4:2, 6).
8. Andre Lacocque, *The Book of Daniel*, translated by David Pellauer (London: SPCK, 1979), p. 199.
9. E. Nestle, "Zu Daniel," Zeitschrift für die Alttestamentliche Wissenschaft 4 (1884), pp. 247-248. His euphemistic approach takes *shiqqutzim meshomem* ("abomination that makes desolate") as a cacophemistic distortion for the official designation of Hebrew *Ba'al Shamen* ("lord of heaven") or Greek *Zeus Olympius*. In this case, *shiqqutzim* serves as a parodic substitute for Ba'al or Syrian Zeus and *shomem* as an allophonic substitute for the consonantly similar *shamen* ("heaven").
10. See Ben Witherington III, *Jesus, Paul and the End of the World: A Comparative Study in New Testament Eschatology* (Downers Grove, IL: InterVarsity Press, 1992), p. 161.
11. See Pasquale De Santo, "A Study of Jewish Eschatology with Special Reference to the Final Conflict" (Ph.D. dissertation, Duke University, 1957), p. 356.
12. Some commentators seek to distance this "apostasy" from its apocalyptic parallels, preferring, as does F.F. Bruce (*1 & 2 Thessalonians*, Word Biblical Commentary 45 [Waco: Word Books, 1982], p. 167), to see a general civil revolt against public order, which in view of Romans 13:1-2 would constitute a rebellion against

"divine authority." Bruce's rejection of a Jewish end-time apostasy is colored by the absence of this teaching by Paul elsewhere, especially in Romans 11:25-27, the only Pauline context to deal with eschatological Israel. However, Paul's purpose in Romans 9–11 has been to present a positive destiny of Israel over against the present failure (and rejection) of the nation to accept Jesus as Messiah. To expect Paul to introduce such a negative picture of Israel's destiny (in desecration) at this point (Paul's climax to Israel's restoration) is contrary to the apostle's logical structure. Nevertheless, Bruce defends the position that it is the eschatological Antichrist that is portrayed here; cf. "Excursus," pp. 179-188.

13. See G. Henry Waterman, "The Sources of Paul's Teaching on the Second Coming of Christ in 1 and 2 Thessalonians," a paper presented to the Midwest regional meeting of the Evangelical Theological Society (Deerfield, IL: Trinity Evangelical Divinity School, March 21, 1975), p. 8.

14. Frank Witt Hughes, "Early Christian Rhetoric and 2 Thessalonians," *Journal for the Study of the New Testament (Supplement Series 30)* (Sheffield, England: JSOT Press, 1989), p. 59. For further study of the character and career of the Antichrist figure in biblical and postbiblical literature, see Bda Rigaux, "L'Antchrist: et l'Opposition au Royaume Messianique dans l'Ancien et le Nouveau Testament," *Universitas Catholica Lovaniensis Dissertationes Seires II,* Tomus 24 (Paris: J. Gabalda et Fils, 1932); W. Bousset, *The Antichrist Legend: A Chapter in Christian and Jewish Folklore,* translated by A.H. Keane (London: Hutchinson and Co., 1896); Ernst Renan, *Antichrist,* translated by W.G. Hutchinson (London: W. Scott, 1899); and Samuel P. Tregelles, *The Man of Sin* (London/Aylesbury: Hunt, Benard & Co., reprint 1930).

15. An apparent exception to this grammatical pattern is 1 Corinthians 3:17. While "a temple" in verse 16 means "the church," the reference to "the Temple" in verse 17 must mean "the Temple [at Jerusalem]" in order for the argument to make sense. There is here an almost a fortiori argument: "Do you not know that you are a temple of God . . . ? If any man destroys the [Jerusalem] temple, God will destroy him, for the [Jerusalem] temple of God is holy, and that is what you are [holy]." In other words, if the Jerusalem Temple is holy and violators will be punished (the greater), what do you think will happen if you violate the church, which, by analogy, is a temple (the lesser)?

16. Another verb for "enthronement" or "usurption" would have been used to express the symbolic sense, had it been intended, rather than the literal act of "sitting." It should be noted that some commentators who admit that a literal Temple is in view nevertheless argue that the activity of Antichrist, "tak[ing] his seat in the temple of God, displaying himself as being God," is nonliteral. This is taken in a metaphorical sense as "usurpation of the honor of the divine."

17. I owe this insight to Dr. Gary Cohen, "The Man of Sin and the Temple," Prophecy Conference, First Evangelical Free Church, Moline, Illinois (March 21, 1993).

18. Desmond Ford, *The Abomination of Desolation in Biblical Eschatology* (Washington, D.C.: University Press of America, 1979) contends that Daniel 9:27 is therefore the source for Matthew and Mark, and bases the deciding factor on the parallels between Daniel 7–9, 11–12 rather than on purely philological grounds (since linguistically, Matthew 24:15 and Mark 13:14 are closer to Daniel 11:31 and 12:11). He also suggests that Jesus' use of Daniel 9:27 (especially in Mark 13:14) may have in view a summary statement of the "abomination" material and therefore may include all the parallel passages in Daniel, including Daniel 8:13-14 (since Luke 21:24 cites this passage).

19. See David Wenham, *The Rediscovery of Jesus' Eschatological Discourse,* Gospel Perspectives 4 (Sheffield: JSOT Press, 1984), p. 178. Wenham argues that in view

of the synoptic references to "holy place" and "where it should not be," as well as the background in Daniel, the Jerusalem Temple is the preferred location.

20. W. Foerster, "bdelugma," *Theological Dictionary of the New Testament* 1 (1964): 598. His references for the *bdelugmata* ("abominations, idols") are LXX Jeremiah 13:27; 39:35; 51:22; Ezekiel 5:9, 11; 6:9; etc. and for the parallel with *anomia* ("lawlessness"), LXX Job 15:16; Psalm 5:7; 13:1; 52:1; 118:163; Jeremiah 4:1; Ezekiel 11:18; Amos 6:8.

21. My interpretation of this verse is based on the alternate reading, which includes the connective "and" before the phrase "those who dwell in heaven." While this reading could support a Tabernacle (Temple) on earth and be a parallel passage with 2 Thessalonians 2:4, I take its association with *God* to be directional as elsewhere (*see* Revelation 16:9, 11, 21).

22. *See* Lacocque, p. 199; Marcel Delcor, *Le Livre de Daniel* (Paris, Gabalda, 1971), p. 201.

23. John E. Goldingay, *Daniel*, Word Biblical Commentary 30 (Waco, TX: Word Books, 1989), p. 263; *see also* Otto Eissfeldt, "Die Flügelsonne als Kunstlerisches Motiv und als Religiöses Symbol," *Kleine Schriften* 2 (Tubingen, 1963), pp. 416-419.

24. G.R. Beasley-Murray, *Jesus and the Future: An Examination of the Criticism of the Eschatological Discourse, Mark 13 with Special Reference to the Little Apocalypse Theory* (London: MacMillan & Co., 1954), pp. 255-256.

25. We have taken the *waw* on *'ad* as pleonastic ("namely"), and *kalah . . . tateka* as a hendiadys, so that the idea is of a decreed or appointed end (Niphal of *haratz*, "things determined" for *shomen*, "the desolator").

26. For a full discussion of this position, *see* George M. Harton, "An Interpretation of Daniel 11:36-45," *Grace Theological Journal* 4:2 (Fall 1983): 205-231.

Chapter 15—The Forgotten Ark

1. A.W. Streane, "The Book of the Prophet Jeremiah Together with the Lamentations," *The Cambridge Bible for Schools and Colleges* (Cambridge: University Press, 1952), p. 25.

2. *The International Standard Bible Encyclopedia* (revised), s.v. "Ark of the Covenant," p. 293.

3. Samuel Terrien, "The Elusive Presence," *Religious Perspectives* 26 (San Francisco: Harper & Row, 1978), p. 175.

4. Charles L. Feinberg, "Jeremiah," *Expositor's Bible Commentary* (Grand Rapids: Zondervan Publishing House, 1986), 6:402.

5. J.A. Thompson, *The Book of Jeremiah*, New International Commentary on the Old Testament, ed. R.K. Harris (Grand Rapids: Wm. B. Eerdmans Publishing Co., 1980). p. 203.

6. John Calvin, *Commentaries on the Book of the Prophet Jeremiah and Lamentations*, translated and edited by John Owen (Grand Rapids: Baker Book House, reprint, 1979), 1:183.

7. Interview with Rabbi Shlomo Goren, Tel-Aviv office, January 24, 1994.

8. Interpretation of Yitzhak Avinari on Jeremiah 3:16 in *Tanakh* edition of *Yedinot Ahranot*, printed for the Israeli Defense Forces under the Chief Military Rabbinate. Interpretive notes by Aaron Dothan and Shlomo Zalman Ariel, Yitzhak Avinari (Tel-Aviv: Adi Publishers, 1986).

9. Brown, Driver, Briggs, *A Hebrew and English Lexicon of the Old Testament* (Oxford: Claredon Press, 1972), p. 795.10.

10. Herbert G. May, "The Ark—A Miniature Temple," *The American Journal of Semitic Languages and Literatures* 52:4 (July 1936): 225.

11. Steve Herzig, *Israel My Glory Magazine* 51:5 (October-November, 1993): 14.

Chapter 16—The Ark Effect

1. Leibel Reznick, *The Holy Temple Revisited* (Northvale, NJ: Jason Aronson, Inc., 1990), pp. 146-147.
2. Interview with Gershon Salomon (by John Ankerberg), Chattanooga, Tennessee, Spring 1993. Printed with permission of The John Ankerberg Show.
3. Interview with Gershon Salomon, TMF office, January 16, 1994.
4. Temple Mount Faithful *Communique*, October 1994, p. 4.
5. Israel Government Press Office "Press Bulletin," August 1, 1988, released by TMF.
6. Letter from Dov Shilansky to Gershon Salomon, February 24, 1989.
7. Most orthodox Jews do not see a return to blood sacrifice in a restored Temple, even though the prophetic texts indicate this will be the case. Even Salomon's own daughter, Aviah, finds the prospect distasteful.
8. In Rabbinic terminology this is called *yediat ha-chetz* ("forcing the hand" [of Messiah]), and is built upon the belief that there is a cause-effect relationship between human acts (the masculine waters) and the divine response (the feminine waters). A rabbinic Midrash observes that "the Red Sea did not part until the Israelites stepped into it." Following this principle, The Temple Mount Faithful argue that the Temple will not be rebuilt until men start making efforts to rebuild it.
9. Interview at the Dome of the Rock, January 20, 1994. Bassam Abu-Lebdah's official position is with the translation office of Al *Haram* al Sharif.
10. Interview with Rabbi Shlomo Goren, Tel-Aviv, January 25, 1994.
11. Interview with Bassam Abu-Lebdah, January 20, 1994.
12. Interview with Gershon Salomon, TMF office, January 23, 1994.
13. David Bar-Illan, "Errors in Arabizing Jerusalem," *Jerusalem Post* (international edition), November 27, 1993, p. 13.
14. This was of immense help to archaeologists in locating ancient biblical place names, since their modern names were relatively unchanged.
15. Carl Hermann Voss, *The Palestine Problem Today: Israel and Her Neighbors* (Boston: The Beacon Press, 1953).
16. The name *Palestine* was first used by the Romans when they conquered Judea and Samaria in A.D. 135. At that time Rome controlled Syria and they considered Judea and Samaria only the southern part of their Syrian district, not an independent state. Therefore the Roman emperor of that period, Hadrian, renamed the region Syria Palestina. The Roman use of *Palestine* probably derived from their identifying the area with the Phoenicians, who had occupied the coastal plain and were ancient enemies of the Jews. Hadrian purposely chose an enemy name to further humiliate the Jews and to disguise their homeland name, Israel, with the intent of removing the Jews from history.
17. Rabbi Yisrael Ariel, *Atlas of the Land of Israel: Its Boundaries According to the Sources*, Vol. 1 (Jerusalem: Cana Publishing House, 1988).
18. *The Near East Report* (October 16, 1994).
19. *See* Joshua Shuman, "Med-Dead Canal Company Revived," *Jerusalem Post* (international edition), October 16, 1993, p. 20.
20. *See* "Temple Mount Yeshiva," *In Jerusalem* (a publication of *Jerusalem Post*), Friday, May 28, 1993, p. 1.
21. Cover page, "Position Paper" (published by The Yeshiva of the Temple Mount, 1993).

22. *See* "Temple Will Be Man-made," *Jerusalem Post* (international edition), August 28, 1993, p. 3.

23. "Position Paper," p. 7.

24. Interview at Temple Mount Yeshiva, Jewish Quarter of Jerusalem, January 16, 1994.

Chapter 17—The Middle East Conflict

1. Moshe Kohn, "Messianic Times," *Jerusalem Post* (international edition), August 22, 1993, p. 13.

2. Rabbi Shlomo Riskin, "The Land and Its Sanctity," *Jerusalem Post* (international edition), October 23, 1993, p. 23.

3. The Jericho district, as defined by Jordanian law (before its capture by the Israelis in 1967), comprised 146 square miles. The 140 miles in question was close to this and was what the PLO wanted the autonomous zone to contain. This eventually included the Allenby Bridge, which was one of two border crossings between Jordan and Israel, although Israel retained rights to monitor the bridge.

4. Felice Maranz, "Palestinians Demand All West Bank Relics," *The Jerusalem Report*, December 16, 1993, p. 5.

5. Adapted from the preface by Baruch Taub in Aryeh Kaplan, *Jerusalem the Eye of the Universe* (New York: National Conference Synagogue Youth/Union of Orthodox Jewish Congregations, 1984), p. 6.

6. As cited in the *San Antonio Express-News*, September 27, 1993, p. 3A.

7. Interview with Teddy Kollek (by Abraham Rabinovich), "This Old Lion Still Has Teeth," *Jerusalem Post* (international edition), October 30, 1993, p. 12.

8. As cited by Clarence Wagner, Jr., "Israel's Defensible Borders," *Dispatch from Jerusalem* 15:4 (1990), p. 11.

9. As cited in "Let Them Speak for Themselves!" *Dispatch from Jerusalem* 18:4 (November-December 1993), p. 8.

10. As cited by Fouad Ajami, "An Old City's Dreams," *U.S. News & World Report* December 13, 1993, p. 68.

11. As cited by Matthew Seriphs, "Present Tense, Past Imperfect," *Israel Scene* magazine (*Jerusalem Post* international edition supplement), May 23, 1993, p. 14.

12. As cited by John Wheeler, Jr., in the *Christian American* 5:2 (February 1994), p. 4.

13. As cited in the sidebar in Nancy Gibbs article (reported by Lisa Beyer and Dean Fischer), "Yitzhak Rabin and Yasser Arafat," *Time* Magazine, January 3, 1994, p. 44.

14. Ibid., p. 49.

15. Jack R. Payton, "Jerusalem Mayor Matters," *San Antonio Express-News*, November 10, 1993, p. 10B.

16. *See* article "Olmert Vows to Prevent Division of Capital," *Jerusalem Post* (international edition), November 13, 1993, p. 2.

17. *See* Jon Immanuel, "Shahal: Law 'Skirted' to Buy Old City Homes," *Jerusalem Post* (international edition), August 22, 1992, p. 24.

18. *Jerusalem Post*, January 28, 1994, p. B4.

19. Reported in the *Guardian Weekly*, January 24, 1988.

20. As cited by Dan Izenberg, "Will He or Won't He? And What If He Doesn't?" *Israel Scene* magazine (*Jerusalem Post* international edition supplement), May 23, 1992, p. 9.

21. As cited in a *Baltimore Sun* Service and Associated Press report, "Israel Closes Holy Site, Fearing Reprisal Attack," March 5, 1994.

22. *New York Times* Service story in the *San Antonio Express-News*, March 14, 1994, p. 1.
23. Ibid., p. 4A.
24. Interview with Adnan Husseini by Ulf Carmesund, September 1991, as cited in his book *Two Faces of the Expanding Jewish State: A Study on How Religious Motives Can Legitimate Two Jewish Groups Trying to Dominate Mount Moriah in Jerusalem* (Uppsala, Sweden: Uppsala University, 1992), p. 86.
25. Ibid., p. 87.
26. *See* Associated Press story, "Israel to Muzzle Jewish Militants to Salvage Peace," *San Antonio Express-News*, March 7, 1994, p. 14C.
27. As cited in an Associated Press report, "Militants Lash Out at Both Sides," December 11, 1993.
28. As cited by Marguerite Michaels and reported by Robert Slater, "Settlers: Violence to Do God's Work," *Time*, September 13, 1993.
29. As cited in Associate Press report, "Riots Deepen Pessimism Over Peace Talks in Mideast," March 3, 1994.
30. As cited by Lisa Beyer and Jamil Hamad, "When Fury Rules," *Time*, March 7, 1994, pp. 51-52.
31. Ibid., p. 52.

Chapter 18—All Eyes on the Ark

1. Interview with Gershon Salomon (by John Ankerberg), Chattanooga, Tennessee, May 1993. Printed with permission of The John Ankerberg Show.
2. Kevin J. Conner, *The Tabernacle of Moses* (Portland, OR: Bible Temple Publishing, 1975), p. 21.
3. Interview with Gershon Salomon, TMF office, January 19, 1994.
4. Interview with Meno Kalisher, pastor, Keyilat Yerushaliyim, Jerusalem, January 21, 1994.

World of the Bible Ministries, Inc. is a nonprofit, evangelical Christian organization promoting the development of local church ministries through education and training of Christians in subjects touching the world of the Bible. "Bringing the world of the Bible to the Word of the church" stands behind a threefold ministry of research, conferences, and tourism:

World of the Bible Research develops new publications and media to educate the church and for a witness to the world.

World of the Bible Seminars is a communication ministry bringing prophetic and instructional conferences to local churches to encourage their understanding of the Bible in its original context.

World of the Bible Tours organizes and conducts inspirational study tours to the Holy Land to give Christians a firsthand and life-changing experience with the world of the Bible.

For more information on these ministries or to schedule Dr. Randall Price for a conference with your church or organization, please write or fax:

Dr. Randall Price
World of the Bible Ministries, Inc.
110 Easy Street
San Marcos, Texas 78666-7326
FAX: (512) 396-1012

In Search of
Temple Treasures
Video

Join author Randall Price in an exciting journey through the places and with the personalities surrounding the search for Temple treasure. Filmed entirely on location in Israel, this fast-paced documentary goes beyond the book to reveal, *in some cases for the first time on film*, current developments that are setting the stage for the fulfillment of prophetic events. Highlighting the Ark of the Covenant, this video provides both a historical overview of this greatest treasure of the Bible as well as an urgent call to audiences to prepare themselves for the coming of Christ. Available from your local Christian bookseller or from Harvest House Publishers.